Prison Stories

Prison Stories

Women Scholars' Experiences Doing Research Behind Bars

Edited by
Jennifer A. Schlosser

LEXINGTON BOOKS
Lanham • Boulder • New York • London

Published by Lexington Books
An imprint of The Rowman & Littlefield Publishing Group, Inc.
4501 Forbes Boulevard, Suite 200, Lanham, Maryland 20706
www.rowman.com

6 Tinworth Street, London SE11 5AL, United Kingdom

British Library Cataloguing in Publication Information Available

Library of Congress Control Number: 2020947255

Contents

Acknowledgments

The idea for this book came about because I had a story to tell. It's a story that has haunted me for the past decade and it changed who I was as a prison researcher, a professor, and a woman. In looking for an outlet to tell my story, I realized that other women prison researchers must have stories of their own they needed to set free, as well—so, this anthology was born. This volume serves as a medium through which we, the authors and the storytellers, are able to critically reflect on the personal moments that have changed us in our careers as women doing prison research. The chapters in this volume brought us out of our comfort zones, they forced us to look back at our experiences and they have allowed us to bring voice to those salient, unforgettable moments that have stuck with us, and strengthened us.

I would like to thank the chapter contributors who opened themselves up to the vulnerability of telling their stories. For many of us, these chapters were not easy to write, and it took great courage and self-reflection to put them down on paper. It should also be noted that the authors wrote their chapters during the peak of a global pandemic when many of our universities closed their doors, and we were left to make sense out of a world where everything seemed to change overnight. This, too, was a challenge and the contributors of this volume persevered, often sacrificing their late nights and early mornings to bring their chapters to life and for that, I cannot thank them enough.

I would like to thank Brandy Holm who worked as my research assistant in the early stages of this project. Without her keen eye for detail and dedication to her work, this book would not be what it is today. I am grateful for my editor at Lexington Press, Becca Rohde Beurer, whose diligence and communication made the publication process run more smoothly than I thought possible. I am grateful, also, to my family whose support over the years has kept me going, even when I wanted to give up. To the families of all the chapter contributors, thank you for your patience and support while your loved one sacrificed her time with you to work on her contribution to this volume.

This book is dedicated first to the incarcerated people who shared their lives with us. We are better because of you, and these chapters should stand as a testament to how deeply you have impacted our lives and to how grateful we are to have experienced these events with you. Second, this book is dedicated to the women prison researchers who are just starting out. When you read our chapters, take comfort in the fact that you are not alone. We stand behind you, we support you, and we will be here to listen when you have your own stories to tell.

Jennifer A. Schlosser, PhD

Introduction

Jennifer A. Schlosser

This is a book of stories; but, make no mistake, this is not a storybook. The chapters presented here contain the experiences of a group of women academics who have dedicated not only our careers to researching prisons and those incarcerated within them, but who have also dedicated our lives to this work. The experience of doing prison research, as readers will learn in this volume, is not the kind of work that can be put aside when the day ends and laptops are closed, field notes are piled neatly (or not) on the edge of the desk, and the kids are ready for dinner. Prison research cannot be left behind while the investigator teachers her classes, sips her morning coffee, or walks the dog. For the prison researcher, navigating the mundanity of her daily life is not separate from her work, because within her daily life is prison research—woven into her thoughts, her dreams, her emotions, and her everyday experiences. As researchers, prison gets inside us—it takes up space, it makes itself known. The experiences we have had in the prison research field are such that the weight of simply being a party to the incarceration experiences of our fellow humans buoys us, anchors us, and sometimes, if we're not careful, can drown us.

WHERE DO WE BELONG? LOCATING WOMEN PRISON RESEARCHERS IN THE LITERATURE

In a field as rich in data, theory, policy, and action, there are countless books and articles written on qualitative research methods in criminology (too many to list here, though Ferrell & Hamm, 1998 is a touchstone for ethnography, see also Noakes & Wincup, 2004; Richards & Bartels, 2011), and there have been many works written on doing research with women inmates in women's prisons (see Hannah-Moffat & Shaw, 2000, for a particularly good example). There are even (to a much lesser extent) scholarly works that address potential issues and provide solutions for new prison researchers entering the field for the first time (Schlosser, 2008; Sandberg & Copes, 2012; Sloan & Wright, 2015). What is lacking in the academic literature are works that focus on the experiences of women *as* prison researchers and the challenges we faced transitioning from novice to expert.

Historically, prison research has been conducted almost exclusively by male researchers. Over the past thirty or so years, an increasing number of women researchers have published articles, monographs, and book chapters reporting on the results of their work in prisons. Entering the male-dominated arena of most criminological institutions, these female scholars have faced unique challenges of their own. Their standpoint as women in these spaces adds layers of insight that deepen their scholarly analyses (Byrne, 2005; Jewkes, 2011; Bucerius, 2013; Abbott & Scott, 2018).

The political, cultural, and gendered constraints imposed on women researchers are entrenched in a hetro-masculine context that extends into their research sites (Gurney, 1985; Schlosser, 2015). These barriers, often acting as gate-keeping devices, are not widely discussed or analyzed in the field of criminology (Martel, 2004; Jewkes, 2011). Correctional institutions particularly engender a male-centered structure of policy, administration, and culture creating structural constraints that make gaining access to prisons as sites of research more difficult for women researchers who may challenge the status quo (Hsu, 2005). Issues such as gaining trust, building rapport with administrators, and accessing inmates abound when women researchers attempt to breach these barriers.

Once access is gained, women prison researchers face a new set of challenges. Our bodies become sexualized, our methods are questioned, and our very presence in prison is often held up as separate from the masculine culture that dominates it (Bucerius, 2013). Inside prison, ideological shifts are regularly required as interactions with staff and offenders change from moment to moment (Bosworth et al., 2005; Nielsen, 2010). We know from Goffman (1961) that the experience of being in a total institution like prison is one in which power structures, languages, norms, codes, and morals exist in a vacuum. The rules in prison are different (though not separate) from the rules on the outside, and anyone coming into that total institution, whether an inmate or a researcher, had better be a fast learner. These rules are structured into the culture and daily operations of the prison place. They allow the prison to seemingly run itself. The inmates learn how to act, whom to trust, what to say and what not to say. The guards and administrators likewise learn how to react, how their particular prison treats their charges, the atmosphere they want to convey, and the culture they have established. Is the warden heavy-handed? Are the guards armed? What amount of corruption is tolerated? How is violence handled? The cultural rules that abound in prison construct the day-to-day operations and require a common understanding among all actors simply for the institution to function.

The precarious balance of common understandings that governs life in prison is, to most outsiders, invisible, quiet, unremarkable—until something enters to disrupt it. We are the women researchers who seek to understand and pull apart those layers of the institution that warrant closer examination. When we enter a prison, our presence disrupts those rules that have churned just below the surface (Rowe, 2014). Our bodies, our minds, our words, our very existence there becomes the disruption that forces those common, unspeakable cultural understandings to finally show themselves (Presser, 2005). What women researchers see as a result of our presence in masculine-dominant places like prisons allows us a unique and (one could argue) privileged standpoint that, when proper attention is paid, becomes highly revelatory. As such, our personal experiences doing prison research are rich sites of data that deserve not only analytic consideration but also a voice.

This book looks deeply at women researchers' personal stories, struggles, and successes within the context of conducting research in the male-dominated sphere of the correctional industry. Their insights provide an analytical resource from which we can better understand the context of doing prison research and the theoretical and methodological challenges that come with it (Liebling, 1999; Byrne, 2005; Jewkes, 2011). Their autoethnographic stories also provide a roadmap for dealing with the novel strategies, methodological landmines, and epistemological challenges for those who will come after them (Schlosser, 2008). Their experiences as investigators are couched in a distinct set of challenges. This book is intended to highlight those researchers' challenges and also to celebrate their successes.

THIS IS FOR YOU: A NOTE TO OUR READERS

What I didn't have as a woman in graduate school, embarking on her first foray into any type of research, but especially prison research, were women mentors. My advisors were men, and while they studied criminology, they'd never done research inside prison. So, I looked to the women who had come before me—Yvonne Jewkes, Alison Liebling, Keramet Reiter, Kate Gooch, Kathryn Fox, and Tobi Jacobi—these women (and others) filled the empty spaces in my education that should have been reserved for women mentors. I read their books and articles, I followed their work and careers, I took strength and confidence from their accomplishments. Whether they knew it or not, these invisible mentors were there with me when I planted my feet (in closed-toe shoes, of course) inside a prison for the very first time, they were with me in the basement of the university library as I sat in my dark study carrel and wrote my dissertation, they were with me when I got my first job as a sociology professor and started teaching others about prison. So, this book is not only *written* by them, but it is also *inspired* by them.

Equally as important as those first trailblazing women who ventured into the prison research world before us are the women who came next, forcing the path to remain open and refusing to let it become overgrown, once again, by the loudness of male voices. These women prison researchers—Beth Easterling, Shenique Thomas-Davis, Abigail Kolb, Lindsey Raisa Feldman, Dallas Augustine, Melissa Barragan, Kelsie Chestnut, Gabriela Gonzalez, Natalie Pifer, and countless others—now do the hard work of making sure that women researching in prison stay relevant and continue to be heard.

As readers might have already guessed, the tone and writing style of this book are different from what is typical in many academic monographs, articles, or other edited volumes. Here, the authors' goals are not to report on data or analyze findings (though some do), our primary goals, instead, are to speak about what we experienced as women doing prison research. We are here to tell *our* stories, and those stories are deeply personal. When I began contacting potential chapter authors and putting this volume together, I didn't quite know yet what direction this book would take. For many of us, after decades of academic training on how to write a research article, the experience of breaking out of that rigorous structure can be difficult at first; and so it was for some of the authors in this book. Over the course of its coming into being, I received many late-night emails from chapter authors struggling to write from a personal perspective. It wasn't that they didn't know *how* to write from the personal, it was that they hadn't yet been *allowed.* This book gave many of us the permission to finally express, out loud, what we've experienced as women doing research in prisons. It provided a medium through which we could finally talk about those deeply important, sometimes life-changing, always impactful, and forever unforgettable stories (Lumsden & Winter, 2014).

Next, I present brief summaries of the chapters in this volume and encourage our readers to proceed with open minds. Here, we have pushed ourselves to think differently, to examine our work and experiences in ways many of us have never done before. These stories didn't come easily, they took hard work and courage to tell, and the women who have authored this book did so with the following question in mind—a question I posed to each of them before they began writing: if you could go back, what advice would you give your former self as a young woman, just starting out on her prison research journey? Their answers live in this text, and our audience now should be clear. We seek to provide new prison researchers with the women mentors they may not have the opportunity to know in person. We seek to illustrate how the experiences of women prison researchers are different from those of men, and we go forward with the hope that some of our readers are inspired by our stories to continue on their path toward making their own name in the study of prisons. We likewise intend that our audience, through reading our stories, takes away some lessons. First, we hope readers are able to better understand where and in what ways male privilege has and continues to impact the field of prison studies for women; and second, we hope our readers take that lesson as a challenge to become emboldened toward change and progress by working to make the field of prisons studies more inclusive, more diverse, and ultimately, more equal for all of us.

THE STORIES

While this volume contains eleven chapters, these chapters contain dozens of stories. Each author writes from her personal experience and, as one can imagine, the perspectives range widely; from reflections on the paths of Yvonne Jewkes's and Alison Liebling's impactful careers, to the specific transcripts of the detailed, nuanced dialogue that took place between Keramet Reiter and her team as they prepared to go to prison. The chapters are arranged in such a way that readers can easily skip around and read each chapter in order of preference, but they are also arranged in complement to one another—so that they can be read mindfully, in order, from the first chapter to the last, through the larger arc of a connected dialogue.

Part I—If We Knew Then: Lessons from the Field

In the first section of the book, three chapters introduce readers to the thought processes, conversations, and "methodological landmines" that colored the initial prison research experience for the authors. The first chapter in this anthology, "The Endlessly Fascinating and Depressing Rabbit Hole of Prisons: Being a Woman Researching in a Man's World" by Kathryn J. Fox, provides a vivid look at her first experiences doing research in prison by giving a boldly honest examination of her place as a woman inside. Fox identifies three main positions she found herself while doing prison research: (1) an invader of male space, (2) a woman being defended by male chivalry, (3) and a mother, mirroring incarcerated mothers. Fox writes, "ruminating on my time researching inside, I am struck by how naïve I was to think my pregnant, female body would be invisible and not play a role in the drama of group therapy; being an educated, middle-class academic was another influential attribute. The combination was formidable. . . . I tried to disappear, but could not be more awkward in such hyper-masculine space." Fox highlights her discussion on positionality with personal stories and reflections, ending with her advice to new prison researchers.

The second chapter "Reflections on Team Research in Carceral Settings" is cowritten by Keramet Reiter, Dallas Augustine, Melissa Barragan, Kelsie Chesnut, Gabriela Gonzalez, and Natalie Pifer. Along with their colleague, Justin Strong, the women authors of this chapter use dialogue to work through the moments in their experiences researching in prisons where gender became a salient and obvious factor. Uniquely written as narrative dialogue, this chapter explores several themes that can also be found reflected in many of the book's subsequent chapters. Through their conversations, the authors discuss how their gender created opportunities for accessing both the physical research sites and the emotional insights that male researchers may not have experienced in the same way. The authors likewise discuss how stereotypes about gender (femininity in particular) that abound in the hypermasculine environment of most carceral spaces were, at once, both frustrating and revelatory. Finally, they identify moments in their research experiences that focus on the interplay between the emotional states of manipulation and empathy. This chapter is one of contradictions (as is the case with most prison research) and the authors masterfully pull apart the layers of the stories they tell to identify those contradictions and reflect on how their encounters in prison shaped the course of their research. Peppered with well-written and personal stories of the memorable moments the authors experienced researching prison as women, this chapter provides an excellent analysis of both the depth and the breadth of issues women researchers often face.

"A Woman's Place: Navigating the Methodological Landmines of Prison Research," the third chapter in this anthology, uses autoethnography to examine the unexpected and surprising challenges that can arise for both women and early career prison researchers. The chapter uses critical theory to investigate the impact of researcher's positionality in the prison field, and how her presence there impacted the culture, actors, and data. Through personal storytelling that recounts sexual harassment, power dynamics, and gender, this chapter reflects on the unseen challenges and "methodological landmines" she faced. The chapter ends with a critical analysis of how researchers' locations in the field site can be examined in an effort to mitigate the effects of those landmines going forward.

Part II—Locating Ourselves: Stories of Belonging

Building on the first part of the anthology, part II features two chapters focusing on the challenges the authors experienced locating and solidifying their own places in the research. Shenique Thomas-Davis's chapter

"Cloaked in Liminality: Negotiating Roles, Identity, and Emotional Labor within and between Prison Walls and Academia" provides a stirring reflection on the author's experiences as a Black woman working in white, male settings. Thomas-Davis allows us a privileged look at her thoughts, fears, and struggles as she navigates both the prison space and academe. Reading Thomas-Davis's deeply personal and honest journey into the transitory, unsolid, and unwelcoming world of prison research and higher education as a Black woman is disquieting—as it was for her. She writes: "I existed behind the wall, replete with complexity, visible, under constant surveillance, as a Black woman, a scholar living in academic liminality, who sought to amplify the voices and range of experiences of the mostly Black and brown men incarcerated at a prison in the Northeastern region of the United States. However, I existed beyond the wall, invisible, as a Black woman, navigating and negotiating multiple identities, marginality, and cultural frames of reference." Thomas-Davis's descriptions of her liminal status are haunting, and for many white folks and men especially, will be new and perhaps surprising. Her call to her readers is clear: to understand the unstable tightrope Black women scholars must walk, and rather than turn away or simply nod and smile—instead: amplify, uplift, and steady.

The second of the two chapters in this section "Just Listen, People!": Narrative as Resistance in Criminological Research" is written by Abigail Kolb. In her chapter, Kolb gives us the juicy data that so many qualitative researchers crave. Reflecting on her interviews with formerly incarcerated female Chicana gang-members, Kolb deftly analyzes how her participants' words (and similarly for all marginalized research participants) should be seen as the definitive narratives of their own identities. Using critical theory, Kolb argues that without reflexivity in both the field, and the narrative moment, researchers run the risk of imposing their own social locations (judgments, experiences, expectations) onto their participants. Kolb writes: "I had to re-frame my own interpretations and view the participants' stories from their perspectives—as active agents who had made choices in their lives based upon their own constrained positionality. In other words, it was crucial that I understood these women as being shaped by their experiences, but simultaneously shaping their own experiences." Kolb's insights give readers a much needed "step back" as we consider how much of ourselves we allow to penetrate the narratives of our participants.

Part III—Blurring the Lines: Tales of Personal Connection

Part III features three chapters focusing on the tricky business of locating our own emotions in research conducted around those with whom we immediately, and personally, identify. Through their direct interactions with their participants, the authors in this section tell stories of entanglement as they navigate the field of prison research with participants whose experiences they see mirrored in their own lives. In "Complicity and Compassion: Meditations on Writing and Researching with Incarcerated Women," Tobi Jacobi describes her near twenty years of work with incarcerated women leading a writing program in prison. Jacobi's chapter is interlaced with poetry, freewriting, and narrative—both her own and those of the incarcerated women with whom she wrote—and a deeply personal analysis into how researchers can practice compassion and care with their participants. Readers can interpret Jacobi's chapter in several ways—it can well serve as a formula for how in-prison writing programs can (and should) be constructed and run, it can be read as a piece of art in itself as her writing is eloquent and nuanced, or it can be read as call to action: for researchers to actively participate in the difficult emotion work that prison demands. Jacobi's chapter gives us permission to humanize our participants and experience our feelings beside them. This chapter, as an introduction to the section on blurring lines and personal connection, gives readers much to consider: "There are times when the echo of one woman's story reverberates so loudly that it overcomes my ability to bring other people into my life, when my own despondency about holding their narrative close slips over into critique of my own family's needs, wants, and desires."

In the second chapter in this section, "Empathy and Identity: Mothers Researching (Incarcerated) Mothers," Beth Easterling puts into words what many of the women in this anthology experienced: the empathetic, emotional, and deeply personal experience of connecting with people who are at once so different from us, but also, painfully similar. Her chapter unabashedly recounts the discomfort that comes with recognizing a deep personal link with our subjects of study, and the privilege and power over them we experience as outsiders. Easterling writes: "I struggled with the responsibility of having to retell these mothers' stories, realizing I connected so deeply with the experiences of motherhood, but so little with the realities of life behind bars." In her chapter, Easterling wrestles with the complex emotions that come with both motherhood, and prison research. She describes feelings of shame, guilt, sadness, and empathy as she struggled to reconcile the differences between herself and her participants, when it seemed that so much of what they felt as mothers, was the same. Drawing on her field notes, Easterling recounts her own emotional highs and lows during her research and, in the end, reminds us that not only is it normal to experience emotions when doing prison research, but that it is, in fact, essential.

The final chapter in this section on blurring lines is written by Lindsey Raisa Feldman, titled "On the Possibilities of Emotional Praxis for Feminist Prison Research." While the title alone is likely enough to intrigue readers, the content most certainly will. Feldman reflects on the fifteen months she spent as a wildland firefighter working alongside a crew of incarcerated men. Like Easterling, Feldman also draws on her notes from her time in the field. Through a recounting of these notes and the lens of feminist critique, Feldman provides incredibly detailed and visceral descriptions of the emotional and highly *physical* experiences she encountered during her research. Feldman's writing gives readers a firsthand glimpse into what most of us will never experience: being a woman, fighting fires, alongside incarcerated men for a year and a half. Her descriptions are mesmerizing and her fluent storytelling makes this chapter an addicting read. Feldman's conclusions, likewise, enlighten readers to the dangers of not thinking critically about our own roles as women in carceral spaces. She writes that we must recognize the masculine, patriarchal rules that have shaped our own views of our femininity and reminds us that "we as researchers are capable of thinking critically about how we choose to move through our field sites, and further, to use this reflexivity to lay bare structures of power and push our research ethics and praxis forward."

Part IV—What We Know Now: Career Reflections and Looking Ahead

The final section in this anthology brings readers a behind-the-scenes glimpse into the storied careers of three women whose work has helped shape the landscape of prison research. In "From *Captive Audience* to Cultural Penology: Reflections on a Career in Prison Research," Yvonne Jewkes describes the trajectory of her career path from first meeting her mentor, Alison Liebling, at the University of Cambridge, to her own surprise at the changes her research interests underwent over the years, to the many other notably influential mentors and colleagues she encountered who helped shape her career path. Jewkes takes us on the journey through her PhD program, her most memorable moments in prison, and concludes by giving us the advice that any good (great) academic advisor would: read more. Her advice is well taken, and the inclusion of her story in this anthology is a good starting place for the rest of us to take up that call.

The second chapter in this section was written by Alison Liebling. Her entry, "Women in our Own Right or 'Honorary Men'? Reflections on a Professional Life in Prisons Research," reflects on her thirty-year career as a prisons researcher. Notably, for this project, she uncovered her old field journals and, along with her sharing of very personal family dynamics and experiences, takes us back to those moments in her career that made her who she is today. Reading her chapter feels somewhat like reading a diary—Liebling gives us a privileged peek behind the curtain. But what she discusses in her chapter is more than a recounting of important milestones, it is the feelings and emotions she experienced during those moments. Liebling's honest look back at how her gender impacted her professional career allows readers to see themselves in her journey. It's easy to relate to Liebling when she writes:

> I was greeted warmly afterwards by a Norwegian Director of the training academy for prison staff, who congratulated me on my "very fine lecture." His first words to me were, "I've read your book." He meant my book on prison officers, which explores what their work consists of, at its best (Liebling & Price, 2001). . . . He had liked the book very much and had used it often in the training of staff. His next words were, "I thought you were a man."

In her stories, many women prison researchers will see themselves. They'll nod along and smile sometimes, reading about how Liebling often surprised herself by what she was able to accomplish—understanding that, despite knowing that gender inequalities exist in this field—we, like Liebling, somehow manage to get it done; and in doing so, often surprise ourselves at just how capable we are.

The final chapter in this book is written by Kate Gooch. Her piece, "'You've Got a Hard Edge!' The Gender Politics, Complexities, and Intimacies Undertaking Prisons Research at the 'Edge,'" is an excellent endcap to the anthology. Gooch's piece touches on many of the issues discussed in previous chapters through the lens of rich interview data and self-reflection. In her chapter, Gooch discusses the experiences in her career where her gender became a salient landmark in her work. Gooch details the ways in which gender politics and identity negotiation in prison and academia shaped her presentation of self, the challenges she experienced, her interactions with participants, prison staff, and colleagues, and how the duality of being "hard" and "feminine" can create both conflicts and opportunity. As Gooch writes, "The most effective way of better understanding ourselves is not, however, gleaned by simply peering longer or closer at our own reflections, but by deliberately asking others to 'hold up a mirror.'" Holding up a mirror for ourselves, for each other, and for those who will come after us, is precisely what this anthology aims to do.

REFERENCES

Abbott, L., & Scott, T. (2018). "Reflections on researcher departure: Closure of prison relationships in ethnographic research." *Nursing Ethics*, *26*(5), 1–18.

Bosworth, M., Campbell, D., Demby, B., Ferranti, S. M., & Santos, M. (2005). "Doing prison research: Views from inside." *Qualitative Inquiry*, *11*(2), 249–264.

Bucerius, S. M. (2013). "Becoming a 'trusted outsider': Gender, ethnicity and inequality in ethnographic research." *Journal of Contemporary Ethnography*, *42*(6), 690–721.
Byrne, M. W. (2005). "Conducting research as a visiting scientist in a women's prison." *Journal of Professional Nursing*, *21*(4), 223–230.
Ferrell, J., & Hamm, M. S. (Eds.). (1998). *Ethnography at the edge: Crime deviance and field research.* Boston: Northeastern University Press.
Goffman, E. (1961). *Asylums: Essays on the social situation of mental patients and other inmates.* New York: Anchor Books.
Gurney, J. N. (1985). "Not one of the guys: The female researcher in a male-dominated setting." *Qualitative Sociology*, *8*(1), 42–62.
Hannah-Moffat, K., & Shaw, M. (2000). *An ideal prison? Critical essays on women's imprisonment in Canada.* Halifax: Fernwood Publishing.
Hsu, H.-F. (2005). "Patterns of masculinity in prison sociology: A case study of one Taiwanese prison." *Critical Criminology*, *13*, 1–16.
Jewkes, Y. (2011). "Autoethnography and emotion as intellectual resources: Doing prison research differently." *Qualitative Inquiry*, *18*(1), 63–75.
Liebling, A. (1999). Doing research in prison: Breaking the silence? *Theoretical Criminology*, *3*(2), 147–173.
Lumsden, K., & Winter, A. (2014). *Reflexivity in criminological research: Experiences with the powerful and the powerless.* United Kingdom: Palgrave MacMillan.
Martel, J. (2004). "Policing criminological knowledge: The hazards of qualitative research on women in prison." *Theoretical Criminology*, *8*(2), 157–189.
Nielsen, M. M. (2010). "Pains and possibilities in prison: On the use of emotions and positioning in ethnographic research." *Acta Sociologica*, *53*(4), 307–321.
Noakes, L., & Wincup, E. (2004). *Criminological research: Understanding qualitative methods.* London: SAGE.
Presser, L. (2005). "Negotiating power and narrative in research: Implications for feminist methodology." *Signs*, *30*(4), 2067–2090.
Richards, K., & Bartels, L. (2011). *Qualitative criminology: Stories from the field.* New South Wales: Hawkins Press.
Rowe, A. (2014). "Situating the self in prison research: Power, identity, and epistemology." *Qualitative Inquiry*, *20*(4), 404–416.
Sandberg, S., & Copes, H. (2012). "Speaking with ethnographers: The challenges of researching drug dealers and offenders." *Journal of Drug Issues*, *43*(2), 176–197.
Schlosser, J. A. (2008). "Issues in interviewing inmates: Navigating the methodological landmines of prison research." *Qualitative Inquiry*, *14*(8), 1500–1525.
Schlosser, J. A. (2015). *Inmates' narratives and discursive discipline in prison: Rewriting personal histories through cognitive behavioral programs in prison.* New York, NY: Routledge.
Sloan, J., & Wright, S. (2015). "Going in green: Reflections on the challenges of 'getting in, getting on, and getting out' for doctoral prisons researchers." In D. H. Drake, R. Earle, & J. Sloan (Eds.), *The Palgrave handbook of prison ethnography.* Palgrave studies in prisons and penology. London: Palgrave Macmillan.

Part I

IF WE KNEW THEN

LESSONS FROM THE FIELD

Chapter 1

The Endlessly Fascinating and Depressing Rabbit Hole of Prisons

Being a Woman Researching in a Man's World

Kathryn J. Fox

The first time I set foot inside a prison was when I arrived to conduct research in one. I had no idea what to expect; I had seen some frightening and dramatic examples on television and in movies. I was surprised by how much less scary it was in reality. In fact, it mostly seemed dull and routinized. Except for the slamming heavy doors. The sound startled me; twenty years later—I am still shaken by the sound. When I think of the challenges of being inside and the prospect of living inside a prison, the heft of the metal doors and the sound they make seem among the most brutal. Still whenever I exit, I let out an enormous breath, relieved that I can leave.

My previous project had been studying an HIV prevention program that reached out to street-based drug users. That research site felt perilous to me, as people on the streets were sometimes volatile. As a woman, I felt vulnerable. Conducting research in a prison sounded easier somehow—more controlled certainly—and the conditions bounded. Because of how structured and regimented the routines inside prison were, it felt easier to understand. At the same time, some of the rules felt so arbitrary, it was tricky to manage to follow the rules. For example, sometimes I was allowed to bring in a notebook and pen; at other times, I was allowed less. Some officers were stricter than others. As Jefferson (2015, p. 169) describes, ethnography—being *in* the prison—reveals the "underside of penal practices." In my case, this does not necessarily refer to pernicious actions, but rather, I would argue that the everyday powerlessness and shifting rules contributed to the sense of being off-balance in the space, even for a researcher. Imagine what it is like to live and work there on a regular basis. Discretion had a powerful effect on my sense of place; it echoed a constant refrain within prisons from those confined.

At a colleague's suggestion, I contacted a higher-up in the Department of Corrections[1] from whom I learned about a prison therapy program for violent offenders. These kinds of programs were popular then and now. This sounded fascinating as a site to see the subjective states of the "fixers" and the "fixed." Other than my rudimentary curiosity, I entered with few preconceived notions about what I would experience or find. As an inductive researcher, I was comfortable with letting the field speak to me. I knew I was interested in observing the exchanges between the group facilitators and the incarcerated, but I did not have a sense of what their conversations would be like. Initially, I imagined I would examine which kinds of therapists were more effective than others. I did notice resistance from participants when therapists took certain positions, but I mostly observed confusion among the participants, as they struggled to explain their motivations, and tried to distinguish (as required but not easily determined) between their thoughts, attitudes, and beliefs.

Ultimately, I became fascinated by the ways that "criminal" or violent selves were constructed through the discourse of the treatment, creating a "looping" effect, as Goffman described—an impenetrable version of truth about the self (Goffman, 1961). For example, the program pressed the idea that criminals were plagued by cognitive distortions; this program was designed to help them understand and intervene in those distorted thoughts. The distortions might be that they were in fact victims themselves (discounted within the therapy discourse), or that their violence was driven by a need for power and control over others. If an incarcerated individual challenged these characterizations of their thoughts, their objections were interpreted as a signifier of their essential criminality or the depth of their distortion. When I would say in private to a facilitator that I thought sometimes the participants' versions of events sounded credible and not distorted, I would be met with a shrug or a sympathetic look about my naiveté. The narrative at the time was that incarcerated individuals were manipulative. Any assertion on my part or theirs that they may have been provoked to violence or that there were structural forces working against them was discounted. I was told once that sociology had been popular in the 1970s but no longer. I was struck by the dominance of psychological discourse, and its impenetrability; that may have been the most interesting story to tell.

GENDER IN THE RABBIT HOLE

Most of the groups I attended were with men; there were fewer women who had committed violence. My experience being an observer, in this predominantly male space, was shaped and constrained by my gender. In other words, my gender affected how I moved within the space and influenced the interactions within the group sessions. As I reflect on this, three main experiences emerge: my role as an invader in male space, as a mirror in the women's darkest hour, and as the woman defended by chivalrous staff. They were all awkward for different reasons. However, most painful for me was identifying with the women, the mothers in the groups.

Perhaps because I knew little about prisons, I did not consider much the gender-fraught conditions entering the men's prison space. I knew of its hypermasculinity from academic literature, and wondered a bit about potential danger. I should have been more aware of my gender (I am a cis-gender woman), and the impact of coming inside visibly pregnant with my first child. Positionality is an issue in any research setting; ethnographers bring in their various statuses. Our bodies, and the various interpretations and experiences that stem from their presence in our field sites, are often considered tangential to the data or the story (Hanson & Richards, 2019). Women ethnographers are often socialized to toughen up if they are going to hang with the guys and to neutralize somehow the impact of gender (Hanson & Richards, 2019). Hanson and Richards (2019, p. 25) write about the "fixations" in fieldwork—that ethnographers are supposed to be fearless and solitary, which places women at particular risk.

What women in the field experience is male power and privilege. Inside prison, this looked and felt real but had a distinctive feel. Prison is such a weird world in many ways: people are literally locked away from public view; they have their own rules, norms, and economies. Power infuses every interaction. That power is masculine, even in low/medium security facilities (Evans & Wallace, 2008). As such, I suppose this is a reflection on being an outsider studying a prison; however, it is essential to note the ways in which the outsider's presence becomes absorbed into and shapes the dynamic inside. Ruminating on my time researching inside, I am struck by how naïve I was to think my pregnant, female body would be invisible and not play a role in the drama of group therapy; being an educated, middle-class academic was another influential attribute. The combination was formidable. Although I did not *really* think I would be invisible or that my positionality was insignificant, I did not know how to acknowledge it or negotiate my embodiment. Because I was an observer, and my role was delimited, I had to determine how much to insert myself in situations anyway, or pretend to be a fly on the wall. I was instructed by Corrections not to share anything significant about myself, so my contributions were innocuous. I tried to disappear but could not be more awkward in such hypermasculine space.

INVADER OF MALE SPACE

As a researcher, working in a male facility, I had to negotiate how to frame my feminine identity, both with those incarcerated and with correctional officers and other staff members. In addition, ethnographers try to develop trust with participants, as a strategy for gaining access to the "real" story. In this case, I wanted to gain trust among correctional staff and incarcerated individuals. Gaining trust is easier if one can reduce whatever divides exist and to be aware of the ways in which the researcher might be threatening. It is good practice, simply as a human being, to be aware of ways to reduce social distance, and to make people feel validated and heard. This was more difficult for me, as I was merely an observer in the group therapy sessions. I wanted to chime in and participate sometimes, but the most I could do is engage in friendly small talk at either end of a session.

Tactically, too, as a researcher, I had to admit what I did not know about prisons, or the perspectives of the officers or other staff members. In my case, this meant taking on a deferential stance. However, working with men and deferring to them created a workable—if problematic—relationship. For example, I often wonder what it would have been like to do the same project if I were a man. I might have been able to bridge that social distance more easily by engaging in "bro" banter. Over time, I may have minimized the gender divide a bit by loosening up, swearing, and joking more. Still—being a pregnant woman engendered a certain protectiveness of me that I would have resented in any other situation. My embodiment was a player in the setting. I can never know the extent of its role in shaping the conversations and interactions.

I was only allowed to observe therapy groups in which all participants agreed to allow me. It usually wasn't a problem—incarcerated individuals are accustomed to a lack of privacy, and tend not to defend it. I have never felt unsafe or threatened in any prison, except for maybe a little once: I went to one therapy group to explain what I wanted to do, why I wanted to do it, and to answer questions. I was about eight months pregnant at the time. I felt vulnerable—not that I might be hurt physically but just exposed somehow in a group of men, many of whom had committed violence against women. In asking questions about my research request, one man suggested that the benefit to me was clear, such as publications and a career boost, but asked what they would get out of my involvement. The answer I provided seemed inadequate then and now. I essentially told him that they would get their voices heard and that it is important for others to understand the way these therapies work. (But of course, their voices would affect a handful of academic criminologists, and not much more, I feared.) This same man was openly hostile toward me. After I left and they voted, I was denied access. I was relieved, as he unnerved me. It was the only moment in twenty years of researching and volunteering in prisons that I felt remotely unsafe.

I have pondered what this hostility was about; was it just that I was a woman? Was it because I was pregnant and perhaps, out of place? Was it my privilege, the imbalance of power—that I was asking things of them while offering nothing in return? I may never know the answer, but I became acutely aware of my own concern about the latter—about the lack of reciprocity in the research relationship inside a prison (Waldram, 2009; see also Given, 2008). This imbalance is magnified inside prison because I could bring nothing inside: no cupcakes, no gifts, no human touch. The incarcerated have given up so much already. Ultimately, I understood the group's willingness to enact the little bit of power they could exercise by denying me access to their inner world.

Most often, prison researchers segregate by gender into gendered spaces (Bosworth et al., 2005). I have spent time in both men's, women's, and mixed prisons. In the therapy groups with men, a somewhat comical dynamic occurred in which the participants would sometimes say that they *would* be willing to describe something (e.g., their innermost thoughts or an incident), except that there was "a lady present." Then in the next sentence or so, they would quickly forget and swear explosively or blurt out something offensive about women or other groups. They were aware that their (somewhat) safe masculine space was being invaded by a woman, but the group code was to be open and honest, and they were sharing their true thoughts; juggling those seemed to add a layer of tension. I assured them that they could act naturally and that their language would not offend me. Many of their stories were about assaults against women. It was a lot to ask that they ignore my presence; over time, this issue dissipated somewhat, as I presented as a neutral party. I did not participate except during "check-in" to say how we were feeling or what was new in our lives.

For me, a challenge I reflected on was how to remain dispassionate about the chronicles of their violent histories. What surprised me most was something I took as a point of pride as an ethnographer—and I am not certain that I should have—that I was able to avoid entirely the judgment of whether their perspectives were accurate or offensive. Instead, because I was focused on the *interplay* between the totalizing therapeutic discourse and the "subjects" of the intervention, I was able to hear these discussions neutrally. In other words, I was being an analytical sociologist, trying to capture the perspective of the speaker. I felt a little robotic and was surprised I was able to maintain that stance.

I felt conflicted then and now about this disembodiment, this objectivity. I consider myself an "underdog" sociologist, seeking to understand the more often silenced, marginalized perspective(s). In this narrow context, the men who committed violence were the underdogs. However, outside of this context, what about the women who were victims? And is "objectivity" a goal or value to applaud? Is judgment to be avoided? For example, the articles I wrote did report the participants' perspectives, and spoke about how their seemingly valid concerns were dismissed as invalid. In groups, they had to recount their violence, and speak about the justifications they used to normalize their acts. I tried to take their accounts at face value, and was remarkably—perhaps inexplicably—able to do so. Once I learned that the interplay was about whether or not their characterization would be reframed as a distortion, or accepted as valid, I was able to focus on the response of the facilitator, and the ways in which they talked back to participants. I accepted, like an anthropologist studying an unfamiliar culture, that women may have been devalued in this particular masculine space (Hua, 2005; Kupers, 2001). I took on a relativistic stance, so as not to be ethnocentric in the space; upon reflection, this seems like an unlikely position for me to be able to inhabit as a feminist and a woman. I steeled myself in the men's groups and remained emotionally detached, except I did sympathize with men who were trying to change their behavior, but found it daunting in a hostile prison setting, and within their other hypermasculine environments.

DEFENDED BY CHIVALRY

I often felt more subject to the whims of correctional staff, who were usually accommodating and helpful, but sometimes appeared threatened or worried about my presence. In all my years of going inside many different prisons in a few states, I have noticed that officers tend not to make eye contact. They become practiced in the art of diminishing the human aspects of interactions—many of them anyway. Working with the facilitators of these therapy groups, who were sometimes contracted social workers or psychologists but often were trained caseworkers or officers, was more complex. Most of the correctional staff were likely to have less education than I did; thus, I tried (consciously and genuinely) to minimize the social distance between us by deferring to their expertise. However, the effect it had was for me to be beholden to their perspective, and I found repeatedly that correctional staff would emphasize the dangers of corrections, perhaps to astonish me. A dynamic emerged, which was one in which the "book-smart" teacher was awed by the "street-smart" officer. A few times, the officers seemed to revel in telling me about how "violent" some people were; my role was to be shocked, I suppose, or impressed that they could handle the work environment. For all I know, their view was accurate and mine naïve, but nonetheless, the dynamic that emerged was one that felt gendered.

Hanson and Richardson (2017, 2019) argue that the standards we set for "good" methodology in ethnography can actually impair women. There is an ethos of cavalier swagger that fails to account for the burdens of being a woman, especially in a male space. In an effort to get the data, we may compromise ourselves, notably by being sexually harassed. I am glad to say I never experienced that in prison, and in fact was treated professionally by every staff person.[2] However, I did experience a certain insinuation that I was gullible, that if I took the incarcerated individuals' pathos at face value, it was because they were manipulative and I was unwise. As a sociologist, I recognize that their worldviews may have been necessary in order for them to conduct their work, as was mine. Perhaps this was not gender as much as it was a contest over expert knowledge. This is a subject I return to repeatedly: what constitutes expertise? What do these knowledges consist of and how do they clash?

As researchers, being open-minded to what we may not know is an important position to take. But it is also a tactic to build rapport. I had opinions about prisons and our punitive climate, but I had only book education, indoctrination, and a bleeding heart. I genuinely understood that my perspective was only one among other legitimate views. Yet, I found the chivalrous dynamic a bit unsettling, although I believe it made my presence tolerable. In addition, my stature is small, which probably contributed to this somewhat.

A MIRROR TO MOTHERS

Later in my research, I had the opportunity to observe cognitive therapy groups for women who had committed violent offenses. Observing women was significantly more distressing for me, as I had more emotions to manage (Bosworth et al., 2005). I identified with the women, and felt self-conscious about my good fortune. Many of the women wanted desperately to see or reunite with their children; that desire motivated their participation and efforts to do well in the program. Some women wanted to chat about whether I was a mother and to bond over it. I felt enormously guilty when they were working hard in groups to be able to see their children, and I was the epitome of a woman who "had it all": a good job, a child in my custody, no state agencies meddling in my life, and a way out the door at the end of the day. The detachment I had cultivated in the men's group was harder to manage with the women. So much of prison conversations center around the ways in which the prison management and staff invoke arbitrary and vague rules enforce them unevenly, and generally make life inside harder than it needs to be. This fact is easy to see in every prison I have ever entered. The powerlessness is the point.

There were women who had done some very violent things; they did not embody the gendered norms of passivity. I could identify with their anger at losing access to their children. They would have jumped through any hoop to get permission to see their kids, but had trouble negotiating the requirements of the therapy program. They would name their violent feelings toward the officials keeping them from their children, but such confession seemed unlikely to help their cause. I could feel their frustration escalate—this happened with the men as well—reinforcing their beliefs that the system is rigged against them. There were also women who refused to engage much in the therapy groups; they were resigned to doing a very long time in prison. Some had done violence to their abusers, and I wondered often about which goal of justice was served by keeping them there.

Sitting in these groups, observing and taking notes, felt absurd at times. I bore witness to some very dark and intense moments in the women's lives. I felt helpless in the face of a desire to help, which was not something I experienced as acutely with the men. My life was wildly different from the women inside, but we were women, we were mothers, and we knew what it meant to feel disempowered at times. I related to their emotions, if not their situations. Moreover, I did not know how to make small talk with them. My expression was impassive, and I hoped my face would not betray my emotion, which included feeling compassionate but helpless. I would often leave swiftly, uncertain how to "be" in that situation.

REFLECTIONS

I was so moved by my experiences inside prison, I never left really. Criminal justice—and in particular, corrections—is a rabbit hole; it is endlessly fascinating. Once inside, there are many riveting dimensions to consider: power and privilege, bureaucracy, punishment and rehabilitation, among countless others. Occasionally I meet people at parties who, when they learn of my passion for prison research and reform, will ask why on earth I would want to spend time in and on prisons. The fascination stems from the many aspects of prison life that demonstrate power. Prisons represent power differences within their organization and within their practices. They are impacted by social class, by race, by gender, by privilege, and by luck. There is no greater site for seeing those issues play out than within the justice system. Being inside a prison is like a step into a private world that most people do not consider, but that is memorable and disturbing. It is even more troubling how hidden the world is. I am not implying corruption or evil intentions, but just that the effects of prison are damaging, to families, to staff, to those confined.

If I could give my younger ethnographer advice going inside, I might suggest that I take more of a stand. In the interest of absorbing information, I think, I deferred too much. It is an interesting predicament in ethnography: the social roles we inhabit on in order to be nonthreatening and open to information may not conform to our politics or positions. In other words, what is the cost of being a blank slate? I might instead consider whether my willingness to defer to others' experiences over my scholarly knowledge was, in fact, gendered. I believe if I were starting anew, I would assert the validity of sociology, and the notion that social structure matters—not in the group therapy settings (I agreed not to disrupt) but perhaps confronting more formally the practices I observed. We tend to write smart-sounding articles for other academics—a project I am less interested in now. Burawoy (2005) proposed that sociologists should engage wider, public audiences, and make our data and perspectives more accessible. I do this now—I engage in public fora that question whether we should abolish prisons. I am doing research that engages incarcerated individuals and staff in the research effort using participatory community-based research. I advocate openly for criminal justice reform, but maintain a positive partnership with Corrections.

I often say that everyone should visit a prison at least once. They should be aware of what we are consigning people to. I still go inside prisons for various activities: I do research inside, I teach inside, I bring students inside to run book clubs and to play sports. I have met some amazing, smart, resilient human beings—working and living inside prisons. It is important to me that the incarcerated know that there are people on the outside who care about what happens to them, and who operate on the premise that they deserve recognition, help, and dignity. I learned that in the rabbit hole of prison.

NOTES

1. The state remains unnamed.
2. However, I have experienced sexual harassment in other field settings.

REFERENCES

Agozino, B. (1995). "Methodological issues in feminist research." *Quality and Quantity*, *29*(3), 287–298. Retrieved from https://search.proquest.com/docview/61406207?accountid=14679.

Bosworth, M., Campbell, D., Demby, B., Ferranti, S. M., & Santos, M. (2005). "Doing prison research: Views from inside." *Qualitative Inquiry*, *11*(2), 249–264.

Burawoy, M. (2005). "For public sociology." *American Sociological Review*, *70*(1), 4–28. https://doi.org/10.1177/000312240507000102.

Carrabine, E., & Longhurst, B. (1998). "Gender and prison organisation: Some comments on masculinities and prison management." *The Howard Journal of Criminal Justice*, *37*, 161–176. https://doi.org/10.1111/1468-2311.00088.

Craven, C., & Davis, D.-A. (2013). *Feminist activist ethnography: Counterpoints to neoliberalism in North America*. New York: Lexington Books.

Crewe, B. (2009). *The prisoner society: Power, adaptation and social life inside an English prison*. Oxford: Oxford University Press.

Evans, T., & Wallace, P. (2008). "A prison within a prison?: The masculinity narratives of male prisoners." *Men and Masculinities*, *10*(4), 484–507. https://doi.org/10.1177/1097184X06291903.

Given, L. M. (2008). *The SAGE encyclopedia of qualitative research methods* (Vols 1–0). Thousand Oaks, CA: SAGE Publications, Inc. https://doi.org/10.4135/9781412963909.

Goffman, E. (1961). *Asylums: Essays on the social situation of mental patients and other inmates*. New York: Doubleday, Anchor.

Hanson, R., & Richards, P. (2019). *Harassed gender, bodies, and ethnographic research*. Berkeley: University of California Press.

Hua-Fu, H. (2005). "The patterns of masculinity in prison." *Critical Criminology*, *13*, 1–16. https://doi.org/10.1007/s10612-004-6110-x.

Jefferson, A. M. (2015). "Performing ethnography: Infiltrating prison spaces." In D. H. Drake, R. Earle, & J. Sloan (Eds.), *The Palgrave handbook of prison ethnography: Palgrave studies in prisons and penology*. London: Palgrave Macmillan.

Kupers, T. (2001). "Rape and the prison code." In D. Sabo, T. Kupers, & W. London (Eds.), *Prison masculinities* (pp. 111–117). Philadelphia: Temple University Press.

Orrico, L. A. (2015). " 'Doing intimacy' in a public market: How the gendered experience of ethnography reveals situated social dynamics." *Qualitative Research*, *15*(4), 473–488. https://doi.org/10.1177/1468794114543403.

Schrock, R. D. (2018). "The methodological imperatives of feminist ethnography." *Journal of Feminist Scholarship*, *5*(Fall), 54–60. https://digitalcommons.uri.edu/jfs/vol5/iss5/5.

Ugelvik, T. (2015). "Be a man. Not a bitch: Snitching, the inmate code and the narrative reconstruction of masculinity in a Norwegian prison." In I. Lander, N. Jon, & S. Ravn (Eds.), *Men, masculinities and the criminological field* (pp. 57–70). London: Ashgate. Retrieved from SSRN: https://ssrn.com/abstract=2553215.

Waldram, J. B. (2009). "Challenges of prison ethnography." *Anthropology News*, *50*, 4–5.

Chapter 2

Reflections on Team Research in Carceral Settings

Keramet Reiter, Dallas Augustine, Melissa Barragan, Kelsie Chesnut, Gabriela Gonzalez, and Natalie Pifer
with additional reflections by Justin Strong

INTRODUCTION

Drawing on experiences working on team research projects in a range of all-male carceral settings, we reflect on our experiences as women, in dialogue with each other and with one additional male team member, in these spaces. The authors all worked together on a team project examining and evaluating reforms to extreme conditions of confinement in a mid-sized state prison system, in which we interviewed hundreds of prisoners and staff. Previously, four of the authors also worked together on a project examining gun markets and arrestees' understanding of gun laws, in which we interviewed dozens of jail detainees in a large county jail. We incorporate and reflect on experiences from both projects in this piece, as well as bringing in other individual experiences conducting research in all-male carceral settings.

As a first step in writing this piece, we each jotted down a description of a moment, an interaction, or an observation when gender seemed especially salient to us, as researchers inside carceral spaces. We generated dozens of examples through this process, and for this piece, chose to focus on a handful that exemplified complex experiences with gender as carceral researchers. In the text that follows, we include many of our individual, original "jottings," along with individual responses of team members to those "jottings" (often either written into a Google Doc, or spoken during a meeting, recorded, and transcribed). Although this is an unusual format for academic writing, and we ourselves had to resist the urge to polish and rewrite original "jottings" and reflections, we also think capturing our initial thoughts and ensuing dialogue more honestly and transparently reveals the actual analytic process in which we as a team engage and seek to make meaning of our qualitative research data, both revealing how we "put reflexivity into practice" while also allowing the reader to generate alternative interpretations of our experiences (Ramazanoğlu & Holland, 2002).

From the shared list of jottings we generated, we each returned repeatedly to one moment, described by coauthor Kelsie Chesnut (KC), as exemplifying the layers of access, emotion, and identity we all wanted to explore in thinking about how our gender has shaped, inspired, constrained, comforted, and frustrated us again and again inside secure confinement facilities. We chose this moment to start this piece; Kelsie begins the dialogue, and one of the coauthors, Natalie Pifer (NP), responds—a formatting of conversation and insight we follow for the remainder of the chapter.

KC: I had just completed the last interview of summer data collection on a project examining experiences of solitary confinement in a mid-sized state prison system. I was the project manager. The emotional stress and exhaustion of coordinating weeks of intensive fieldwork weighed down on me. And the interview I had just finished with a prisoner had been disturbing. As a convicted sex offender, he had made the instrumental choice to threaten a staff member in order to ensure his placement in solitary confinement, rather than face (what he believed to be) certain violence from prisoners in general population. He had been in solitary for seven months at the time of our interview, and he planned on staying in solitary until his release the following Christmas Eve—a total of nineteen consecutive months. His skin was sickly pale, and he cleared his throat often, being out of practice talking to anyone. He told me he had no pictures in his cell, because he was "unloved." He no longer took his rec time, because he "had no one to call." The only mail he received was a sporadic chess move from a civilly committed sex offender he'd known previously. He was the most pitiful human I had ever met: aware that he was in the discard pile and no one cared. I needed a minute to get my crap together. I went into the women's staff bathroom, past the sink, and ducked into one of the stalls. The bathroom and adjoining locker area were empty. I had the place to myself. After a couple minutes, I heard the door open and someone come in. I held my breath and immediately stopped crying. I could hear the person standing near the sink, and then struggling to choke back sobs of their own. There were ten of us conducting interviews that day. We were mostly women, so I figured I was overhearing one of my team members doing the exact same thing I was doing in the women's bathroom—seeking a private retreat from the otherwise heavily male-dominated and surveilled setting. I was about to open the stall door and commiserate. Then I heard keys jangle. I froze. I wasn't in the bathroom with another researcher. I was listening to a CO [correctional officer]. I didn't want to embarrass the CO. I was sure she also had thought she was alone in the bathroom. But I didn't want to remain silent and further invade her private moment. I swallowed, then began to shuffle around the stall, making obvious noise to alert the CO of my presence, and then walked out to the sink. The CO was a blonde woman about my age, early-thirties. I had seen her escorting a prisoner through the unit earlier in the day. We made eye contact, our puffy eyes betraying each of our outbursts. She asked me if I was alright. I told her I was fine—"hanging in there"—and asked her the same. She replied: "Just never gets easier." I didn't see her the rest of the trip. I don't know if she was upset about something a prisoner said to her, something that had happened to a prisoner, or if it was about the stress of the job and coworkers who didn't want her there.

NP: This story is emblematic of the compartmentalization that I employ as a researcher when I do fieldwork, especially fieldwork in carceral spaces designed to inflict the "pains of imprisonment" on all those who live, work, interact with, and conduct research there. I remember learning to focus in the few minutes I had between interviews—taking a couple minutes to process the incredibly heavy things I experienced and the data I collected in one interview before I put on my proverbial game face and went back to consent the next interview subject.

KC: In that moment in the bathroom, I was trying to just collect myself at first. And then I thought I was sharing the space with another researcher, who could relate from that perspective. When I heard the keys jangle and realized it was a CO, I shifted emotionally. My first thought was of being a prisoner; prisoners told me that the sounds of keys jangling signaled staff coming down the tier in solitary confinement, and, later, even in general population, the sound would "trigger" memories of being in solitary. But then I felt safe, sharing space with another emotional deviant. Ultimately, we were both in the women's bathroom, escaping from the hypermasculine and emotionally repressed world of prison, and we had both been crying.

Running through all the possible scenarios of who the person on the other side of the bathroom stall might be—fellow researcher, imposing officer, or just another woman—Kelsie's encounter illustrates how she, and many of us, had to constantly negotiate our assumptions about other people (and the places we were in) and other people's assumptions about us. In this chapter, we explore how our sympathies align at different points with each other, with prisoners, and with staff, and how these alignments, in turn, position us alternately as competent, warm, caring women, as subservient, naïve, and vulnerable women, or as something in between. In this sense, we implicitly engage with the sociological debate asking "whose side we are on": the liberal side that is often critical of a given institution, or the conservative side that tends to be more supportive of that institution (Becker, 1967; Liebling, 2001; Gaborit, 2019). Rather than firmly position ourselves on either side of the binary, however, we focus more on the personal question of how we navigated the process of "taking sides" with particular subjects or particular stereotypes in a given moment, how we reflected on this process after the fact, and how we think the sides we took affected the data we collected.

By reflecting in this way, we join a growing body of literature attending to reflexivity generally, especially in qualitative prison research (Bosworth et al., 2005; Jefferson & Schmidt, 2019; Jewkes, 2012), and to gendered reflexivity in particular (Golde, 1986; Markowitz, 1999; Mahler & Pessar, 2001; Perrone, 2010), specifically in relation to ethnographic work in prisons (Crewe, 2014; Gaborit, 2019; Kruttschnitt & Gartner, 2004; Padovani et al., 2019; Philipps & Earle, 2010; Piancentini, 2004; Rowe, 2014). We also attend to the challenge of navigating how to present intersecting characteristics of race, gender, and class in qualitative interview and ethnographic work (e.g., Harrington, 2003; Gaborit, 2019; Jenness, 2010). Through the following dialogue we hope to not only contribute to this literature, talking openly about how we experienced our gender and discussed those experiences as a team, but to model the importance of being transparent about the complexity of research decisions and processes, to explore the benefits and challenges of team research, and to reflect on what these insights reveal about the people and institutions we study.

ON METHOD AND FORMATTING

In order to convey our process of identifying, engaging, and analyzing issues as a team, we write much of this piece "in dialogue" with one another, anchoring each section with one author's (indicated by initials) description of a particular research moment when gender was especially salient. Other authors (again indicated by initials) then react: adding details, describing similar situations, or complicating the analysis with other examples of observations or interactions that suggest alternative interpretations. We say "dialogue" in quotes, because we started this piece by talking about our experiences as women in carceral settings and transcribing our comments, but we then went back and edited this dialogue: trimming some examples, expanding on others, and layering in additional comments as we each reflected on what the others had written. As we did this, we organized our dialogue around three central, descriptive themes, which had emerged through this interactive process: how gender opens doors; how we later leveraged assumptions about our gender to maintain access; and how self-protection and over-protection awkwardly coexisted in many of our interactions, especially with staff.

We each went back to original transcripts of interviews we had conducted in order to bring in quotations to illustrate our reflections. Where you see dialogued text in quotation marks, these are exact quotes from transcriptions of recorded interviews.

Through this iterative process, we were able to attend to prison ethnographer Lorna Rhodes's argument that, in the field, "our attention can be *caught*, illuminated by the unexpected and serendipitous" (2015, p. 273). Essentially, each of us identified moments that had caught us individually, and then we explored those moments together. The dialogues capture the process of working in collaborative and team-based projects and highlight the importance of supporting fellow researchers in engaging with emotionally intense and draining research sites (Liebling, 1999; Jewkes, 2012; Reiter, 2014). Moreover, the dialogues reveal how both secondary analytic insights and central research findings emerge over the course of conversations. In the beginning and end of each section, we present a more polished (and traditional) description of the analytic conclusions we reached through our dialogues, explaining how our dialogue produced our interpretations, and connecting these interpretations to existing literature about research in prison.

THEMATIC DIALOGUES

First, we discuss how gender has structured our access, concluding that being a woman in a male prison generally opens both literal doors into institutions and cells, and figurative doors into emotional insights. However, this door-opening access comes with awkward moments and ethical challenges, as when Kelsie both had the opportunity to share a moment of empathy with a female correctional officer in the bathroom, but struggled with how to present herself and how to interpret the officer's response. Second, we discuss how negative stereotypes about gender and femininity, however frustrating and exhausting, can actually be leveraged in various interview settings to build rapport and further access. We explore situations in which we leverage the assumptions others make about us as part of the process of maintaining research access. Third, we explore the pervasive concept of "manipulation" and how the (not wholly unjustified) assumptions around women's susceptibility to men's flirtations in prison settings shapes everything from access to daily interactions to the kinds of data ultimately collected. In this section, we focus on how gender frames interactions not only with prisoners but also with staff, allowing for surprising moments of empathy, again, as in Kelsie's opening narrative, but also generating frustrating moments of staff overprotectiveness; both kinds of moments provide insights into the ways paradigms of masculinity dominate the prison setting. Finally, we each reflect on what we learned in dialogue together, leading into our conclusions about how gender dynamics provide a lens for better understanding both research methods and prison power dynamics.

OPENING DOORS: GENDER AND ACCESS

Prisons, and male prisons specifically, are notoriously hypermasculine settings (Crewe, 2006, 2014; Sabo, 2001; Thurston, 1996)—where any sign of weakness can make one vulnerable to psychological and physical abuse (Crewe, 2014; Newton, 1994; Skykes, 1958). Prisoners may, therefore, be hesitant to disclose personal details with other prisoners or staff—even those directly involved in their well-being, such as mental health providers (Warr ND). Researchers may, in turn, encounter prisoners who are reluctant to provide insights about certain phenomena, or who simply decline to participate altogether (Comfort, 2008, p. 202; Bosworth et al., 2005). However, in our experience, our gender identity as women has served as a brokering factor encouraging prisoners (and staff, as it turns out) to participate and spend the time—often hours—talking with us about topics they purposefully keep hidden from other prisoners, staff, and often even family.

Gabriela's (GG) experiences anchor this section: she reflects on a series of interactions with prisoners that not only made her acutely aware of her identity as a woman in a hypermasculine space but also led to prisoners being willing to talk with her in the first place, and then willing to talk about especially personal details as the conversation progressed. Natalie (NP) and Kelsie (KC), who anchored the introductory dialogue, respond, as well as coauthors Keramet (KR) and Dallas (DA). In this section, Justin (JS), our one male team member, also reflects on how gender shaped his experiences.

GG: Sometimes the sign that gender facilitated access was explicit, such as when an interviewee commented that he was only willing to participate because the interview presented an opportunity to talk with a woman: "I don't interact with people, let alone women, so being able to talk to a pretty woman is ridiculous and cool. I like it. So, thank you for coming here to talk to me. I appreciate it."

NP: I explicitly asked a subject once if he would have done the interview with me if I had been a man. He had already told me, in talking about correctional staff, that he generally did not talk to them. But: "If it's female staff and they want to be cool, I mean, yeah for females, I'll talk to them . . . to me, it's like this—if you're not flirting with me or doing me special favors, then I'm just going to treat you like you're not even there." Then he commented on me specifically and how my presence changed his mind about doing the interview in the first place. He had not intended to do the interview, because it conflicted with a TV show he had planned to watch that day. But then, he changed his mind: "To tell you the truth when I first seen you, I seen you had a real nice smile, and I was just thinking in my mind, I was generally, I was like, man, I've just seen a pretty smile today." Then I asked if he would have done the interview if I had been a man. "No," he said, reiterating "I wasn't going to originally do this interview."

GG: In other cases, for me, the way my gender encouraged prisoners to talk was more subtle. Like when an interviewee said: "What you ladies do, you care about other people, so you sacrifice your time to come into this environment to work, whereas you could probably be somewhere else where it smells better and there's more sunshine."

KC: I think prisoners see us as champions voluntarily trying to improve conditions, in contrast to prison staff, whom they see as adversaries trying to make things worse. However, for me, prisoners ascribed this perceived benevolence to my femaleness, rather than my being a researcher. While as a researcher I was genuinely interested in listening to them, participants experienced that professional interest as caring and kindness, characteristics tied to femininity. This certainly works to my advantage in men's prisons, where emotional withdrawal is survival 101, and I [as a female researcher] could be a safe outlet.

JS: Your point about "adversarial prison staff" makes me think about different expressions of masculinity in prisons, how these expressions clash (e.g., COs vs. prisoners), and how this further complicates the gender dynamics of interviews. I remember an exchange I had with a participant who asked me if I had been to jail before. I told him, "No." He responded that I just looked like someone who had been incarcerated. I was glad he thought I looked like a prisoner, rather than a CO. Had other participants I interviewed thought something similar? Had it positively influenced my rapport building? The majority of my interviews broached sensitive topics, and several participants commented they felt relief after being able to voice to me their struggles and frustrations. Perhaps my gender presentation was read as a more favorable form of masculinity—masculinity closer to that of the prisoners than that of COs—working to my benefit as a researcher, even if some participants might never want to interview with me as a male. At the same time, given the emotional labor required for this sort of research, I also consider how doing this work requires some gender bending. My engagement with masculinity might have helped to establish rapport, but my femininity in the form of caregiving, empathy, and listening is what allowed for participant vulnerability.

KC: In a sense, you accomplished the same work we did, but your gendered, coded "stamp of approval" was: "Have you done time, too?"

KR: Our prisoner subjects frequently tried to find gendered reference points for us as researchers: "pretty woman," "caring" listener, even fellow "prisoner." But, in my experience, prison staff also navigate these reference points with researchers. Not only have staff commented to me about how men in prison are likely to be happy to see me—"a young, attractive woman," or some other lightly complimentary phrase—but male prison staff also appreciate seeing women in the male-dominated spaces of prison and jail. One sergeant, assigned to escort me for the day while I was conducting a survey in a large jail facility, commented that it was a "nice break" to have a "young woman" to escort for the day. And another lieutenant, assigned to escort me at a different facility, noted that if he tried to survey his staff colleagues, he would not expect to get a good response rate, but, he said, looking me up and down: "someone like you will certainly do better," implicitly acknowledging our differences in gender, dress, and approachability.

GG: I think my gender also played a role in opening figurative doors to at least a few subjects' most intimate secrets. I particularly remember an unusual interview where a prisoner labeled as male by the prison system was candid about his sexual orientation, sharing with me his journey toward discovering his (non-hetero)sexual orientation and his struggle to come to terms with this. He subsequently reflected on what he'd told me: "I've said some things to you that I probably wouldn't tell a lot of people because you know it's dangerous to tell people [who I'm attracted to]. Right? That kind of shit gets you beat up in here." As the prisoner in this interview acknowledged, he assumed a risk in disclosing information about his sexual orientation with the *wrong* person. Gender, and the overall assumption that women are more empathetic and sensitive than men, therefore, works in our favor not only to open literal doors and gain access to study such an isolated segment of society, but it also encourages the degree of vulnerability prisoners are willing to expose themselves to in interviews.

DA: I had an experience like this, too, but where the prisoner spoke openly about his depression, self-harm, and past trauma. He hinted that these were not topics he ever spoke about otherwise—something that was reinforced as he frequently paused during moments of notable vulnerability to say, "I don't want to say too much," but then continued his story. Interestingly, he also sprinkled in reminders about his masculinity, to be sure that I didn't interpret his emotional openness as feminine. For example, he explained "I kind of break down, I'm not going to lie. I'm a man, but I break down sometimes." This reflected not only the hypermasculinity of the prison space but also reinforced the way in which my gender created space for him to speak about his emotional struggle.

KC: I remember a similarly vulnerable moment on a completely different topic. I was conducting a one-year follow-up interview with a young man, who told me he hadn't talked to anyone else about his recent stint in solitary confinement since being released to another, general population housing unit. Even though he thought about his time in solitary confinement "every single day," he explained his restraint, not talking about it, as necessary for self-preservation, since any sign of weakness would leave him vulnerable to attack in prison:

"I don't really like telling people what bothers me. Because I feel like they'll exploit it. I try not to give people a weapon to use against me." I asked if he ever tried talking about it with other people he might trust more, like his mother, who he described as "always there" for him. But, he said, he only shared positive updates with her, like classes he was taking. He didn't want his mom "stressing out about it" and feeling burdened. The interview with me, then, was a unique opportunity for him to safely talk about pent-up feelings. "You are the only one [I can talk to]," he said. This prisoner ultimately described feeling physically relieved about having been able to talk with me: "Actually, I feel comfortable right now. . . . It feels good to actually have this conversation and let some things out. . . . Shoulders feel lighter."

NP: On the other hand, I think there are limits to how our identities shape the answers people give, or how much they talk. Thinking back to that interview with the prisoner who decided to do the interview with me because I "had a real nice smile," he repeatedly engaged with my gender identity in answering questions. For instance, he described himself as "a talented singer and lyrist, that he was able make people smile on a bad day, and that he could give and get 'insight and influence that's beneficial.'" He gave an example referencing me: "So let's speak hypothetical—let's say that you told me that you were having problems with your boyfriend. . . . So I would be like, if you know that this is not the man that you want to be faithfully committed to, then you should basically not engage in any further relationship until you know what you want." This was a man who liked talking to women (especially white women, he told me), and I was a white woman with a lot of questions for him. My identity as such didn't change that he felt he had a special talent for giving advice, or that he felt like the CO's sometimes went of their way to threaten to write him up for silly things, like singing a song over the intercom; it just gave him a reason to give very specific examples to demonstrate his point.

Reflecting on our collective experience doing research inside carceral settings, each of us recalls specific instances where our gender identity framed our experience: providing access to data and reframing our understanding of how prisoners and staff alike experience the space of prison. In some cases, our gender opened literal doors for us, encouraging prisoners to participate in interviews. But gender also facilitated rapport building. Subjects implicitly or explicitly associated us with other female caregivers in their lives (or whom they wished were in their lives), like girlfriends or mothers. These associations, in turn, at least to our perceptions, increased the level of detail and depth of interview data we were able to collect.

As qualitative researchers in carceral settings, one of our main objectives was, of course, to document prisoners' experiences and opinions. But, also being women, our femaleness was foremost, and prisoners perceived our authentic interest as emotional caring, rather than as us being skilled at our jobs. Thus, we *as women* cared about *them*, rather than as *researchers* that cared about the *work*. Still, even though our gender identity may have helped to facilitate initial access and ongoing rapport building, this identity is inseparable from our research identity, and our training as qualitative researchers, which also enabled us all, male and female, to conduct lengthy, substantively similar interviews with prisoners and staff.

THE LITTLE LADY TROPE: MANIPULATING GENDER STEREOTYPES

As interviewers, we were frequently aware of the assumptions, preferences, and motivations projected onto us (Gaborit, 2019; Jenness, 2010; Piancentini, 2014; Rowe, 2004). In this sense, gender is something that happens to us. Sometimes the projections are flattering—friendly, caring women with whom prisoners want to engage. Other times, the projections are less flattering—naïve, subservient women whom prisoners and staff want to "school." But these projections, too, can be useful. In this section, we reflect on how we actively leverage our positionality when interviewing staff and prisoners alike to probe for more details. We are experts on prisons, but as interviewers, we seek our subjects' expertise, which can mean that sometimes we have to pretend to know very little when asking questions. Luckily, men are usually more than willing to explain things to women, and having things explained to us is often precisely our goal as interviewers.

Natalie (NP) and Kelsie's (KC) experiences anchor this section, while coauthors Gabriela (GG), Justin (JS), and Keramet (KR) also interject reflections. We reflect on a series of interactions with prisoners in which prisoners assumed that, as women, they lacked both substantive knowledge of traditionally gendered topics, like guns or violence, and the practical authority of traditionally gendered authoritative leadership roles, like manager or professor. Although these assumptions were frustrating, they also repeatedly proved useful in gaining and maintaining access. While femininity might make participants more willing to open up, as we discussed in the previous section, it can also generate gendered assumptions to be negotiated.

NP: The "little lady" trope is a label I assigned in my head to an experience I had again and again conducting interviews with people detained on firearms-related charges about a variety of firearms-related questions. I play into the "little lady" trope when I say, in an interview, *tell me more*, with an imaginary hair twirl. I'm actually quite unexperienced with firearms—in fact the first (and only time) I've handled a firearm was during a research team trip to the local police department's "gun unit." A police escort took our team of female graduate students into the gun unit's storage room to stand in a circle and pass around a selection of weapons from a collection of seized firearms. Kelsie, on the other hand, is not clueless about firearms. On rides home from jail, she would reflect on how often interviewees assumed that she knew nothing about firearms. I remember her describing how this frustrated her as a person, but intrigued her as a researcher.

KC: We learned early on in that study that people obtain illegal guns for many reasons, including for their materialistic value as a status symbol. For the men we interviewed, the size and power of guns was inherently tied to manhood (e.g., only females carry "small, pink, hand bag" pieces). So even though I had some previous experience with firearms going into that study, shooting out in rural Nevada with my family, I recognized right away that it was more beneficial to essentially "play dumb" during interviews and let the male respondents I interviewed be the authority on guns. In practice, this "tell me about your big guns" approach drew out information from them in a non-threatening manner by allowing them to symbolically show off their guns to me, a young woman.

NP: Even now that I'm a professor, I'm often misidentified as a college student or a social worker when I am in the field. But I find that makes my presence in criminal justice spaces natural, or at least unobjectionable. This facilitates my access to spaces and insights, especially from criminal justice practitioners, who might interpret me as a student who wants to "grow up" and work in the field, and is on a field trip to explore her job prospects. In other words, subjects experience me as a blank slate, ready and often in need of their insights as mentors, rather than subjects.

GG: I remember one interview with a prisoner, who hesitated to share details about his prior gang membership with me. He said, "It's a long story . . . you want to know the story about that?" I reminded the prisoner he didn't have to talk about it if he didn't want to, but he did start describing the violent history of the gang he had been affiliated with. Then he paused to make sure I was not going to tell anyone in the prison what he had told me: "I'm no longer a part of that, for me it's over so don't [repeat this] . . . because they'll send me to a different prison." At this point, I reminded him that I did not work for the department of corrections, that I was, in fact, "a student in California." And he seemed reassured: "You're here to do your job. To do your things for your exams ok." Although we had established rapport at this point, my status as a young woman, and a student, seemed "unpowerful" or "unthreatening," and, I suspect, encouraged this subject to share potentially compromising information with me.

JS: I experienced these kinds of stereotypes and assumptions manifesting in ways that were openly oppositional or dismissive of research, too. I am reminded of how COs at one prison put up politically conservative propaganda (signs and news stories) in anticipation of our visit—a gesture of defiance against us as Californian "intruders" in another state prison system. In these cases, it is not so much our naïveté as researchers that is assumed, but our status as outsiders, meddling in matters we cannot possibly understand by virtue of the fact we are not staff.

KR: In that case, I have to think that the gender of our team members—predominantly female, except for you, Justin—also contributed to exaggerating our outsider status.

NP: Now that I have started running my own prison research project as a PI, I have learned to cultivate these research identities as student and outsider and deploy them strategically in order to facilitate access and foster rapport with my subjects. For instance, I tend not to challenge the assumption that my older, male colleague is my boss, because presenting as a subordinate can unlock the Little Lady Trope's advantages for data collection. And this identity, in turn, has also been instrumental for me in decompressing with team members after data collection.

In reflecting on these experiences with gender stereotypes and assumptions about our knowledge, or lack thereof, we all experienced both appreciation—for the access we were able to gain in leveraging stereotypes—and frustration—with assumptions about our lack of competence inherent in these stereotypes. Indeed, femininity produces both capacity and contradiction in carceral spaces. It can inspire assumptions about authority or lack thereof, which, in turn, can be leveraged into making subjects more comfortable opening up. On the other hand, gender can also activate dismissive assumptions about our capacity to navigate and understand the prison environment, because we are both women and outsiders (Gaborit, 2019, p. 13; Perrone, 2010, p. 718).

Reflecting on the capacities and contradictions of being women in all-male carceral spaces also helped us to identify two important benefits of working on team research projects. First, we appreciated the inherently wider variety of potential stereotypes available among multiple team members. Sheer diversity of identity facilitated research access: students leverage their identities to gain access more senior project managers might struggle to gain, while more senior project managers (especially of the older male variety) can lend an element of authority and trustworthiness in hypermasculine contexts.

Second, we appreciated the opportunity to reflect on these varied identities together, as a way to make sense not only of our experiences but of their impacts on our identities. Our dialogue here (as Natalie and Kelsie describe at the beginning of this section) grew out of initial conversations we had traveling to and from carceral settings. As we have all experienced, long days of interviewing in high-security jails or prisons (often sitting on a steel stool, talking to someone through glass) are frequently compounded by long drives to and from homes or hotels, since prisons are often located in geographically out-of-the-way and isolated areas (Gilmore, 2007). These trips, however, provided both critical transitional spaces and important moments of analytic insight. Identifying—and also laughing about—moments where we leveraged the Little Lady Trope, or felt it being applied to us, helped us transition between the identities of researchers collecting data in spaces that deny humanity back to human beings that have born witness to the places and the people that live and work in those spaces. But fellow research team members are more than sounding boards and empathic people experiencing the same secondary trauma of incarceration and hearing stories of abuse, they are also instruments of methodological reflexivity, helping us to explore how our presence is experienced by our subjects and how our identities translate in the field, as we hope our dialogue captures.

SELF-PROTECTION AND OVER-PROTECTION: BEING MANIPULATED

In addition to gendered assumptions about our lack of knowledge and authority, as female researchers working in carceral spaces, we regularly navigated various kinds of paternalistic efforts meant to protect us from ourselves and from others—especially prisoners. Staff assumed that we, as female researchers, were constantly vulnerable to manipulation by prisoners, who might deceive us into thinking they were "good" people, convince us to engage in a romantic relationship with them, or, even, physically harm us. This well-established tendency to think prison outsiders, and especially women, need special protections sometimes creates access challenges (Gaborit, 2019), sometimes is simply annoying or awkward (Jenness, 2010), and other times, of course, opens the door to a better understanding of the power dynamics underlying day-to-day prison interactions (Kahn, 2011).

Dallas (DA) and Melissa's (MB) experiences anchor this section: they reflect on multiple points at which they were warned, often in ways that made them bristle with offense, about the possibility that prisoners would manipulate them into engaging in some surreptitiously romantic way. The assumption that male prisoners would manipulate any woman in their presence, came up so frequently, in so many different contexts, that we began to think more carefully about what role this assumption was playing within the institutional and relational dynamics of the carceral spaces we entered.

DA: Outside of the interview space, prison staff—correctional officers in particular—frequently made comments warning us to be careful of manipulation by our prisoner participants. I am well aware of the common trope of the woman drawn in by a charismatic (but ultimately very bad) male prisoner (e.g., prison pen pals turned wives, "Bundy-philes," and the cast of the sensationalist reality show *Love After Lockup*). But while the warnings I heard again and again may have been warranted in some instances, they also felt weighted with assumptions about my perceived vulnerability as a female outsider. I was being warned not only about prisoners' tendencies toward "goal-oriented behavior" (i.e., manipulation), but also about my own *manipulability* as a woman. The warnings strongly implied that I, or at least other women like me, would be naïve to men's intentions, unable to resist male romantic advances, and desirous of a romantic connection with a "bad boy." In these moments, my role as a professional capable of executing an established task seemed subsumed by the imposition of a romantic or sexual positioning relative to men (in this case, the male prisoner). Staff assumed my eagerness for male attention would blind me to prisoners' nefarious intentions. So they assumed the role of protective guardian, managing me along with the prisoners.

GG: I've had experiences conducting interviews with incarcerated persons where a CO took it upon himself to create a physical barrier between me and the respondent, literally shielding another body from mine. As if sitting across from me might generate some sort of sexual gratification for the prisoner—and thereby endanger me.

JS: I think officers are also protecting a certain sense of self, too, as protectors rather than caretakers. More than once, I heard male COs working in solitary units criticize their job as a form of "housekeeping." For some COs, delivering food, laundry, and toiletries to male prisoners challenges their masculinity, because it is viewed as a more feminine, and for them, a degrading form of work.

MB: I also heard assumptions about female manipulability relayed by prison staff about their *own* female colleagues. A male CO said in an interview: "I don't know why a female would want to work in a male prison anyway, but—[a female relative] used to work here, too, and after I started here, I thought, why would you? I mean, it's a very demeaning place, and I don't know how they ever get used to it. . . . And then there's those . . . a certain faction of them [women] that enjoy the attention." These warnings about manipulation seem to be more about how the female body is positioned within a predominantly male (and hypermasculine) institution than about any specific woman. This CO perceived female staff as either too weak to handle the stress and dehumanization within the prison environment, or too self-absorbed, choosing to work in a prison only for "the attention." This crude binary of female staff as either impressionable or hungry for attention leaves little room for female staff agency or power. Perhaps female staff choose to work in a prison because it provides one of the better paying jobs in the area, or because they have an interest in establishing a career in corrections more broadly. This exchange also made me think of how the female researcher is often viewed and treated in the same light: we are vulnerable to a fault, and it is incumbent on the staff to "protect" us from ourselves. Like the female staff unable to cope with the harshness of the prison setting, the female researcher is somehow less capable than male researchers of engaging in ethical practice and, thus, must be made aware of the threat of prisoner manipulation. Personal experience may have taught some male staff to be wary of female outsider relationships with male prisoners, yet these assumptions, nonetheless, operate from a frame of hypermasculinity: men are objective—women are subjective; men are strong—women are weak; men are the enforcers—women are the protected.

KR: There is an irony to the assumption about women researchers, or women staff, being so exceptionally vulnerable to male prisoners' manipulation and advances, given the proliferation of investigations across the United States into prison officers (usually male), who traffic drugs and phones into prison in order to get financial or other benefits from prisoners they are charged with protecting, or engage in ongoing sexual relationships with female prisoners, or nonconsensual relationships with female colleagues.

JS: An interview I did with a female staff member helped me to see how the same protectiveness that performs a paternalistic function, reinforcing correctional officers' masculinity, also, ironically, excludes female staff experiences of vulnerability and threat. This female staff member was well into a successful twenty-year career, having worked her way up to a supervisory position. Before being promoted, she had worked as a correctional officer in a sex offender treatment unit for over five years. In this unit, she had felt constantly at risk. Distinguishing between what she termed "thugs" and sex offenders, the participant said that "sex offenders are very, very, very, sneaky and calculating in some regards." A looming threat of gendered violence, very different from the victimization that might worry her male colleagues, directly informed this categorization between "thugs" and "sneaks." Of course, we could critique the construction of such a crude binary—which operates similarly to the gender binary—but such a critique would obscure the work the thug-sneak binary does. In the context of immense stress and a constant threat of violence not experienced by male colleagues, this schema might be a response to a lack of professional protection and consideration for female COs. The same paternalism that questions female COs' place in the prison ultimately neglects and excludes the professional challenges they face: female COs must navigate threats and vulnerabilities posed by both prisoners and male officers.

DA: I noticed that staff didn't just worry about female desire for male attention, but also about male desire for female attention. In some instances, staff expressed concern with who received *my* attention, treating female attention as a desirable commodity sought out by male prisoners, and even working to limit prisoner access to this commodity. For example, although I had been conducting interviews one-on-one as part of a team project evaluating reforms to extreme conditions of confinement, male staff insisted that, to interview death row prisoners, I pair up with another interviewer, even when it was logistically burdensome to do so. I insisted I would be fine conducting a death row interview alone, but a male staff member countered that the prisoners would "enjoy it too much." Here, the staff member treated female attention as a commodity that could not only be given to someone but also denied to someone. Rather than reward especially reviled death row prisoners with undivided female attention, the staff member withheld the possibility of that direct attention as an additional form of punishment to the prisoner.

MB: For me, the really challenging part in processing this is how to ultimately balance these very gendered statements about female capacity, or what I can or cannot handle in prison, against some of the realities of the prison setting. I, as woman, am outnumbered, and, because of that, out of place. There is also the reality that some prisoners do indeed experience female attention as a commodity, as this quote highlights: "Sometimes the females, they don't care or [maybe] they just ain't getting enough attention at home. With this female [redacted] . . . I've heard dudes talk about, 'oh, I love you' this and 'love you' that, and she would respond to them . . . to tell you the truth, man, to some extent, I felt a brush of jealousy. It's not about I didn't think it was appropriate because, I mean, at the end of the day, you got females that are cool that will talk to you about whatever. You don't mind the flirtation. But the people that it was happening with was actually dudes I didn't get along with." Though I was not entirely surprised with this prisoner's frustration, as interactions with women were, indeed, in limited supply within the male prison, I was still struck by how he objectified the female staff. He viewed them primarily in terms of their gender—and what that gender could or could not do for him—and not in terms of their occupation or position of authority.

KC: In this moment, I feel myself empathizing with the female staff member. As a researcher, too, my femaleness is foremost, the dominant relational identity.

MB: Juxtaposing the prisoner's comments about the attention-attracting female staff member with the comments of the female staff member Justin described experiencing fear of the thugs and sneaks in the sex offender unit, I can see why someone might question a woman's rationale for working in a prison setting. Women correctional officers face doubt about their fit and capacity to serve from their own colleagues, and an increased likelihood (at least as compared to their male staff counterparts) that they could be put in very uncomfortable situations by prisoners *because* of their gender. However, the assumptions made by staff and prisoners about women are exactly why the prison can so often feel unwelcoming to the female body, and to female authority. These assumptions also made me question how I, as a female researcher, was perceived by staff.

> Researchers are already viewed with an air of suspicion in the carceral setting, as we are there to ask questions, investigate, and understand what most of the public is rarely able to see. Entering the prison as a *female* researcher seems to invite another layer of suspicion or concern, similar to how female staff are perceived. Understanding this dynamic, I tried to be extra vigilant about any displays of sensitivity or empathy for prisoners, as I did not want to give staff any additional reason to doubt my objectivity. In doing so, however, I was left wondering if I then became complicit in reinforcing the gender binaries that help make the prison a hypermasculine place.

Through exploring the pervasive assumptions we encountered from male correctional staff—that we, as female researchers, talking with male prisoners were at risk of inspiring and succumbing to romantic overtures and that other female staff at the prison faced similar risks—we raise a number of questions about how these assumptions structure our research. In some cases, concerns led to changing our standard interview protocol, diverting multiple interviewers to one subject. In other cases, concerns led us to act more restrained and less empathetic than we would have preferred, leaving us wondering if we had conducted the best interviews possible. In still other cases, we were surprised by the similarities between the assumptions made (by prisoners and staff alike) about us as female researchers and the assumptions made about female staff working in the prisons. Assumptions about female desire for male attention seemed to underlie both male staff members' beliefs that female staff only work in prisons "for the attention" and their continual warnings to us as female researchers about potential prisoner manipulation. Likewise, just as prisoners experienced us (female researchers) as caregivers bestowing our time temporarily, so too they described female staff members as commodities to be monitored on an ongoing basis for opportunities to attract attention.

Reflecting on both the gendered assumptions we encountered and our reactions to them helped us to better understand both the gendered power dynamics at play in the prison environment, between staff and among staff, prisoners, and us as researchers, and the way these dynamics shaped our interpretations of our data. Correctional officers, charged with ensuring the safety and protection of both prisoners in their custody and us as outside researchers, asserted and reasserted to us their role as protectors. Statements about both prisoners' manipulative intentions and our own manipulability as female researchers were made in the context of this assertion of the protector role. And male staff members' focus on rules—like where we sat during interviews or how many people participated in interviews—helped to differentiate their enforcement-focused protector roles from more traditionally feminine caretaking roles, like maid or babysitter (roles that certainly have some parallel with correctional officers' daily tasks and obligations). Warnings about manipulation, justified as protective claims, also, at least potentially, undermined prisoners' claims of being uncared for, or worse, abused. In sum, assumptions about gender (and specifically manipulability) were deployed in drawing firm boundaries around institutional capital such as belonging, legitimacy, and capacity. In carceral settings, where borders are constantly reified between inclusion/exclusion, un/worthy, and im/moral, masculinity becomes a site of power and meaning, as well as threat and anxiety. In this way, we could trouble the theme of protectiveness as the work done by male correctional officers to protect a certain sense of self—a self that is knowable, capable, and in control.

LEARNING IN DIALOGUE

Through both conducting intensive qualitative research as members of collaborative research teams, and then subsequently reflecting together on the role of gender in our research, we have each gained insights about how our identities affect our research and how engaging with the relationship between identity and research produces insights about the institutions we study. We hope these insights have made us more precise methodologists, collecting more robust and rigorous data, as well as more insightful theorists, integrating reflexivity and transparency into our analyses.

To conclude this process of analyzing our experiences and our data in dialogue, each of the coauthors on this piece articulated what they learned individually through this process, both as an exercise in identifying what we would do differently in the future (or what others might learn from us) and as a first step toward developing our concluding thoughts. Again, we present this is a dialogue, each reflection responding to and building on the prior ones.

MB: I've learned how our outsider status as academic researchers does not protect us from experiencing the insecurity, doubt, frustration, and anger that often animates social relations within prisons. I'm also increasingly aware of how particular identities become more or less salient in prison as a means of both survival and strategy—whereas in everyday life, I see my ethnicity as most salient; in prison, it is my gender. While I did not necessarily choose for my gender to be dominant, it allowed me to see gender in a way that might have otherwise remained hidden or less focused, and to capitalize on the assumptions made about my gender (whether I agreed with those assumptions or not).

GG: I generally leverage both my gender and ethnicity as a form of relating to participants, whether male or female. Both as a qualitative researcher and due to the nature of my research with marginalized populations, I've learned how to present myself (through dress, makeup, and speech) as non-threatening in order to create a safe space for individuals who typically avoid interacting with any government or formal institutions to feel safe in sharing their experiences with me. In the prison setting, I learned that the parts of me I leverage so well on the outside are often the reasons why staff assume I will be easily manipulated by prisoners. This forced me to reconsider the ways in which I engage with them and use their perceptions about me to better inform the research process.

KC: This work has taught me that carceral settings are intensely performative; staff, prisoners, and outsiders alike are continuously navigating optics in order to function in this extremely antagonistic and hypermasculine space. Rather than fight against that reality, I've learned to anticipate and leverage assumptions about my identity to the benefit of my work.

NP: This team has made me a better interviewer and the process of reflecting on our process and what we think our gender means has clarified its value for me. Keramet, as my mentor, trained me in interviewing as a methodology and her team (this team, our team) has given me the opportunity to do this work in a way that feels safe and supported—which is exactly how we've argued some of our subjects experience us as interviewers. This makes me a better interviewer not only because my subjects will share more with me but because it empowers me as a researcher to show up to interview after interview with that energy. Fieldwork is exhausting, and I tend to slip into my compartmentalized researcher identity to get through the process of experiencing other people's stories and emotions all day, but in the moments between interviews, and at the end of the day, this team was there to support me, process with me, and bring me back to myself so I could show up again authentically for the next interview.

JS: I have been left thinking about all the barriers and constraints that work against reciprocity in carceral settings. Is there ever a moment in which I truly share in unmediated presence with another? The very terms of my interactions are directed by the goals and efficiencies of research. And then there's the physical and institutional barriers of the prison, such as the plane of glass in the visiting booth or the paramilitary organization of correctional officers. Complicating all of this is the symbolic economy of masculinity within prison that devalues intimacy and vulnerability. For me, at least, the weight and exhaustion of doing this work are felt in attempting to truly be with another when the very relationship is structured by estrangement.

KR: Writing this piece together with doctoral and former doctoral students has made me appreciate anew the importance of teamwork, not only in conducting emotionally intensive research but in reflecting on and analyzing the data collected as a result. Working from our dialogue to articulate themes and conclusions has helped me to see more clearly the individual perspectives of each team member and think concretely not just about each individual's methodological skills and strengths in conducting interviews but about each individual's analytical skills and strengths—asking questions, contradicting, reconciling—in a way that I think will make us better collaborative writers on future projects. All of this has made me wish that I had done more earlier not only to create space for but also to document this kind of reflective engagement on team research projects.

CONCLUSION

The carceral setting is frequently resistant to the presence of women. As women researchers in male-dominated prisons, we are forced to navigate volatile assumptions about our abilities, worldviews, and intentions. This produces negotiations between gender and power at crucial stages of research: gaining access, rapport building with key participants, project leadership, and reflexivity. Our dialogue reveals important gendered tensions of doing prison research. As women researchers, our positionality can grant us increased access to prisoners, who frequently see us as benevolent caregivers. With prisoners and staff alike, presumptions about our naïveté and lack of authority can lead to substantively interesting exchanges and rich insights. Both sentiments produce knowledge, revealing how femininity overlaps and blends with epistemology.

We've considered what prisons might tell us about gender and femininity, but what do gender and femininity tell us about prisons? How do we make sense of institutions that punish through opacity, yet open themselves up to the researcher's gaze? Our gendered experiences also reveal substantive insights about punishment. The fact that so many of our subjects craved a caring listener reveals how prisons inherently disrupt relationality, gendered or not. The fact that staff and prisoners typologized each other—as thugs and sneaks, as females in need of attention, as protectors—reveals how the institutional structure of prisons generates irresolvable differences between prisoners and staff, differences we as researchers can only observe and analyze. The gender typologies staff struggle with often reveal alienation from their jobs; the gender typologies prisoners struggle with often reveal dehumanization and civil death. The lens of gender helps to reveal these structural positions and, at least, provides glimpses of moments of empathy that might allow transgressions across power divides, as in the experience Kelsie described at the beginning of this piece.

Through dialogue, reflection, and analysis of our gendered experiences, we see how prisons both produce and restrict gender, and how prison research, in turn, produces its own forms of femininity, which alternately reinforce and resist the gendering of the institution under study. In team research especially, important opportunities exist to resist the gendering we encounter. Space to decompress with each other is critical to identifying moments when we expressed "in-authentic" selves (when, for instance, we accepted assumptions of naïveté or incompetence), reasserting our authentic selves, and rearticulating our honest opinions about gender stereotypes. In sum, we have appreciated this opportunity to reflect on the gender stereotypes we encountered in our prison research and look forward to continued analysis of how and how much to resist gender stereotypes encountered during the course of observations and interviews.

REFERENCES

Becker, H. S. (1967). "Whose side are we on?" *Social Problems*, *14*(3), 239–247.

Bosworth, M., Campbell, D., Demby, B., Ferranti, S. M., & Santos, M. (2005). "Doing prison research: Views from inside." *Qualitative Inquiry*, *11*(2), 249–264.

Comfort, M. L. (2008). *Doing time together: Forging love and family in the shadow of the prison*. Chicago, IL: University of Chicago Press.

Crewe, B. (2006). "Male prisoners' orientations towards female officers in an English prison." *Punishment & Society*, *8*(4), 395–421.

———. (2014). "Not looking hard enough: Masculinity, emotion, and prison research." *Qualitative Inquiry*, *20*(4), 392–403.

Gaborit, L. (2019). "Looking through the prison gate: Access in the field of prison ethnography." *Cadernos pagu*, *55*, e195500. Epub December 2, 2019. http://www.scielo.br/scielo.php?script=sci_arttext&pid=S0104-83332019000100305&lng=en&nrm=iso&tlng=en.

Gilmore, R. (2007). *Golden gulag: Prisons, surplus, crisis, and opposition in globalizing California*. Berkeley, CA: University of California Press.

Golde, P. (Ed.). (1986). *Women in the field: Anthropological experiences* (2nd ed.). Berkeley, CA: University of California Press.

Harrington, B. (2003). "The social psychology of access in ethnographic research." *Journal of Contemporary Ethnography*, *32*(5), 592–625.

Jefferson, A. M., & Schmidt, B. E. (2019). "Concealment and revelation as bureaucratic and ethnographic practice: Lessons from Tunisian prisons." *Critique of Anthropology*, *39*(2), 155–171.

Jenness, V. (2010). "Getting to know 'the girls' in an 'alpha-male community': Notes on fieldwork on transgender inmates in California prisons." In S. Fenstermaker & N. Jones (Eds.), *Sociologists back-stage: Answers to 10 questions about what they do*. New York, NY: Routledge Press.

Jewkes, Y. (2012). "Autoethnography and emotion as intellectual resources: Doing prison research differently." *Qualitative Inquiry*, *18*(1): 63–75.

Kahn, J. (2011). "Safety concerns of a prisoners rights lawyer." *The Daily Journal*, February 4. https://gspp.berkeley.edu/assets/uploads/research/pdf/executive_summary_08142018.pdf.

Kruttschnitt, C., & Gartner, R. (2005). *Marking time in the golden state: Women's imprisonment in California*. New York, NY: Cambridge University Press.

Liebling, A. (1999). "Doing prison research: Breaking the silence." *Theoretical Criminology*, *3*, 147–173.

———. (2001). "Whose side are we on? Theory, practice and allegiances in prisons research." *British Journal of Criminology*, *41*(3), 472–484.

Mahler, S. J., & Pessar, P. R. (2001). "Gendered geographies of power: Analyzing gender across transnational spaces." *Identities*, *7*, 4, 441–459. https://dx.doi.org/10.1080/1070289X.2001.9962675.

Markowitz, F. (1999). "Sexing the anthropologist: Implications for ethnography." In F. Markowitz & M. Ashkenazi (Eds.), *Sex, sexuality, and the anthropologist* (pp. 161–174). Chicago, IL: University of Illinois Press.

Newton, C. (1994). "Gender theory and prison sociology: Using theories of masculinities to interpret the sociology of prisons for men." *The Howard Journal of Criminal Justice*, *33*(3), 193–202.

Padovani, N. C., Hasselberg, I., & Boe, C. S. (2019). "Anthropological engagements with the prison: Gender perspectives." *Cadernos Pagu*, *55*, e195500. Epub December 2, 2019. https://dx.doi.org/10.1590/18094449201900550000.

Perrone, D. (2010). "Gender and sexuality in the field: A female ethnographer's experience researching drug use in dance clubs." *Substance Use & Misuse*, *45*(5), 717–735.

Phillips, C., & Earle, R. (2010). "Reading difference differently? Identity, epistemology and prison ethnography." *The British Journal of Criminology*, *50*(2), 360–378.

Piacentini, L. (2004). "Penal identities in Russian prison colonies." *Punishment & Society*, *6*(2), 131–147.

Ramazanoglu, C., & J. Holland. (2002). *Choices and decisions: Doing a feminist research project*. London: Sage Publications Limited.

Reiter, K. (2014). "Making windows in walls: Strategies for prison research." *Qualitative Inquiry*, *20*(4), 417–428.

Rhodes, L. A. (2015). "Ethnographic imagination in the field of the prison." In D. H. Drake, R. Earle, & J. Sloan (Eds.), *The Palgrave handbook of prison ethnography* (pp. 271–283). London: Palgrave Macmillan.

Rowe, A. (2014). "Situating the self in prison research: Power, identity, and epistemology." *Qualitative Inquiry*, *20*(4), 404–416.

Sabo, D. (2001). "Doing time, doing masculinity: Sports and prison." In Sabo, D., Kupers, T. A., & London, W. (Eds.), *Prison Masculinities* (pp. 61–66). Philadelphia, PA: Temple University Press.

Sykes Gresham, M. (1958). *The society of captives: A study of a maximum security prison*. Princeton, NJ: Princeton University Press.

Thurston, R. (1997). "Are you sitting comfortably? Men's storytelling, masculinities, prison culture and violence." In M. Mac An Ghaill (Ed.), *Understanding Masculinities* (pp. 139–152). Buckingham: Open University Press.

Warr, J. (n.d.). "Quid pro quo in prison research. Guest Blog." *Comparative Penology*. https://www.compen.crim.cam.ac.uk/Blog/blog-pages-full-versions/blog-18-jasonwarr.

Chapter 3

A Woman's Place

Uncovering the Methodological Landmines of Prison Research

Jennifer A. Schlosser

I was a young, twenty-something graduate student, just beginning the data-gathering phase of my dissertation work. I'd successfully defended my proposal to my committee and had written revision after revision of my research plan for the Institutional Review Board (IRB). I was asked to appear before the full board to defend my proposal, which included going to a men's, medium-security prison and conducting interviews with thirty convicted felons to better understand how their experiences in prison related to mandatory classes allegedly designed to help them be successful upon release (Schlosser, 2015).

Walking into the full-board IRB defense meeting I felt prepared. I knew my methodology, and I knew that I had the unspoken support of all the female prison researchers who'd come before me. I'd immersed myself in their articles, pored over their findings, read between the lines of their published works, and found the secret messages they left there; painting the picture of the methodological challenges they'd faced as women doing research in prison.

As I entered the room, I noticed that the lights were dimmed. Twenty or so faculty and professionals from across all colleges at my Research I university sat at conference tables, arranged in a circle. I was directed to a swivel chair in the center of the circle. As I sat, I realized that the arrangement of the room made it impossible for me to see everyone at once; my back was always to one group or another, depending on where my chair was facing. It took years before I realized that this arrangement was intentional.

The questions came quickly and relentlessly. I couldn't see who was speaking to me unless I swiveled my chair to face them. They asked what

I would do if an inmate told me something insidious. They asked what I would do if my notes were subpoenaed and I had to testify in court on what I had been told. I hadn't considered the possibility of a subpoena, but I promised that I would go to jail if I had to in order to protect the confidentiality of my participants. I insisted that if I were held in contempt of court that I would gladly uphold my promise to protect their voices at all costs and refuse to surrender my field notes. They asked what I would do if an inmate sued the university because my questions had triggered them and caused psychological damage. I insisted that I would explain my consent forms fully and remind my participants that their participation was voluntary (as voluntary as anything is in prison). They said that in order to protect the university, they were denying my request to tape-record my interviews (this is not uncommon, see Byrne, 2005; Reiter, 2014). What if the tapes got out? Handwritten notes were easier to destroy.

I walked out of the room, blinking in the bright lights of the hallway after an hour and half of fielding questions from people I couldn't see. I stepped into the elevator victorious, confident that I had passed their test . . . and immediately burst into tears. But that test, passing the gauntlet thrown by the IRB at my university, was *nothing* compared to the one I was about to face.

LESSONS BEFORE THE FIELD

In this chapter, I aim to systematically address several of the unforeseen challenges I experienced as a young scholar doing prison research for the first time and the lessons I have learned as a result. Some of the challenges I experienced (and discuss in this chapter) were related to my gender as a woman as I experienced relentless sexual harassment in the field, some were related to my youth, and some were related to my lack of experience. My career doing research in prisons has spanned the past fifteen years across five different states and numerous correctional institutions. I am, however, still surprised by the new challenges and "methodological landmines" that arise while doing this type of work. In my 2008 *Qualitative Inquiry* article, I used the term "methodological landmines" to describe the moments in qualitative prison research that arise unexpectedly. These landmines have the ability to affect one's data, to send the project in an entirely new direction, or to stop it in its tracks before it even begins (Liebling, 1999; Jewkes, 2011). Likewise, encountering certain methodological landmines can also affect how the researcher herself responds to her participants and, as I explain later in the chapter, how the research field responds to her. In an attempt to retrospectively identify some of these landmines, I use a reflexive analysis of my experiences in prison through storytelling to illustrate the unexpected moments in my own research that surprised me, caught me off guard, affected my data, and in some cases, forever changed me.

Qualitative prison research is different from other types of criminological research, in that it is not common nor easily done (Patenaude, 2004; Reiter, 2014). Doing work in prison requires a mix of both openness and restraint; it compels the researcher to be both emotional and reserved while seeming available, yet also remaining distant (Wincup, 2000). Prison research is one of contradictions. There is certainly no singular way to conduct qualitative research in carceral spaces. Each interview is different—even if a researcher asks the same question to the same participant, the moment has changed, and thus, so have the data. For this reason, it is difficult for IRBs to understand (nay, approve) qualitative research in prisons because, by their nature, they tend to favor quantitative methods (Patenaude, 2004; Reiter, 2014). In fact, as Bosk and De Vries (2004) note on using ethnographic methods in prison:

> For some types of social science research—the laboratory experiment, the fixed-item survey, the longitudinal panel study—the relationship of researcher and subject closely tracks the biomedical model that informs IRB procedures: a highly structured, objective relationship. But ethnographic research fits this model poorly. For ethnographers, the primary data-gathering tool consists of the relationships that we forge with those whose lifeworld we are trying to understand. (p. 252–253)

Understanding that challenges will present themselves before one even enters the prison research field or can even begin to think of collecting any data is an essential first step to being able to take those challenges head-on. My first experience with a Research I IRB, while harrowing, was also rich in lessons. I know now that IRBs are ill-equipped (in many cases) to adequately evaluate the type of research that qualitative prison investigators propose. In my case, for instance, there was no one serving on the university's IRB with any prior experience in prison research. There was no outside community member familiar with criminal justice (there should have been), nor was there a sociologist on the IRB (again, there should have been). The IRB members on the board I stood before were from the Business School, the Nursing School, the Psychology Department, the Biology Department, the Medical School, and the School of Agriculture. Professionals and experts who conduct experimental research in a laboratory, while certainly highly qualified experts in their own fields, are not equipped to evaluate research on human subjects that will require the amount of flexibility and adaptability that does prison work. Therefore, prison researchers must prepare themselves for having to answer questions that are, at least in the short-term, unanswerable. The primary lesson I learned from my experiences with IRBs over the years is that while it is noble to attempt to have answers to all of their questions prepared beforehand, being able to think quickly and creatively is essential to being successful. When I promised that I would be willing to be held in contempt of court and go to jail if my research notes were subpoenaed, I meant it; but I also hadn't had time to think through the implications of that promise. Below, I list a several questions new prison researchers might consider before seeking research approval from an IRB:

Do I need to record my interviews, or can I take notes by hand? How will this affect the data I receive? How will it affect my rapport with participants?

Where will I keep my recordings or notes? In a lockbox? On a password protected computer?

Would I be willing to turn over my research notes if compelled by a legal order?

If I am not willing to turn over my research notes, can I accept the consequences that may follow?

What is the minimum amount of personally identifying information I can collect from my participants while protecting their anonymity and without compromising my research goal?

When composing my written consent forms, at what reading level should they be written to ensure that all of my participants can understand them considering that some may not have completed high school?

What if I encounter a participant who doesn't speak English? Can I afford to hire a translator?

What will I do if a participant tells me they are planning to harm themselves, someone else, or that they are being harmed in prison?

Is there an administrator I trust at the prison? Do I have easy access to their contact information? How much do I trust this person?

What if someone confesses committing a crime that they have not been charged with? What will I do with that information? What is my moral and ethical obligation if I receive such information?

The IRB requires that I give my name and contact information to my participants if they have questions after the interview. How comfortable am I in giving that information?

What will I do if a participant becomes angry, or agitated?

What will I do if a participant makes sexual advances toward me?

What is my plan for assigning pseudonyms?

How much personal information am I willing to divulge in the interest of building rapport?

How might my gender, race, or age affect the interview dynamic?

How can I best show my participants respect and humanity while asking them to answer difficult, personal questions?

How do I explain that participation is optional, when nothing in prison is truly voluntary?
What kind of shoes should I wear?

These and many other questions may arise in the course of doing prison research. Being prepared to answer them beforehand will save valuable time and resources, particularly for first-time prison researchers.

As much as the IRB is a gatekeeper to doing research, it is also important to consider that the state Departments of Correction or the Federal Bureau of Prisons (in the United States), along with the director of research and the specific prison warden, are also capable of granting or denying access to the field site. My best advice here is to be persistent—sometimes, to the point of becoming an annoyance. If you are new to prison research, it is important to begin contacting representatives of the relevant agencies you wish to access early and often. It is often not in the best interests of the DOC or the prison for researchers to breach their barriers and come "poking around." Many may see it as an unnecessary disruption to their precariously balanced power structure, and some may even see a researcher as an intruder with nefarious intent. Understand that, as an academic, a scholar, and a member of a university, ties to higher education may actually become a barrier in themselves both to the gatekeepers of the institution and to the participants. As Reiter (2014) reminds us, "Prison administrators not only resist public accountability by keeping civilians out, they also resist public accountability by keeping information in" (p. 421).

After receiving IRB approval to conduct my dissertation research at a state prison near my university where I had gained access, I was given a list of rules to follow once I got there, and on each visit. My research for this project involved interviews with thirty men, incarcerated for various offenses, all of whom were set to be released within a year to six-months (see Schlosser, 2015). Before I arrived for my first set of interviews, my contact at the prison sent me this list:

No open-toe shoes
Wear shoes you can easily run in
No weapons
No tight clothing
No tops exposing your midriff
No tank-tops or shirts exposing your arms
Wear socks
Do not wear your hair in a ponytail
Do not wear jewelry
No shorts

No electronic devices
No food or drink
Wear little or no makeup/ perfume
You will be accompanied by a staff member at all times
You must ask to be escorted to the bathroom
You will carry an alarm on you at all times
Do not speak to any inmate unless you are interviewing them

Several of the rules I was sent seemed obvious—clearly I wouldn't bring any weapons or expose my midriff—but others were less clear. I learned that wearing my long hair in a ponytail was against the rules because, according to one officer, "a ponytail is an invitation to be yanked to the ground." I quickly learned how to twist my hair into a tight bun. Before receiving these rules I had never thought about whether the amount of makeup I wore was excessive, nor had I ever considered which of the pairs of professional shoes I owned would be the easiest to run in, should I need to flee on foot. Over the years and across the many correctional institutions I've visited, similar rules have applied. Some are standard—no shorts, no jewelry, no flip-flops—but others, I now know, were very specific to me: a young, woman. Would a male doctoral candidate have been given the same list? Would a man have been told not to wear perfume, or to be sure his clothing wasn't too tight? I doubt that he would. So, what did this list of rules, tailored by my prison contact specifically to me, say about how they viewed my presence there? I soon found out that not only was there no way I could have prepared myself for what I experienced, but there was also no way out of it once I was in.

LESSONS FROM THE FIELD

The story I am about to tell I have uttered countless times aloud, both to small audiences (individual family and friends; numerous criminology and corrections classes I've taught over the years) and to large audiences—filled auditoriums and lecture halls. However, this is the first time I've ever written it down. It is perhaps best introduced with the following, highly understated point: "Being in a fieldwork setting and gaining initial access to a site is no guarantee of acceptance much less trust or even popularity" (Samspson & Thomas, 2003, p. 174).

It was summer, and I had successfully defended my dissertation proposal to my doctoral committee, passed the gauntlet of the IRB, revised my methods dozens of times, constructed (and reconstructed) my consent forms, prepared my interview instrument, and practiced my interviewing skills with my advisors. While it was not the first time I'd ever been to a prison (the one and only other time being a year earlier when I was a Teaching Assistant in a Criminology class), it was the first time I'd ever entered one alone, as the principle investigator. I was twenty-three years old. I'd read and reread the list of rules given to me by my prison contact—I'd taken great pains to choose the perfect outfit—a button-up, collared shirt under a cardigan, under a sweater (I was foolishly attempting to hide the fact that I was a woman), not tight slacks, the least attractive most "easily runnable" shoes I owned, tinted moisturizer only (no mascara, no lipstick), glasses that I didn't really need to be able to see, and my long hair, tightly wound atop my head and secured with a plastic clip. I took a selfie and was very pleased.

It's worth noting at this point that I was the only graduate student in my academic department doing (or who had, in recent memory, ever done) prison research. My advisors, while experts in criminology, had not conducted interviews in prison themselves, so I was as green as they came. Nevertheless, I'd read (a lot) of research, I'd spoken at length with my prison contact, and I felt prepared. I'd thought a lot about what types of feedback I'd receive walking into a prison, as I was. I anticipated being catcalled—I wasn't *that* naïve—I assumed it came with the territory, that a twenty-three-year-old white woman coming into a prison full of men wouldn't realistically be able to remain invisible. I anticipated the looks, the leers, the comments, the names I'd be called as I walked past, the whistles. I convinced myself that I would be objectified and gawked at, that it would be bad—and, it was.

The first day I entered the prison I was met at the front door by an armed correctional officer. This was not the person I'd been in contact with for several months prior, it was someone I'd never met before. I put out my hand to shake his—I looked him in the eye (as my dad had always taught me) and squeezed hard (not too hard), attempting a firm but friendly grip. He took my hand and immediately his fingers went slack. His hand turned slightly to the side and he ended up only pinching my fingertips with his, giving my hand one weak pump before he dropped it. It was the type of handshake that every woman has encountered at some point in her life—the one that says: "We are not equals."

I processed in, received a "visitor" badge, and a small alarm that I was informed would emit a high-pitched noise if I pulled the pin. I was instructed to keep the alarm on me at all times and, should I need help, to activate it and dozens of guards would coming running to my rescue. I clutched it tightly, next to my non-spiral bound notebook and pen—the only other things I was allowed to take with me. I was glad that the badge they gave me only said "visitor" and wasn't an actual nametag because I'd thought long and hard about whether I should give my real (or full name) out to my participants. After lengthy discussions with my advisor, analyzing the risk of providing my full name and office location to prison inmates who were about to be released, we decided that I would only give my first name and the general contact information of the IRB on the consent forms. I felt good about that decision and had even practiced introducing myself with my first name only, as I would when I met my participants.

The correctional officer had a gun holstered on his side next to a large club (the kind I thought only existed in movies). He wore a crisp, white uniform and sported a lavish mustache. He was in his mid-fifties, he was white with strawberry blond hair, and he was stoic. He barely spoke to me at all as he led me out of the processing area, through the metal detector, and out into the main prison yard. He told me I'd be "taking over" his office for my interviews, and he didn't seem happy about it. I thanked him and assured him that I would take up as little space as possible and try not to disrupt his day more than was necessary. I was deferential and polite—I realize now that I wanted him to like me because if he liked me, he might be able to make things easier for me.

The officer and I passed through two heavy double doors and walked outside, into the bright, hot sun of the rural Midwest in late June. I immediately regretted the triple-layer cardigan/ sweater combination I'd chosen. Behind us was the front building with the intake desk, waiting room, and visitor area. To our left, he told me, was the "crazy building—the one where they keep the druggies and the nut jobs when they can't be in gen pop." To our right was building that held the warden's office and other administrative areas. Straight ahead, about a football field's length away, was the building where we were going—the Transitional Housing Unit. This building was where the prisoners lived—the ones who were transitioning out of the prison back into society in a couple of months. I hoped it was air conditioned.

As we walked the length of yard between the intake building and the THU, groups of inmates also walked "freely." Some were in orange jumpsuits, some in faded khaki, all wore socks and slip-on sandals. The prison was medium-security so no one was walking around in shackles or dragging chains behind them. It was recreation time in the yard for one of the units. As we closed the distance to our destination, we approached a basketball court. A dozen or so inmates in brown jumpsuits were playing a game, under the watchful supervision of four correctional officers posted up on the retaining wall on one side of the court. The four officers stood together, casually leaning against the wall, arms crossed in front of them. As we approached, I was surprised when my escort didn't begin walking around the game, but instead, became quickly horrified as he led me directly *into* the basketball court. The game stopped (it had to), the inmates dispersed, all backing away like they were afraid they'd catch something from me. One of the guards on the wall stood up a little straighter. "This is Jennifer Schlosser" said my escort, "she's a *doctor* at the university" (I wasn't). He'd just given out my full name. My heart was pounding and sweat poured off my face. "Well, good luck, *doctor*," said the other officer, emphasizing the word. The other officers chuckled. We walked on, toward the THU. The game resumed behind us, but I didn't look back.

And, so it was—nearly every day I was at prison, three days a week for two months, the same officer met me at the intake gate, we walked up to the basketball court, and it started. Everything I feared and anticipated happened. The catcalls, the leers, the eyes moving over my body, hands on chins, nodding their approval. Their tongues licked their lips, their hands drifted toward their crotches, they called me "baby" and "girl." I was asked if I had a boyfriend, I was asked for my number, I was asked if I needed a date. Most days, at the exact time of this standing basketball game, I was paraded through the court. And, every single time I was publicly humiliated—by the guards.

Never, in all the times I was walked through that game, did an inmate utter a single word to me. They stopped playing, dropped their eyes, and let me pass. And every time it was the same with the guards, which surprised me, because I thought eventually they'd get tired of it—those men with guns humiliating me. When I tell this story in talks at universities and in my classes, people are horrified and, in fact, some question me about whether it really happened the way I interpreted it (I assure them that it did, I've lived with the memory for over a decade). Some people wonder aloud if I'm possibly exaggerating how bad it was (I wish). I'm asked why I didn't report them. Why didn't I tell my contact at the prison, or even the warden, that these guards were abusing me? I've even had wardens at other prisons tell me that if they found out their officers were doing something like that, they'd fire them on the spot. So, why didn't I say anything? Why didn't I put a stop to it?

I have asked myself these questions many times as well and, as McCorkel and Myers (2003) note, it is important to self-interrogate in this way because "strong objectivity must coincide with strong reflexivity and this requires the researcher to subject herself to the same level of scrutiny as she directs to her respondents" (p. 205). So, my answer is that of a researcher: it was never about me. The catcalls, the laughter, the name-calling—none of it was for me. I was not the audience the guards were performing for—I was not even the intended target of the abuse, I was a convenient tool they found useful in asserting their power and authority over the convicts. It is my strong belief that if any inmate had joined in by making a crude gesture or a lewd remark, the guards would have had him on the ground in seconds. I was simply an ancillary figure in this event, not even a main player. I know this now, after over a decade of thinking about it, analyzing it, questioning myself, wondering if I should have done something differently. Now, though, I've forgiven myself for any guilt I felt in allowing it to happen to me (and to the inmates). I've stopped beating myself up over the thought that because I didn't say something, the guards may have been allowed to continue to abuse their power in even worse ways, behind closed doors because, after all, if this is how they acted in front of an outsider, what did they do when I wasn't around? I've had to let go of that and forgive myself for just wanting to get it over with because I wanted to graduate. Looking back, I still believe I made the right choice for myself at the time. I can't know what would have happened if I had used my voice to stop the officers—maybe they would have been fired or, maybe they would have been provoked into amplifying their tactics against the inmates later, when no one was looking.

I tell this story now not to emphasize how difficult prison research is for young women (though it is), but rather to illustrate the nuances, layers, and complexity of the prison field site. Because so many women prison researchers have stories to tell about their time in the field, it is essential that we heed the call of engaging in critical self-reflection, reflexive self-analysis, and autoethnographic narrativity. Lumsden and Winter (2014) put forth this call:

> Criminologists must openly acknowledge, reflect upon, and share their experiences of research in various settings, crucially highlighting instances where internal or external power dynamics are at play, and problematizing such relations and knowledge production. It is crucial that as criminologists we reflect upon the research we do, whom we do it for, and to what purpose it will be used. (p. 3–4)

Likewise, in their 2017 article on sexual harassment in the field, Hanson and Richards discussed the importance of critical self-reflection. The authors identified three "fixations" that become prominent, particularly for women researchers, in the development of ethnographic knowledge. Through interviews with (mostly) women ethnographers, the authors found that "solitude," "danger," and "intimacy" held central places in the way the researchers experienced not only the filed but also academic standards of doing "good" ethnography. In my case, Hanson and Richards's concept of "solitude" best explains what I experienced. Like many of their interviewees, I also felt isolated and alone as a woman in a male-dominated space believing that if I asked for help or collaboration, it would weaken my status and, subsequently, my research. I believed that enduring the sexual harassment in solitude was necessary to maintaining the integrity of my study. Hanson and Richards (2017), however, argue that we must interrogate the epistemological underpinnings of ethnographic knowledge that lead many women researchers to stay silent about sexual harassment experienced in the field. So, it is not simply enough to jump through all the hoops, "lean in," or "persist" as women researchers. We must also critically reflect on the impact of the circumstances and contexts of our investigative environments as well as how the structure of academic "standards" in academic research contributes to our silence and further victimization.

LESSONS AFTER THE FIELD: CONCLUDING REMARKS

I mentioned earlier in this chapter that it wasn't until well after I had left the research field that I recognized the correctional officers' responses to my presence were not about me, but rather, about displaying their power to the inmates in their charge. The literature in social psychology on the group dynamics of prison guards supports this point:

> Under conditions of stress or "external danger" created by threats to the *status quo*, the subcultural values and group solidarity around these anti-inmate and anti-administration values are capable of mobilization. Guards emerge as a group in response to threats from the outside, while they act as isolated individuals under normal circumstances. (Lombardo, 1985, pp. 87–88)

In this case, I was the threat from the outside. I wasn't someone's girlfriend on visiting day, and I wasn't a fellow officer who happened to be female (see Farnworth, 1992; Crew, 2006). I had entered the prison as an outsider and would remain an outsider. I disrupted their daily routines, upset the power structure, and threatened the officers' authority. But, if a twenty-three-year-old, five-foot-two-inch white woman could walk into a prison and undo all the hard work they had accomplished to make the prison theirs, it begs the question: just how solid and deeply entrenched was that culture to begin with? If their authority could be so easily threatened to the point where the officers were willing to repeatedly publicly humiliate and sexually harass an outsider, it's worth taking a closer look at how the context of our field sites impacts our studies and our participants.

The great prison researcher Lois Presser (2005) argued that if we are going to actively participate in reflexive feminist methodologies, we cannot simply interrogate the narratives of our participants, we must also dissect how both the interview setting and ourselves as investigators, reproduce power, agency, and serve to alter the situated stories we are told. In my case, the experiences I encountered leading up to my actual interviews with offenders—from the power asserted in the IRB hearing, to the rules I received before my first prison visit, to the sexual harassment I experienced at the hands of the guards almost daily—tell the *story* of my research. But, the story of my research is, because of who I am, inherently gendered. To ignore the effects that these events had on my ability to conduct good interviews, or to "objectively" analyze data is to do a disservice to the research as a whole. For Presser (2005),

> If methods are to cohere with critical theories of power, we must integrate research-situated dynamics into data analysis. This sort of strong reflexivity will better illuminate how gender is "continually being forged, contested, reworked and reaffirmed" (Jackson, 1991, p. 210) (p. 2087).

While Presser is mostly discussing our role as investigators in the interview setting and in the construction of the narratives we help create with our participants, her call can also be applied to our critical self-evaluations of how our presence disrupts the larger cultural habitus of the prison (Schlosser, 2013). Using critical theory to examine how our mere existence in prison affects the overall social structure of relationships, roles, and behaviors of actors will allow us to get closer to understanding the lived experiences of the actors there. In this way, we can engage in what Jeff Ferrell (1997) called *criminological verstehen*: an examination of how our total immersion in a criminological field not only impacts the field itself, but also how our lived experiences and emotions as researchers in that space can help us better understand, empathetically, the lived realities of the actors.

Yet, it is not enough to consider gender alone as the "great catalyst" that allows for these types of critical methodologies to emerge. To improve ourselves as researchers—to more fully entrench ourselves in the messy work of critically analyzing our own roles in the research field and how our presence affects the habitus of that research field—we must require ourselves to engage in *intersectional* reflexivity (Hunting, 2014). What is meant by that is the following: race, age, social class, education, titles, religion, culture, sexuality, whether we are parents, accents, marital status, and of course, gender all *matter* in the field (Couture et al., 2012). But those intersecting identities don't just matter for us, the researcher, they matter for our participants and, perhaps most importantly, for the field itself. The spaces we enter—prisons, jails, detention centers, parole offices, courtrooms, treatment centers, and halfway houses—these spaces exist because of (and sometimes in spite of) their organizational identities; the norms and cultures that create the habitus of the space. So, our identities as humans-who-are-also-researchers can and do impact the organizational identities of the spaces we study.

For Gaborit (2019), one way we can view the intersection of our various identities and how they impact the organizational balance of the field site is to consider how our positionality may open up certain *vantage points*. Gaborit notes:

> Simultaneously, as I study "the field" it becomes part of my own trajectory, which when visible to others affects the way I am seen but also the way I see my subjective experience (Holzkamp, 2013). I saw the field through a specific lens colored by the stories I previously heard from former prisoners and prison staff. (2019, p. 12)

Gaborit argues that because of (rather than in spite of) her presence as a white woman researching imprisonment in Myanmar, she was offered certain vantage points from which she could observe elements of the field that others might not. By seeing the research field, with all of its layered complexities as a factor that impacts our identities and, thus, our research, we can better position ourselves to take advantage of our unique positions. For instance, my presence as a young, white, single, female graduate student with a Midwestern accent, long hair and petite stature *mattered* when I walked into the full-board IRB hearing and it especially mattered every time I walked into the prison. It disrupted the everyday routines and silent understandings that allowed that particular prison to operate the way that it did. Now, however, when I walk into a prison as a not-so-young, married, child-free, white woman with a PhD and fifteen years of prison experience under her belt, my presence still disrupts, but it does so in a different way. For that reason, researchers are never finished engaging in critical self-analysis—it will be an ongoing challenge, but it is an important one to undertake, each and every time we enter the research field.

I contend that we cannot begin to understand our participants if we do not first understand the prison where they live. To understand the prison, then, we must accept that every institution is different and reject sweeping generalizations made by some that attempt to examine or explain prison "as a whole." Further, we must walk in with our eyes open, ready to accept and understand that our momentary, situated, subjective existence in the prison *will* change it. The changes may be subtle, or (as in my case) severe, but the changes we enact there should be included in our analyses *as data*. As criminologists, sociologists who study prison, and qualitative researchers, we should actively view the research field itself as another source of data. In this way, the myth of researcher total objectivity can be exposed, and we can truly undertake the hard work of critical self-analysis and reflexivity. Only when we can view *ourselves* as "methodological landmines" in our own research journeys will we be able to truly begin the hard work of listening, observing, and learning.

REFERENCES

Bosk, C. L., & De Vries, R. G. (2004). "Bureaucracies of mass deception: Institutional review boards and the ethics of ethnographic research." *The Annals of the American Academy of Political and Social Science*, *595*(1), 249–263.

Byrne, M. W. (2005). "Conducting research as a visiting scientist in a women's prison." *Journal of Professional Nursing*, *21*(4), 223–230.

Couture, A. L., Zaidi, A. U., & Maticka-Tyndale, E. (2012). "Reflexive accounts: An intersectional approach to exploring the fluidity of insider/outsider status and the researchers' impact on culturally sensitive post-positivist qualitative research." *Qualitative Sociology Review*, *8*(1), 86–105.

Crewe, B. (2006). "Male prisoners' orientations towards female officers in an English prison." *Punishment & Society*, *8*(4), 395–421.

Farnworth, L. (1992). "Women doing a man's job: Female prison officers working in a male prison." *Australian & New Zealand Journal of Criminology*, *25*(3), 278–296.

Ferrell, J. (1997). "Criminological verstehen: Inside the immediacy of crime." *Justice Quarterly*, *14*(1), 3–23.

Gaborit, L. S. (2019). "Looking through the prison gate: Access in the field of ethnography." *Cadernos Pagu*, *55*, e195505. Epub December 2, 2019. https://doi.org/10.1590/18094449201900550005.

Hanson, R., & Richards, P. (2017). "Sexual harassment and the construction of ethnographic knowledge." *Sociological Forum*, *32*(3), 587–609.

Hunting, G. (2014). *Intersectionality-informed qualitative research: A primer.* Vancouver, BC: The Institute for Intersectionality Research & Policy, SFU. ISBN: 978-0-86491-357-9.

Jewkes, Y. (2011). "Autoethnography and emotion as intellectual resources: Doing prison research differently." *Qualitative Inquiry*, *18*(1), 63–75.

Liebling, A. (1999). "Doing research in prison: Breaking the silence." *Theoretical Criminology*, *13*(2), 147–173.

Lombardo, L. X. (1985). "Group dynamics and the prison guard subculture: Is the subculture an impediment to helping inmates?" *International Journal of Offender Therapy and Comparative Criminology*, *29*(1), 79–90.

Lumsden, K., & Winter, A. (2014). *Reflexivity in criminological research: Experiences with the powerful and the powerless*. Basingstoke: Palgrave MacMillan.

McCorkel, J., & Myers, K. (2003). "What difference does difference make? Position and privilege in the field." *Qualitative Sociology*, *26*(2), 199–231.

Patenaude, A. L. (2004). "No promises, but I'm willing to listen and tell what I hear: Conducting qualitative research among prison inmates and staff." *The Prison Journal*, *84*(4), 69S–91S.

Presser, L. (2005). "Negotiating power and narrative in research: Implications for feminist methodology." *Signs*, *30*(4), 2067–2090.

Reiter, K. (2014). "Making windows in walls: Strategies for prison research." *Qualitative Inquiry*, *20*(4), 417–428.

Sampson, H., & Thomas, M. (2003). "Lone researchers at sea: Gender risk and responsibility." *Qualitative Research*, *3*(2), 165–189.

Schlosser, J. A. (2008). "Issues in interviewing inmates: Navitaging the methodological landmines of prison research." *Qualitative Inquiry*, *14*(8), 1500–1525.

Schlosser, J. A. (2013). "Bourdieu and Foucault: A conceptual integration toward an empirical sociology of prisons." *Critical Criminology*, *21*(1), 31–46.

Schlosser, J. A. (2015). *Inmates' narratives and discursive discipline in prison: Rewriting personal histories through cognitive behavioral programs*. Abindgon, Oxon: Routledge.

Wincup, E. (2000). "Feminist research with women awaiting trial: The effects on participants in the qualitative research process." In K. Gilbert (Ed.), *The emotional nature of qualitative research* (pp. 17–33). London: CRC Press.

Part II

LOCATING OURSELVES

STORIES OF BELONGING

Chapter 4

Cloaked in Liminality

Negotiating Roles, Identity, and Emotional Labor within and between Prison Walls and Academia

Shenique Thomas-Davis

INTRODUCTION

I wasn't supposed to be there. In this carceral, controlled space, at least, not on this side of the wall or in this context. Not in a position where limited authority and domination could be exercised. Modest privilege and power allowed for the preservation of most of my rights. I was on the side of the wall where those in uniform were forced to *see* me despite my social status reflecting similarly to those who were confined and denied their "perceptual salience" (Breyer, 2015). Typically, there were few circumstances in which a woman fitting my characteristics visited prisons: contact/connect with a loved one or as a state employee. To note, the prison administrator offered up the employment opportunity as a corrections officer on multiple occasions. Given these two scenarios, the power dynamic of the advantaged and disadvantaged was clear. However, my role, as a researcher, was primed with ambiguity. Agents of the criminal justice system were unable to completely control my body and behavior or shape my thoughts. I existed behind the wall, replete with complexity, visible, under constant surveillance, as a Black woman, a scholar living in academic liminality, who sought to amplify the voices and range of experiences of the mostly Black and brown men incarcerated at a prison in the Northeastern region of the United States. However, I existed beyond the wall, invisible, as a Black woman, navigating and negotiating multiple identities, marginality, and cultural frames of reference (Diggs et al., 2009; Stanley, 2006; Viernes-Turner, 2002).

The yearning to climb the ivory tower and conduct prison research while cloaked in a mask of colonized conformity was rooted in the tradition of

Black women's activism and resistance—group survival and institutional transformation (Collins, 2000). There is much to be considered in the discussion on the uniquely gendered experiences of women, specifically through the lens of Black women, who conduct research in the carceral setting. Neglecting to call attention to the distinct lived experiences of women active in this work threatens the collective leveraging of women's power and voice in the discipline (Lorde, 1984).

Intersectionality presents a framework to understand and analyze "the complexity in the world, in people, and in human experience" (Collins & Bilge, 2016, p. 135). Audre Lorde (1984, p. 120) acutely describes her own reckoning when "encouraged to pluck out some one aspect" of her full self. She remarks,

> But this is a destructive and fragmenting way to live. My fullest concentration of energy is available to me only when I integrate all the parts of who I am, openly, allowing power from particular sources of my living to flow back and forth freely through all my different selves, without the restrictions of externally imposed definition. Only then can I bring myself and my energies as a whole to the service of those struggles which I embrace as part of my living.

Black women often feel compelled to deny or censor their "full selves" as each aspect of self is entangled and necessary to present the meaningful whole. Anchoring work with an intersectional lens provides an opportunity to holistically examine the lived experiences of Black women using an asset-based model opposed to a fragmented or deficit structure. Not surprisingly, these "experiences of intersectionality have not been common subject for anthropologists of any cultural experience to explore" (Haldeman, 2009, p. 210). Historically, scholars of color have been excluded from participation in these academic spaces and the complementary rituals. Instead, they contend with critiques of lacking scientific judgment, having appropriate discernment, and practicing constant management of self (Dickson-Swift et al., 2009), often regarded as too proximal to the topic of inquiry, forced to reckon with the legitimacy of the selected methodological approach, and prove the validity and reliability of their research findings (Bartlett, 2019).

The study of social sciences views subjectivity as philosophical trouble; "it's what pollutes objective knowledge" (Shapin, 2012, p. 171). Emotional detachment and suppressed emotions are preferred to induce the illusion of neutrality (Bellas, 1999). Yet, in a broader sense, there is significant value in acknowledging the inherent subjective nature of social scientific research, the difficulty in disentangling researchers' vulnerabilities from the analysis and perceived findings, and the accompanying messiness. Reevaluating the traditional expectations of research objectivity require social scientists to see that "every view is *a* way of seeing, not *the* way" (Wolcott, 1999, p. 137, italics in original).

Hence, the intention of this autoethnography/autobiographical narrative is to highlight the interconnectedness of multiple existences and present the wholeness of my experiences as a Black woman engaged in prison research while simultaneously navigating liminal space in the academy and life (Turner, 1964, 1979). Emphasizing the need for centering Blackness and womanhood in our crafts, Collins (2000) begs the question, "If U.S. Black women cannot put ourselves in the center of our own intellectual and political work and claim identities as Black women, then who else will?" (p. 239). In maintaining race, gender, and even class as prominent threads, this narrative aims to create space and expose the dynamic identities held by researchers, routinely buried as research limitations (Ellis & Bochner, 2000). Acknowledging the persistent and disparate experiences of women makes it possible to recognize the common "problems and pitfalls facing us as women" (Lorde, 1984, p. 118). Further, in an effort to deny erasure, silencing, and exclusion of the cultural identities and voices of researchers of color, in scholarship, particularly of Black women, this work is positioned to rally these scholars to embody the power of their voice and narratives.

ROOT CAUSE: THE JOURNEY TO PRISON RESEARCH

I must've been about six years old when I first visited a jail. The family gathered at my grandmother's house, Black matriarchs are long-known for being the cornerstone of the family, followed in a caravan, on the main local highway, to visit my uncle in the county jail. It wasn't his first time behind the wall and it wouldn't be his last. For years, he struggled with substance use (now twenty+ years sober). Honestly, I do not remember much about the visit but the memory and feeling continue to live with me. A few things were evident—children were not supposed to be there, and our visit was to be kept a secret. Despite these ideals, my mother, a single mother, had limited sitter options. Though several other men in my family would find themselves seized by the criminal justice system, that would be my last visit to a jail, until interning at a correctional facility as an undergraduate psychology major.

Over the years, the idea of jails and prisons frightened me. Family members who spent relatively short periods of time in jail, for a first-time minor offense, and had yet to be convicted, died in county jails—not just a social death, but physical death. My nineteen-year-old stepbrother passed away while on the rec yard, and twenty-something old cousin didn't receive his prescribed diabetic medication in enough time. I suppose this is the entry point that solidified my interests in examining how people experience the carceral setting in addition to other myriad criminal justice issues. I owed it to my stepbrother, cousins, and uncles, to amplify their stories.

Following my own interests and experiences with/in the context of the criminal justice system and bearing witness to the direct impact of incarceration on the persons who were confined and their families, I decided to explore how incarcerated men construct and enact familial roles over the course of their imprisonment. Specifically, the research examined the strategies used to manage the synchronous enactment of the role as "prisoner"[1] and familial roles within the geography of prison (Crewe et al., 2014), during visitation sessions when directly faced with conflicting role expectations, and over the longer imprisonment period. Because the carceral environment, social landscape, and role as an incarcerated person have many restrictions, it is without argument that only limited aspects of familial roles are able to be expressed.

In being granted permission to conduct this research in the correctional facility, I recognized the necessity of being prudent and meticulous in my actions and behaviors to avoid mistakes and missteps. Any error would undermine the work of and limit access to future researchers seeking to lead research within the agency's jurisdiction. Scholars who identify as women were already believed to pursue relationships with participants. As a Black woman, I needed to defend my moral integrity. Black women have long been defined as a "jezebel," hypersexual, sexually deviant, promiscuous, and supposed manipulative seductress (Epstein et al., 2017; West, 1995; Wyatt, 1997). My actions would reflect researchers generally, but more so, all Black scholars. Black people carry the weight of accepting responsibility for the actions of *all* Black people.

Data were drawn from twenty-five in-depth, semi-structured interviews with incarcerated men at various stages of their sentence, twelve hours of observations at prison visitation sessions, and a focus group with incarcerated men, over a nine-month period. Participants were selected from a random sample of the general population of incarcerated men, excluding those in special units of the prison such as the gang units, administrative segregation, and the psychiatric stabilization units, because prison officials considered interviewing these men to be a security risk. Interviews, lasting sixty to ninety minutes with each participant, were conducted in a small, private room. During the interviews, the door was closed. Officers maintained surveillance through video cameras and frequently, physically, glanced in the small window.

I worked earnestly to conform to expectations and regulations to prove my legitimacy to the corrections officials and administration, but also to the ivory tower and myself. Conformity was compulsory. Lorde (1984) suggests Black women adapt to the language, behavior, and decorum of the oppressor as an "illusion of protection" (Lorde, 1984, p. 114), because the "mask of behavioral conformity" conceals acts of resistance (Collins, 2000, p. 107).

At the initial onset of this project, officials permitted laptops in the facility, but this changed less than three months into the study. Unexplained policy changes resulted in the banning of laptops in the facility. Capturing participant responses and other notes during the interview session was easier with a laptop, yet, it hindered the process of building rapport and trust. Moreover, it was difficult to advance the conversation with the steady sound of keys being ferociously attacked. Audio-recording was also prohibited; therefore, responses were recorded by hand.

Interviews were not forced to follow and fit into a standard protocol due to the exploratory nature of the research. Open-ended questions focused on life prior to and during incarceration, strengths and deficits in family relationships, perception of their familial roles, and experiences with family contact through phone, letters, and visits (Thomas, 2011; Thomas & Christian, 2018). Participants were encouraged to "describe and reflect upon his experience in ways that seldom occur in everyday life" (Charmaz, 2006, p. 25). The participants candidly stated that, although important, they rarely critically thought about themes of the posed questions. For a brief moment, they allowed me to enter their world.

For me, the research (Thomas, 2011; Thomas & Christian, 2018) was personal and in some way mimicked my own internal struggle of negotiating roles, conflicting worlds, and contrasting norms. Here I was, constantly engaged in "code-switching" (Sadao, 2003), as I navigated home life in tandem with academic life and life as a prison researcher. In any given day, I existed in and transitioned through these different worlds, multiple identities, and cultural frames of reference. Stanley (2006, p. 7) conveys that such frequent transitions require considerable "time and effort that can tax the psyche and lead to occupational stress." I was at war with consistently living in my truth.

MUSING ON COMPLEX (IN)COMPETENCE

The significance of the prison research rested in a broader purpose of centering the voices, lived experiences, life histories, and authentic accounts of incarcerated Black and Brown men. Criminal justice/criminology research often superimposes narratives onto people who are imprisoned similar to a conviction or sentence. Common areas of investigation include categorization of incarcerated people, explicating the prison subculture, outlining the effects of incarceration (often on family members and children), and coping strategies, to name a few. Extant research, with exception (Arditti, 2005; Christian, 2005; Comfort, 2008; Pierce, 2015; Thomas, 2011), ignore the crucial reality that despite the restrictive requirements of corrections agencies; the barriers put in place to force the removal and separation from society to ensure the "curtailment of self" (Goffman, 1961, p. 14); and prisons general incompatibility with the function of family—people continue to engage in role enactment and performance within the carceral context.

Here I was, seeking to uncover how incarcerated men manage the conflicting role obligations and expectations and the strategies used to negotiate the incompatibility of these roles (Thomas, 2011), while confronting my own identity crisis. A role is expressed as the "culturally expected behavior" of an individual who occupies a particular position within the social system (Cottrell, 1942, p. 617). It is what an individual's surroundings expect from him or her and what he or she ought to do or be (Allen & van de vliert, 1983; Moerings, 1983). The obligations and expectations of my roles were not my own. I was denied the opportunity to tell my story. I believe that I sought to uphold the humanity of these men and present the depth and richness of their stories because I desired the same.

The research participants were not that different from me. We shared a likeness—a quiet suffering that mirrored our collective oppression. I was removed from the prison culture, yet connected to it and possessed an in-group understanding of the experiences within the culture (Johnson, 1984). The discipline of criminal justice was not anthropology or even sociology, from which it draws its roots from; the academy made that clear. The program where I pursued my doctoral degree was the "School of Criminal Justice." At one point, there were rumblings that faculty and the administration toyed with the idea of adding "criminology" to the title, but apparently the issue was not ever seriously contested. The school was to maintain its position as a pillar in studying the system, with limited attention on individuals and behavior. Nevertheless, systems, such as the institution of criminal justice, are created by people. It is impossible to hold a system accountable without learning about the motives of the people who perform in it.

Now, I am not arguing that scholars in the discipline (though mostly sociologists studying issues akin to criminal justice) have not produced seminal works grounded in an ethnographic approach. Conversely, I can name relatively few women who did not draw criticism for similar works (maybe rightfully warranted[2]). Nor am I suggesting that these criminologists did not practice some forms of qualitative research. Nonetheless, as a graduate student in this program, you knew to expect intense and extensive scrutiny when stating your intention to employ a qualitative methodological approach to mark your transition (i.e., complete your formal rite of passage, the dissertation research) instead of "rigorous" quantitative analysis, with the exception of white men studying elephant poaching in Africa (Lemieux, 2014). Nielson (2010) finds that ethnographic research is embedded with "uncertainty and insecurity, because the participation of the researcher, as an informed and involved outsider, requires shifting social engagements in relation to which the researcher constantly has to guard and disguise information and positioning to observe confidentiality and build trust" (p. 307).

For most graduate-school students, the many shifts that occur in status, responsibility, and expectations and pseudo-initiation hazings can be anxiety producing and destabilizing, and result in traumatic memories. To endure as a Black woman, engaged in qualitative research anchored in grounded theory (as I was told this approach was reserved for the most competent and confident of scholars), in prisons was even more crippling. "I dreamed of being competent" (Cottom, 2019, p. 77). In her collection of "thick" essays, Cottom (2019) poignantly describes the myriad complexities that accompany being a Black female public intellectual, as she exists in and beyond the ivory tower. She plainly states, "For Black women, racism, sexism, and classism have always made us structurally incompetent" (p. 81). Academia is one of the many institutions that eagerly worked to reaffirm feelings of incompetency and of not belonging. The twenty-five men included in the research represented my father, grandfathers, uncles, brothers, cousins, and lovers. *My* conducting of this research and recounting of their stories would not result in accolades or features on national platforms.

The incarcerated men welcomed me. Most appreciated the opportunity to reflect on their life history and parts of their background missing in official prison records or presentence investigation reports or the state's public prison database. Some were delighted to simply converse with a visitor, who was not a representative of the state, and presented at the very least to be empathetic and willing to listen.

Twenty-one of the participants were Black (84 percent), with the mean age of thirty-eight years, ranging from twenty-nine to sixty-two years. Fourteen of the interview participants were under the age of twenty-five at the start of their current incarceration, and four of these participants were under the age of eighteen years. The participants had a wide range of time served, from eighteen months to twenty-seven years. On average, the men served eleven years in prison and faced sentences ranging from five years to life. I made every effort to authentically describe their diverse, rich, and dynamic stories with emphasis on their vulnerabilities, strength, struggles, and humanness. The participants were intentionally afforded some power, even if symbolic given the setting, as they controlled the narrative. There were only their words and voice.

I'm unsure if these men would say that I did right by them or that my re-telling of their captivating stories was an equitable exchange; follow-up interviews were limited, and the corrections agency policies on research permissions were rapidly changing. I was unable to provide any compensation, not even the postal stamps as initially planned. And, selfishly, I did not contact them via mail due to concerns of protecting my reputation as "researcher and scholar" capable of imparting objectivity in a study anchored in a grounded theory methodological approach—*to expect the researcher, as "human instrument" proximal to participants and issues to impart objectivity was oxymoronic and nearly impossible.* However, upon the completion of the study, I taught in a state prison, as a way of returning the many gifts (their time and stories) shared with me. Despite not being able to provide any tangible sentiment of thanks, I vowed to tell their stories, and that I did do.

PARKING LOT BLUES: THE RETREAT FROM THE RESEARCH AND PROCESS

Prison research days required mental and physical preparation. These days were long, arduous, tense, stressful, and exhausting. Denying my dance with subjectivity and struggle to hold on to their stories would be deceitful, dishonest, and insincere.

I rotated three suits—black and gray—and sports bras on interview days, making sure the jacket covered my posterior, wore little makeup, and minimally styled hair. On observation days, I usually sported jeans and a long button-down shirt with a casual jacket or cardigan. These were my prison outfits. I purposely downplayed any features that I thought officials would interpret or mistake as an attempt to entice those involved in the research or draw the attention of curious officials.

I had to prepare for whatever would might come my way on research days. On few occasions, I was denied or delayed entry because someone forgot to add my name to the approved visitor list. Or, the person randomly selected for participation in the study decided not to leave the tier, since they were not formally briefed on the research project until our face-to-face meeting. Or, a "code" could be called in the prison, disrupting the daily routine. In one instance, alleged rival members of a gang became involved in a violent altercation, resulting in one person being shepherded away on a gurney; I was there to witness the aftermath of the ensuing disorder.

> Saturday, February 23, 2008
>
> 12:45 p.m.
>
> When walking up to the prison, I heard someone announce something over the prison intercom system. When I entered the facility visitors, around eighty people were in line waiting to be processed. I informed the CO why I was there, and she said to have a seat because a CODE was called. The code was called because one incarcerated person slashed (possibly stabbed) another's throat. The alleged perpetrator was supposedly a Latin King and the other a Blood. The alleged perpetrator walked up on the other while in the "mess line and stabbed him from behind about five times from the back."

> Because of the incident, the visitation did not have the usual number of COs when the visiting session started. Many COs were sent to secure different areas of the prison, leaving the visitation program with few officers.

Or, the prison could sound a "lockdown" and restrict all movement due to a possible escape—no one enters or leaves the facility until authorities locate the missing individual and the count clears. This day was not fun, but fortunately, I was in the administrative unit reviewing records and the person who escaped was located within the span of three hours. Or, your otherwise intriguing research participant could become overly excited by your conversation and decide to interrogate your marital status and dating life while blocking the small window used by the officer to keep a watchful eye. Or, officials could badger you on why you want to be bothered with and study these "jokers" as they reveal personal information about people under their supervision and their visitors. I was fatigued by the process and burdened with their stories.

In the case of thirty-three-year-old Christopher, incarcerated since the age of eighteen years, I was there as he grappled with the recent arrest of his son. He just learned about the incident a few days prior to our interview. He spoke about regretting his absence and the example he set for his children.

The first time fifty-one-year-old David *saw* his son was in prison. They never met. Imprisonment defined a good portion of David's life. He was first incarcerated as a juvenile and, later, as an adult. David completed four jail and three prison terms over the course of three decades.

> I got locked up in 1981 and released in 2003. My son was locked up here in the ______unit when I left. . . . I didn't know he was here. He was born in 1982, so he wasn't even born yet when I was locked up. The first time I seen him . . . was here, that's the first time I seen him. I was working in the kitchen and feeding the _____unit, he had a stepbrother on _____unit, and he told me he was here, I didn't see him until three months after, didn't even speak to him.

Reflecting on his life, David remarked,

> I stayed with my mother 'til I was 13. I started getting incarcerated and doing bad things since I was 13. I've been in jail and prison, since I was 13. All of my adult life, I say I've been in prison.

Sixty-two-year-old Roberto and his son are codefendants, both serving thirty-five-year prison sentence.

> For the first time in 20 years, we are on the same unit. He locks with me. We were together at _____[another state prison], but I rarely saw him. The first time in 20 years that we've been in such close proximity.

> Our relationship . . . well, he still calls me Dad. The guys on the tier get a kick out of that. He is smart, intellectual, a prolix and argumentative. There's love there, but communication wise, I'm very intolerant of his way. I try to let him know that there's more to being a man than being of age.

Best friends Vincent and Amir, both thirty-one years old, have been incarcerated since the age of eighteen. In boasting about his frequent family visits and strong support network, Vincent disclosed concerns about his ambiguous identity and confronted never having the opportunity to stand on his own.

> I don't know any other position. I mean, I got locked up at 18. I went from being taken care of by parents to being taken care of by state.

Amir toiled with allowing his family into his life inside, that is, until his mother was diagnosed with terminal cancer. He reflected,

> Man, once the cancer came on, something happened. I gave her the green light. . . . I can't let much time go by without seeing her.

These are snippets of the stories that I secretly carried with me. The participants unloaded in unexpected ways. I traveled a short journey with these men, processing their heartbreak, regrets, disappointment, and grief. Some stories were defined by dysfunctional familial interactions and relationships and traumatic life experiences entrenched with physical, verbal, and sexual abuse as children, alienation, abandonment, absent parental figures, and poverty.

I sat in my car, in the prison parking lot, on prison research days. I sat there to mentally prepare for what might come my way that day. I remained there to process and digest the entirety of what unfolded in that small room. Ironically, I couldn't escape the prison fast enough, yet, I sat paralyzed in the parking lot. I couldn't muster the strength to ever leave, immediately.

IN VIVO: PERIODS OF FLUCTUATION AND BECOMINGNESS

> *Twenty-five interviews with incarcerated men is not enough. She must do more.*
>
> —Remarks of graduate-school faculty

The research was guided by a pilot study with thirty-three incarcerated men (twenty-five interview participants, twelve focus group participants inclusive of few interview participants) and employed a mixed-methods approach (i.e., interviews, observations, and focus group). Accordingly, the proposed data collection and analytical strategy were not enough. Persistent feelings of inadequacy rooted in others perception of who I was supposed to be, guided my thoughts and actions. The period of transformation was marked by uncertainty, ambiguity, and despair and throughout this critical rite of passage process (and beyond), I battled with imposter syndrome.

When I left the prison, I teetered on the side of invisibility. I lived in a constant state of transition. I wasn't supposed to be there—a twenty-something-year-old Black woman in a doctoral program, conducting research to learn about the lived experiences of people convicted of crimes. This role was not reserved for people like me. It was presumed that most of the Black and Brown students completed their stint in the academy at the master's level. We weren't supposed to *still* be there, becoming familiar with the practices and rituals required to earn the PhD. The initiation phase, which was crowded with exams, required yet ungraded research papers, frequent microaggressions, comments about our delayed progress (i.e., length of time from prospectus to defense) and shaky statistical skills, explicitly stated preference for international students, preferably from the UK, and minimal funding opportunities were supposed to be enough to push us out and discourage our pursuit.

The transitions were typified from perceived and experienced invisibility as a first-generation college graduate from humble beginnings to increased visibility as a Black woman with an upgrade in social status and a newly procured PhD. In addition to shifts in roles in the academy, there were also changes taking place in my home life. My maternal grandmother passed away while I was nearing the end of the data analysis phase. I was approaching important doctoral graduation deadlines and needed to commit to finishing the project. Yet, I now owned the role of manager of her estate. Clearly, the obligations and expectations of executrix conflicted with doctoral student, but I needed to prove to the academy that I could merge the two and own these new temporary identities. I fluctuated from subject to researcher, and from student to expert. Behaved in ways that at times reflected an actively involved family member and then that of distant relative who had to meet mandatory academic demands. Grieving granddaughter to pseudo-lawyer and realtor. One without power to asserting power. Invisible to visible. My existence was fluctuating and slowly becoming "legitimatized" and "validated."

AFTERTHOUGHTS

Undoubtedly, these experiences in the academy and in prison anchored my commitment to scholar-activism, the telling of complex and complicated stories, and the amplifying of neglected and marginalized voices. In this chapter, I explored my emotional response to conducting prison research and shifts in, and at times, dissolution of my sense of identity. But this journey also highlights the navigating of external biases that were internalized and allowed to define my identity and behavior, specifically in the academy. As a Black woman, who embarked in prison research early in my academic career, I would have found the following advice to be advantageous:

> Stand firm in your conviction to conduct the research of your choosing. You will have to stand by this work for the rest of your career. Although prominent and established scholars will attempt to sway your focus area or methodological approach or question your competency and capabilities, do it anyway. Research is activism. Own your power. Along this same vein, trust yourself and your voice. Believe that you are the right person at the right time to carry out this work. Prepare for the emotion work (Dickson-Swift et al., 2009; Nielson, 2010). You will need to rely heavily on a supportive network for sustenance. Identify a community of people, part of the academy or not, who understand your intentions and transitions. Despite my family being cognizant of the difficulties facing people who were incarcerated and their loved ones, at no point did they truly grasp why a twenty-something-year-old would voluntarily spend her days in prison. Moreover, they panicked at the thought of me in a small room with people who were convicted crimes. . . . Develop a connection with others, a communitas, who face the same or a similar liminal experience or initiation/rite of passage (Turner, 1964, 1979). Vital to my matriculation in the doctoral graduate program and completion of the highlighted research project was the support of peers and my advisor, who were all women of color who shared in the experience of liminality and were at the tipping point of crossing over from student to expert; or, newly minted PhD to respected scholar. As a collective we engaged in emotional vent sessions that provided a safe space for us to remove the layers and expectations. With my chairperson, I was able to discuss and unpack the emotional aspects of conducting prison research and develop strategies for addressing potential fatigue and bias. Still, at times, even with faculty of color, I found myself having to constantly demonstrate my commitment to complete the project and process. Connect with a therapist or counselor to help you place your experiences in context. Prison research and existing in the academy are equally emotionally and physically taxing. Acknowledge and respect the lens that accompanies you in the data collection process and analysis phase. Be willing to adapt to change, quickly, particularly when the prison is a main "subject" in your research. Don't forget to give back to the community of people who willingly divulged their life stories. As Rios (2011) poignantly remarks about a discussion on his research journey with a graduate-school professor, "I took your advice and went native in the academy, but I made sure to go back to the community where I come from" (p. 15). The one true regret I hold is not being able to directly give

back in a tangible, reciprocal manner, to the men who freely gave their stories to me and helped to strengthen and hone my voice. Lastly, in echoing the sentiments of civil rights activists, Ella Baker and Fannie Lou Hamer, seek liberation opposed to validation or legitimacy from systems (or people)—when we liberate and speak up and out for ourselves, we move to transform the world, and liberate others.

NOTES

1. The author uses person-first language when referring to people with criminal justice involvement. The use of the term "prisoner" is to explicitly state the limitations of the role(s) under study.

2. See critics of Alice Goffman (2014) On the Run: Fugitive Life in an American City and other similar works, referred to as "jungle-book trope" (Rios, 2011, p. 14). Would a Black woman conducting research chronicling community life similar to "6th Street" receive the same support, accolades, or platform?

REFERENCES

Allen, V. L., & van de Vliert, E. (Eds.). (1983). *Role transitions: Explorations and explanations*. New York: Plenum Press.

Arditti, J. A. (2005). "Families and incarceration: An ecological approach." *Families in Society*, *86*, 251–260.

Bartlett, T. (2019, September 24). *The criminologist accused of cooking the books*. "The Chronicle of Higher Education." https://www.chronicle.com/interactives/20190924-criminology.

Bellas, M. L. (1999). "Emotional labor in academia: The case of professors." *Annals of the American Academy of Political and Social Science*, *561*, 91–110.

Berger, M., & Guidroz, K. (Eds.). (2009). *The intersectional approach: Transforming the academy through race, class, and gender*. Chapel Hill: University of North Carolina Press. www.jstor.org/stable/10.5149/9780807895566_berger.

Breyer, T. (2015). "Social visibility and perceptual normativity." In M. Doyon & T. Breyer (Eds.), *Normativity in perception* (pp. 140–160). Basingstoke: Palgrave Macmillan.

Charmaz, K. (2006). *Constructing grounded theory: A practical guide through qualitative analysis*. Thousand Oaks, CA: Sage.

Christian, J. (2005). "Riding the bus barriers to prison visitation and family management strategies." *Journal of Contemporary Criminal Justice*, *21*(1), 31–48.

Comfort, M. (2008). *Doing time together: Love and family in the shadow of the prison*. Chicago: University of Chicago Press.

Cottom, T. M. M. (2019). *Thick and other essays*. New York: The New Press.

Cottrell, L. S. (1942). "The adjustment of the individual to his age and sex roles." *American Sociological Review*, *7*(5), 617–620.

Crewe, B., Warr, J., Bennett, P., & Smith, A. (2014). "The emotional geography of prison life." *Theoretical Criminology*, *18*(1), 56–74.

Dickson-Swift, V., James, E., Kippen, S., & Liamputtong, P. (2009). "Researching sensitive topics: Qualitative research as emotion work." *Qualitative Research*, *9*, 61–79. https://doi.org/10.1177/1468794108098031.

Diggs, G. A., Garrison-Wade, D. F., Estrada, D., & Galindo, R. (2009). "Smiling faces and colored spaces: The experiences of faculty of color pursing tenure in the academy." *The Urban Review*, *41*(4), 312–333. https://doi.org/10.1007/s11256-008-0113-y.

Ellis, C., & Bochner, A. P. (2000). "Autoethnography, personal narrative, reflexivity." In N. K. Denzin & Y. S. Lincoln (Eds.), *Handbook of qualitative research* (2nd ed., pp. 733–768). Thousand Oaks, CA: Sage.

Epstein, R., Blake, J. J., & González, T. (2017). *Girlhood interrupted: The erasure of Black girls' childhood.* Washington, DC: Georgetown Law, Center on Poverty and Inequality.

Goffman, A. (2014). *On the run: Fugitive life in an American city*. Chicago: The University of Chicago Press.

Goffman, E. (1961). *Asylums: Essays on the social situation of mental patients and other inmates*. Garden City, NY: Anchor Books, Doubleday and Company.

Haldeman, K. (2009). "The 'burden and blessing' of being a Black woman: Engaging intersectionality through an anthropology of pregnancy and motherhood among African American women." In M. Berger & K. Guidroz (Eds.), *The intersectional approach: Transforming the academy through race, class, and gender* (pp. 210–228). Chapel Hill: University of North Carolina Press.

Hill, C. P. (2000). *Black feminist thought: Knowledge, consciousness, and the politics of empowerment*. New York: Routledge.

Hill, C. P., & Bilge, S. (2016). *Intersectionality*. Malden, MA: Polity Press.

Hine, C. (2020). "Strategies for reflexive ethnography in the smart home: Autoethnography of silence and emotion." *Sociology*, *54*(1), 22–36. https://doi.org/10.1177/0038038519855325.

Johnson, N. B. (1984). "Sex, color, and rites of passage in ethnographic research." *Human Organization*, *43*(2), 108–120.

Lemieux, A. M. (2014). *Situational prevention of poaching*. New York: Routledge, Taylor & Francis.

Lorde, A. (1984). *Sister outsider: Essays and speeches*. Trumansburg, NY: Crossing Press.

Moerings, M. (1983). "From society into prison and from prison into society." In V. L. Allen & E. van de Vliert (Eds.), *Role transitions: Explorations and explanations* (pp. 153–168). New York: Plenum Press.

Nielsen, M. M. (2010). "Pains and possibilities in prison: On the use of emotions and positioning in ethnographic research." *Acta Sociologica*, *53*(4), 307–321. https://doi.org/10.1177/0001699310379143.

Pierce, M. B. (2015). “Male inmate perceptions of the visitation experience: Suggestions on how prisons can promote inmate–family relationships.” *The Prison Journal*, *95*(3), 370–396.

Rios, V. M. (2011). *Punished: Policing the lives of Black and Latino boys.* New York: New York University Press.

Sadao, K. C. (2003). “Living in two worlds: Success and the bicultural faculty of color.” *The Review of Higher Education*, *26*(4), 397–418.

Shapin, S. (2012). “The sciences of subjectivity.” *Social Studies of Science*, *42*(2), 170–184. https://doi.org/10.1177/0306312711435375.

Stanley, C. A. (2006). *Faculty of color: Teaching in predominately white colleges and universities.* Bolton, MA: Anker Publishing Company, Inc.

Thomas, S., & Christian, J. (2018). “Betwixt and between: Incarcerated men, familial ties, and social visibility.” In R. Condry & P. Schraaf Smith (Eds.), *Prisons, punishment, and the family: Towards a new sociology of punishment* (pp. 273–287). Oxford: Oxford University Press.

Thomas, S. S. (2011). *Negotiating family and prison behind the wall: Incarcerated men‘s role management strategies* (Doctoral dissertation, Rutgers University-Graduate School-Newark). Retrieved from Rutgers University Community Repository.

Turner, V. W. (1969). *The ritual process: Structure and anti-structure.* Chicago: Aldine Pub.

Turner, V. W. (1974). “Liminal to liminoid in play, flow, and ritual: An essay in comparative symbology.” *Rice University Studies*, *60*(3), 53–92. https://hdl.handle.net/1911/63159.

Viernes Turner, C. S. (2002). “Women of color in academe: Living with multiple marginality.” *The Journal of Higher Education*, *73*(1), 74–93. www.jstor.org/stable/1558448.

West, C. M. (1995). “Mammy, Sapphire, and Jezebel: Historical images of Black women and their implications for psychotherapy.” *Psychotherapy*, *32*(3), 458–466.

Wolcott, H. F. (1999). *Ethnography: A way of seeing.* Walnut Creek, CA: AltaMira.

Wyatt, G. E. (1997). *Stolen women: Reclaiming our sexuality, taking back our lives.* New York, NY: John Wiley & Sons.

Chapter 5

"Just Listen, People!"

Narrative as Resistance in Criminological Research

Abigail Kolb

> *What the community can do . . . the community can listen, because a lot of people need to talk, but they're afraid to talk; they're afraid to express their feelings because they feel like they're gonna be rejected*
>
> —Diane

Diane, age fifty-seven, was the mother of nine and a former member of a local Latinx street gang in the Los Angeles area. An abusive childhood led her leave home and seek the "protection" of an alcoholic, abusive, gang affiliated partner who introduced her to street life. In her home and on her streets, she was objectified and viewed as a commodity, responsible for having children and supporting the men in any way necessary. After deciding to leave her husband and the street lifestyle, she became pregnant with her eighth child, but found it impossible to support herself and her children. As such, she turned to the only means she believed she had to make money to survive: drug trafficking for a Mexican-based cartel that controlled the drug trade in her community. Diane, a single mother trying to support her children, and now pregnant with her ninth child, was arrested and taken to a federal detention facility two-and-a-half hours away from her family. She agreed to participate in this research as a means of "finding" her voice.

My interest in studying the experiences of Latinx women in gangs was twofold: (1) I was familiar with East Los Angeles, and various Latinx communities in Los Angeles in general, due to my former employment as a social worker in that area, and noticed the myriad challenges that women in these communities faced; and (2) my experience working with Latinx youth who were at risk for gang involvement led to my interest about what gang affiliation means and how it is perceived by women. I sought out Homeboy Industries in East Los Angeles as the desired site for the research because of the large, diverse clientele they serve.

The founder of Homeboy Industries, Father Greg Boyle, started the organization in 1988 to provide support to and improve the lives of formerly gang-affiliated individuals in East Los Angeles. Since its inception, the organization has become the world's leading model for gang intervention, rehabilitation, and community reentry. Homeboy Industries provides intensive and diverse programming for thousands of gang and formerly gang-affiliated individuals in Los Angeles, including tattoo removal, substance abuse treatment, mental health treatment, job training, and even employs participants whenever possible. Homeboy Industries was thus an ideal location to conduct research and gain a better understanding of programming, services, and resources necessary to aid individuals hoping to leave, or stay away from, gang activity.

Gaining entry to the organization for my research was a process, though fairly straightforward. I was granted permission to conduct research with clients and employees at the organization by the former director of External Affairs. Both she and her assistant were initially responsible for selecting participants for me to interview. During my second and third trips to Homeboy, participants began to refer their friends—also affiliated with the organization—to me. The director and her assistant chose participants based upon the criteria that I provided and participants' availability. Their goal, they said, was to allow me to interview as many women as possible who met the criteria I had outlined. As such, I did not have any reason to believe that certain participants were selected based on social desirability or that they best represented the agency and would reflect the agency's goals in a positive manner. In fact, I did interview some participants who were ambivalent about moving away from the gang and gang lifestyle despite their participation in programs at Homeboy. After three trips to the organization and spending several weeks talking to Homeboy staff and clients—both informally and during the formal interview process—I was informed that I had interviewed all of the women who both met my criteria and wanted to participate.

For my doctoral research, I conducted twenty-four in-depth qualitative interviews—each lasting an average of two hours—with women who were currently or formerly gang affiliated. Participants all identified as Latina or Chicana, and were between the ages of eighteen and fifty-six. I was initially interested in understanding how Chicanas involved in gangs acquire and perform agentic behavior through language use, corporeal expression, and negotiation of space. I had some ideas about how they might engage in corporeal expression and use space in order to negotiate agency despite the constraints, which they faced in their lives, and indeed these issues emerged somewhat, though they were not as relevant in the lives of the participants as I previously thought. What I unexpectedly learned was that my understandings of these women's experiences were not their understandings. In fact, the issues I was most interested in uncovering and developing were essentially nonissues in the lives of these women. They had far more salient experiences and issues they brought to the interviews and upon which they expounded. For example, of the twenty-four women interviewed for this study, fifteen admitted to having spent time in jail or state or federal correctional institutions in California. This led to some unexpected findings in my research, as these women offered insight into street and prison life, the complexities involved in doing time, and thus discursively constructed their identities, in part, through their retelling of these experiences. In other words, these interviews were demonstrative of how a marginalized group of individuals can and do use counternarrative as a form of resistance against identities imposed upon them by mainstream society.

When I was not conducting interviews, I spent time talking to staff members and anyone else with whom I could strike up a conversation while milling around the organization. Additionally, I spent a couple hours each day walking around the neighborhood, sitting in the crowded lobby or at the Homegirl Café, a restaurant in the organization run by formerly gang-affiliated women, observing people's interactions with one another, their tattoos, hand gestures, and listening to their fears, challenges, and aspirations. One day, one of the participants in my research, Little One, even took me to her neighborhood in the Ramona Gardens housing projects to provide more history and context to her life and experiences. Ramona Gardens has a long history of heavy gang presence and violence. It is one of the more notorious communities in Los Angeles, and one in which I would not have been welcome without my guide. Having the opportunity to not only interview people but also observe their communities and interactions with one another in these settings was invaluable, as I was able to gain a more holistic understanding of the spaces that shaped their lives and identities and that they simultaneously helped shape.

While conducting previous research and discussing the direction of future research interests, I was asked whether it is possible or even justifiable for an educated white woman from a middle-class background to undertake a project to which she cannot and never will be able to relate on a personal level. I argue that undertaking this type of work—particularly because it has, in part, been framed within a critical context—is not impossible, but only if the researcher is able to maintain an appropriate reflexive stance. My own location as a white woman involved in academia has allowed me various privileges in life, specifically the privilege to be able to speak out about issues such as sexism, racism, classism, and Eurocentric, hegemonic practices and be heard. Why should my voice be privileged over the voices of those who have truly struggled? Why should their voices only be heard through my work? What strategies of resistance can be used to disrupt the privilege I have and allow these women's voices to stand on their own? In order to advance academia socially, politically, and methodologically, academics and activists alike must take these questions into consideration, incorporate a reflective and reflexive position, and critical perspectives to accurately reflect the participants' voices. Research, such as mine, does not do anyone justice if its sole purpose is research. Instead, it is imperative that critical research involving marginalized and oppressed individuals and groups be shared with community activists and community members so that these important issues can be addressed. Working within a social justice-based model is a collective process in which everyone with a vested interest in community-based issues must participate. Indeed, change and empowerment are processes that do not occur within the bubble of academia, but through collaboration within communities.

Throughout this chapter, I will use the stories that these women shared in order to argue that gang identity is not only about "getting high," "robbing people," and "doing time." Though these activities are certainly facets of a gang lifestyle, it is important to recognize the ways in which other factors, such as socioeconomic status, systemic inequality, and relational patterns, are communicated as playing a role in the construction and reconstruction of identity for and among gang-affiliated Latinas in Los Angeles.

A NEED FOR GENDER-SPECIFIC EPISTEMOLOGY AND CRITICAL EVALUATION

Studying the lived experiences of women in general and women of color specifically requires more than traditional "masculinist" theories of criminality. Gender-neutral theories tend to compare women's experiences to those of men and, in doing so, pathologize women like Diane and the other women who participated in this research. In order to gain a more complete picture of my participants' experiences, I draw generally upon feminist criminology, and I specifically emphasize the importance of intersectionality—the ways in which race, class, gender, and other identity markers intersect and play a role in identity construction (Chesney-Lind & Jones, 2010; Crenshaw, 1989). Chesney-Lind (1989) argues that it is not sufficient to use existing theories that explain male delinquency and "add women and stir." Instead, we require a feminist approach that incorporates the roles of "patriarchal arrangements" and the multitude of other ways in which women, specifically women of color, have traditionally been oppressed and marginalized in order to explain the unique ways in which participants in this study came to understand their unique lived experiences. Development of a feminist approach to delinquency requires scholars to take women's raced, classed, and gendered experiences into consideration. It is necessary to acknowledge the role that patriarchy plays in this process and how it is manifest in women's lives.

Understanding identity construction requires a critical lens that not only acknowledges the role of the embeddedness of patriarchy and white supremacy but simultaneously acknowledges that we cannot rely only on patriarchy or "white-washed" explanations to understand individually situated behaviors. There is a tendency in feminist-based research to use patriarchy as the defining factor in women's socialization, thoughts, values, and behaviors. While it certainly should not be ignored, using it to describe the totality of women's experiences blinds us not only to women's multifaceted experiences as raced, classed, and gendered subjects, but also to the ways in which women are active agents in their own lives. Women are not simply victims of social and systemic inequalities but are also agents who create and perform identities for and among themselves and others, respectively. As such, it is important to place participants' narratives within their relevant social, historical, and political context.

Employing critical theory, then, allows us to critique and question hegemonic norms, ideas, and relationships that we often take for granted. It helps us to analyze power relations between those who have power and those who do not. Because the purpose of this study was to examine formerly gang-affiliated Chicanas' understandings of their own identities as racial/ethnic minorities, women, mothers, "inmates," and as individuals from disadvantaged socioeconomic backgrounds, using an intersectional framework was most appropriate. Acknowledging the implications of various identity markers opened up space for participants to explain how they interpreted the impact of these markers within their lives, and allowed for an understanding of the fluidity of identity, which created a more complete picture of the women's lived experiences.

For example, Marissa (age twenty-one) talked about her experiences during her numerous stays in juvenile detention. She explained that she used to shave her head in order to look more "gangster," or "like one of the guys" (Miller, 2001) in order to command respect on the streets. However, at the age of seventeen, the sentencing judge ordered that she let her hair grow to look more "like a girl."

> Anyway, so this judge, he was my judge for all these times I went to court and he seen I shaved my head, he seen I cared less, and I didn't care, I was more into the gang and I would act like a boy. I was like, "yeah, I'm hard." And so he made a court order for me to grow my hair. He said I was doing it to be gang-related and he said for me not to shave it . . . while I was in the institution. So I could not get no shavers or nothing, I had to let my hair grow while I was in there. . . .

> You don't have to look like a boy to be a gangster; girls can be gangsters too. And I said "alright." So I stopped shaving my head; I didn't do it again.

When probed further about this incident, Marissa stated that she soon realized she had been a "hypocrite" for trying to behave "like guy" when she was, in fact, a girl. Despite the fact that Marissa's new identity was imposed upon her through the practices of a paternalistic system, she constructed herself as agentic because she "realized" her actions were in contrast to social expectations and thus agreed to make this change. Patriarchal attitudes are expressed in many ways, one of which is through the perpetration of physical, sexual, and emotional abuse at the hands of the carceral state. Marissa's story serves as just one example of how strong macro-structural factors, such as race, gender, and sexuality impact poor communities of color, and community members' everyday lives.

In addition to helping account for the implications of intersecting identity markers, critical theory examines power within relationships and allows us to better understand the nature of insider and outsider groups, the meaning of the unequal power distribution that ensues as a result of these groups' formation, and how that power is negotiated by both parties. Indeed, it is important to note that the distribution and negotiation of power plays a role in the ways in which individuals' identities are constructed for and by them. Importantly, even "out" groups recreate power-imbued hierarchies and are responsible for physically and discursively distancing themselves from others who are considered to be part of the same marginalized group. The use of critical theory allows us to recognize the matrix of power and power relations that are inherent in our everyday lives (Crenshaw, 1989). Using a critical lens allows us to critique this distribution of power in order to better understand how and where human agency lays and how it can be achieved (Kincheloe & Mclaren, 2002).

Collins (1991) points out that we must create space in order to understand and allow for the emergence of agency among women of color. She argues that there is no monolithic "black woman" culture (or any monolithic culture that only takes into account one or two identity markers), but "rather there are socially constructed black women's cultures that collectively form black women's culture" (p. 44). Expanding upon this idea, one objective of this research was to provide a better understanding of the social construction of a Chicana gang culture that is culturally relevant within a particular space. Using the results to explain a "Chicana culture," "female gang culture," or even "gang-affiliated Chicana culture" in other locations, not only would be problematic because doing so would essentialize an entire group of people, but it also would dismiss other socio-spatially, politically, and economically relevant factors in these women's lives. If women of color play an active role in defining themselves, rather than allowing hegemonic discourse to uniformly define them, then they are, arguably, rejecting objectification and acting on their own behalf, on behalf of their communities, and women of color as a whole. In other words, using a critical approach allowed participants to define and construct themselves as agentic beings, and develop an individual and collective consciousness based on oppression.

Acknowledging the role of power and its embeddedness in identity (re)construction was central to interpreting and ultimately understanding participants' perspectives of their positions within the larger social environment, their communities, their gangs, and in prison. Allowing participants the space to discuss their role—both active and constrained—in the public and private sphere helped capture the dynamic nature of their ontological positions. In other words, participants explained the unique ways in which power dynamics are created and recreated for and among them and how this was related to agency. Thus, doing research from a critical framework helped participants claim discursive space to explain the impact of power on and within their lives. Likewise, engaging with people from this framework forced me to move beyond my myopic, academic position in life and better understand how this group of women negotiated theirs.

NARRATIVE AND QUALITATIVE RESEARCH

One of the most important themes of this project was narrative construction and the role of voice. I addressed the importance of participants' narratives by critically evaluating what they said and how they told their stories. Narrative is a tool that allows individuals and groups to make meaning of and organize their thoughts and experiences (Bruner, 1991). While narratives are informed by experiences, they assist in shaping individuals' understanding(s) of their experiences (Ochs & Capps, 1996). Schiffrin (1996) argues that "the self neither preexists all conversation nor arises just from interlocutors' responses; rather it arises within conversation" (p. 169). In other words, because the individual is defined through the narration of experiences, and meaning is made of experiences through the telling of a story (or sequence of stories), narrative is necessarily a representation of the self (Ochs & Capps, 1996). Thus, it is important to acknowledge that the discursive construction of one's "experience" does not necessarily constitute a true "reality."

Fragmented narrative and narrative asymmetries are commonplace. The problem with ignoring these narratives is that the researcher exerts her power as researcher over the interview process and the interlocutor, thus privileging certain individuals while discounting others. This process creates and maintains a power differential and leads to what Ochs and Capps (1996) refer to as "linguistic oppression" whereby one person has the power to decide what is relevant and what is not (p. 34). They further contend that "differential control over narrative content, genre, timing, and recipiency is central to the constitution of social hierarchies. Narrative practices reflect and establish power relations in a wide range of domestic and community institutions" (Ochs & Capps, 1996, p. 34). During the course of this research, I did not necessarily seek out dominant stories that would lead me to give preferential voice to one participant over another, nor was it my intent to look for absolute consistency in stories from all participants. In fact, some scholars have argued that researchers should look for "messy cases," or outliers to construct a more complete picture of "reality" (See Becker, 1998). In her analyses of narratives, Byrne (2003) argues that narrative should be a "coherent story of the self" (p. 47). She proceeds to discuss the manner in which her participants' narrated their stories and suggests that a lack of coherence, or lack of chronological order, was indicative of a "disruption to her narrative rather than giving direction and meaning to an unfolding story" (p. 47). This argument is problematic for two reasons. First, it implies that a coherent interview can only be attained if the participant follows the researcher's linguistic protocol. This type of reasoning may lead the researcher to only account for dominant stories and silence certain participants. The second problem lays in the idea of authority. If the researcher decides what constitutes a coherent or an incoherent interview, she runs the risk of imposing her beliefs on the data rather than allowing the data to speak. The question then becomes: "Who has the authority to determine how 'meaning' is constituted within narrative?"

Riessman (1987) and Ochs and Capps (1996) argue that stories are not necessarily told in chronological order. Participants make meaning of their lives through their stories even if their narrative is not presented in chronological order. When an individual narrates his or her story, the story makes sense to the one telling it. Hesse-Biber and Leavy (2011) further argue that "communication strategies may differ based on the intersection of race, ethnicity, class, gender, sexuality, religion, and nationality" (p. 146). That is, while narratives may be told in chronological order, there are different types of narrative structures that do not correspond with traditional modes of communicating one's narrative (Hesse-Biber & Leavy, 2011, p. 146). Different forms of narrative are significant to consider because they may be reflective of how the participant views themselves, their experiences, and their worlds. It then becomes the researcher's task to locate the context in which the narrative is being told. For example, during my interview with one participant, Little One, it was difficult to follow the order of her stories. Little One frequently moved from topic to topic and decade to decade. At first, I was confused and often encouraged her to walk me through a timeline that made sense to me. It took me hours of data analysis to understand that she was telling me a story that made sense to her. Throughout the interviews, she made meaning out of her own experiences and was, in fact, conveying an intricate story to me. After listening to the interviews several times and reanalyzing the transcripts, I realized that, in a round-about way, Little One was clearly making very important points by focusing on themes that were relevant and present throughout her life.

NARRATIVE CONTRADICTIONS AND AGENCY

From participants' accounts, it appeared as though some of the narratives were riddled with contradictions. Researchers have argued that gang members tend to exaggerate their experiences and present a glorified image of themselves as either more or less deviant (see Campbell, 1984; Hagedorn, 1996). While this is likely true (as I suspect was the case with a number of the narratives in my research), the way in which a story is told is arguably just as important as the story itself, as it provides insight into the interlocutors' understandings of their worlds. Ochs and Capps argue that "narratives are versions of reality" that reflect feelings and beliefs about one's life (p. 21). Despite interlocutors' possible exaggeration about their actual experiences, their narratives serve to tell the listener what she has heard, seen, or what she hoped had happened; all of which are integrated into their understanding or perception of their reality. The constitution of individuals' or a groups' reality is reflected in how they make meaning out of situations, whether those situations have happened to them directly or not. Understanding and appreciating this phenomenon helps researchers gain a more complete picture of the main idea(s), or concepts being communicated.

For example, eighteen-year-old Alma was taught to dislike and distrust African Americans because they were different from Mexicans: they were more violent, and were abusive toward their *jefitas* (girlfriends/wives), and mothers.[1] "We were raised different . . . we're just different," she stated. Even "when you going to jai, when you go into the penitentiary, there's politics involved which is that you have to go to the South Side, to *raza*. You have to go kick it with your *raza*. You are Mexican. Latino. You have to be with your race." She then continued to talk about growing up in a community and home where her step-father sexually abused her, and physically abused her mother. Eventually, she left home to be on the streets with her homeboys and homegirls, where she carried a gun, and engaged in gang activity because it made her feel more powerful. When probed, Alma admitted that Mexican men are equally abusive to their *jefitas*, as African American men because they subscribe to *machismo*, a form of hypermasculinity:

> Well I'm not gonna lie 'cuz Mexican moms they come from abusive homes a lot of the times 'cuz Mexican guys, they're used to that whole power thing. Seeing your mom get beat, that's probably sometimes . . . not for me though, but for the homegirls. . . . It was accepted . . . 'cuz if you mouth off to the man of the house, you need a slap.

Instead of interpreting Alma's narrative as dishonest, her statements are one example of how contradictions within narratives can be viewed as meaning-making, and a simultaneous reclamation of power. In other words, this discussion of racialized and gendered violence allowed Alma to construct herself as an independent and self-sufficient Mexican-American woman who did not "need a slap" because she was stronger than the other women in the neighborhood and those in prison.

Similarly, participants reported that they saw themselves as equal to the guys in their respective gangs because they spent the majority of their time hanging out with them rather than with the other women. They distanced themselves from the other women whom they referred to as "hoodrats" because they did not want to be associated with partying too much, being too promiscuous, or being disloyal (Kolb & Palys, 2016). While they reported that they had equal status as the men, some women also reported that homegirls had to work harder than the men to be seen as being "down" and achieving that status (Kolb & Palys, 2012). One way of demonstrating that one was a true homegirl was not snitching on one's homeboys, even if it meant serving time in prison. Likewise, Michelle, who identified as a true homegirl, stated that risking one's freedom by smuggling drugs into the prisons was another way for a woman to prove her loyalty to her homeboys.

> The women gangs are trying to be like the men gangs, so for a homeboy to tell you you're down then that means everything, you know? Like, I've been the type of female that's been to the prisons to take drugs to the homies. I've tooken drugs to my brother; sneaking them in through my mouth. You know, dropping off balloons of heroin in the system.

Interestingly, many of the women simultaneously reported that their roles were to support the men and that they did not engage in the same types of gendered crime as the men. Despite this, they argued they were still considered homegirls because of their closeness and loyalty to the homeboys. While this is contradictory, in relaying their stories, these women were responsible for (re)constructing a tough, homegirl identity dichotomously opposed to the stereotypical hoodrat image.

Throughout the interviews, Little One frequently shared traumatic stories from her childhood and adulthood. Even when the topic moved away from these periods in her life, Little One would come back to the traumatic events that had left her physically, sexually, emotionally, and psychically disempowered. Interestingly, however, she also followed up each event that left her disempowered by discussing her strength and perseverance.

For example, Little One frequently recounted traumatic incidents she experienced at the hands of her emotionally and physically abusive ex-husband. When she talked about her role as "the aggressor" during her interviews, she prefaced her story by recounting how her husband physically attacked her first while her "aggressive behavior" was simply her attempt to fight back.

> You know, he was a very possessive man. He's from Mexico so he believes in that controlling, macho-ness. But I'm not. I'm from here and I'm from the projects so I really don't give a fuck what you're saying. Like, no, no, no, that's not how we do it over here in California. But he was a womanizer. He was abusive, but I became the aggressor. You can do this . . . you be Chucky and I'll be Chucky's bride. Because I ended up stabbing him like four or five times after I stood there and let him slap me about 20. Are you done? He said, "yeah." I said, "okay," went to the drawer, got a fishing knife and stabbed him four or five times. I don't even remember because I blacked out. So, it was just back and forth, back and forth and I got sick of it because, see, my mom and dad went through all that and I'm like, I'm not gonna go through this no more. Never again. I don't have to. You can't go to school. You can't work. You can't do this. It was all "you can'ts."

Both Little One and her husband were arrested for participating in this incident. Little One suggested that she was not only guilty of committing acts of violence against her abusive husband in order to protect herself and fight back but that she "became the aggressor." Interestingly, she never acknowledged that she was the victim, only the perpetrator, suggesting that relaying her story this way, allowed her to reclaim power she had lost on account of her race and gender at the hands of her husband, and society at large.

Collins (1998) draws a parallel between ideals created and standards employed by families and nation-states. She uses the idea of birth order in order to understand hierarchal differences. Just as birth order in families tends to determine the amount of "freedom" a family member will have (i.e., an older child may have more freedom than his or her younger siblings), citizenship also determines the amount of freedom one may possess. This means that white, heterosexual, European-Americans who have resided in the United States for decades or centuries have more freedoms and are more entitled to benefits than immigrants or the children of immigrants. Here, Collins argues, is where violence has the potential to occur. Violence can be physical but can also be expressed through sanctions used to maintain unequal power relations. Violence is often exerted by those in power toward those with little or no power and, therefore those with little or no power fail to recognize their own oppression. For example, violence in the form of hate crimes is routinely overlooked by police (and may even be perpetrated by the police) and other criminal justice officials and is underreported by the media. Middle- and upper-middle-class whites do not recognize their own privileged status within American society and, therefore, question why racial and ethnic minority groups cannot pull themselves out of poverty. Underreporting of "family secrets" is commonplace because of fear of retribution or sanctions.

Collins (1998) also explains how the hierarchies that exist within families mirror those that exist within society at large. The nation-state lays the foundation for hierarchal ideals within its "family" at a macro level, which, in turn, influences familial patterns operating at a micro level. For example, society, like the family, socializes children to understand their raced, classed, and gendered position within society. Children are conditioned to view the world through a particular schema, and people are thus socialized to acknowledge and point out racial and cultural difference.

Little One's statement that she was not from Mexico, but rather "from here," is a rhetorical technique whereby she distances herself from being "Mexican" by constructing her ex-husband as an outsider. This rhetorical distancing technique has important implications from a raced and gendered standpoint. Little One was oppressed by her husband—a non-American Mexican, or foreigner—because of his "macho-ness" because she was a woman. The implication is that "macho-ness" is an undesirable trait associated with Mexican culture, but that it is not as prevalent among American-born Mexicans/Latinos. In other words, abuse stemming from "macho-ness" is the result of unsophisticated, or uncultured individuals.

In Little One's case, she equates her ex-husband with the sadistic movie character, Chucky. If he behaves like Chucky, she will behave like Chucky's bride. In other words, Little One constructs herself as being the equally violent opposing character from the movie. Through this juxtaposition, she suggests that she has actively chosen to step into the role of Chucky's bride who, at the end of the movie, attained control over her counterpart. Thus, she demonstrates her role as an agent in her relationship with her ex-husband specifically, and her relationship within the larger social world and criminal justice system in general, because it was her *choice* to be the perpetrator of the violent behavior that ultimately led to this particular incarceration.

NARRATIVE AND MORAL AGENTS

The construction and sharing of narratives is one way in which individuals exert agency. In this sense, agency, or the capacity to act, is a crucial component of (self)-empowerment, particularly for those who have been rendered marginalized and disempowered through institutionalized practices. Narrative, then, becomes a tool through which the "storyteller" is able to exert power by (re)defining and (re)constructing the self to the listener. Moral agency, on the other hand, refers to an individual who chooses to behave in a "moral" fashion, according to social norms and expectations. Thus, moral agents know the difference between right and wrong and actively choose the "right" path. But, moral agency may also be discursively constructed through counternarrative. That is, marginalized individuals may use counternarrative to (re)define or (re)construct oneself as a moral agent, through their telling of their story.

Rymes (1995) argues that "social roles, social identity, and moral agency are reconstituted collaboratively through the narrative and in turn construct the narrative. Narrative analysis therefore is an invaluable resource for the study of resistance and the formation of identity and moral agency within a resistant group" (p. 497). Little One discussed her time in and out of prison for engaging in criminal behavior with her homeboys. She was adamant, however, that during one of her longer—seven years—incarcerations she "took care of" her mother and son from prison by paying for their groceries, clothing, and rent. Whether or not this was the case, her telling of story can be interpreted as admirable to the audience, and empowering for her for two reasons. First, in her narration, Little One situated herself as pushing back against gender-based marginalization inherent in American and Mexican culture by engaging in the "masculine" role of caretaker and provider. Similarly, Little One demonstrates a reclamation of power by discursively demonstrating her resistance to the totalizing, disempowering, and coercive carceral setting. Second, she shows that despite committing a crime for which she received several years in prison, she was still a "good" person. In other words, her narrative is indicative of her resistance to the ways in which the state dehumanizes people, particularly women, through incarceration. Little One's case was just one example of how the creation of discursive space for counternarrative allows marginalized individuals share their experiences, and thus co-construct their identities, all of which are morally agentic practices used by those who have traditionally been denied a voice.

Similar to Little One, Charlie actively constructed herself as being different other incarcerated women. She frequently mentioned that she, unlike many of the other women with whom she was incarcerated, took better care of herself, had more respect for herself and others, and did not engage in prison politics or "drama":

> I was very accepting of people. Let's say they fuck with me, I'm not going to fuck with them unless they fuck with me. That's how I've been all my life. If I can help you out I'll help you out. I'm not asking for nothing in return. If I

> could help you with something I'm gonna help you, just don't fuck me over or else I'll never help you again. I'm a good person. Prison was just easy, it was easy for me.

She continued to state that she was "able to respect myself. And a lot of girls know that about me, too. They like that. They see that I carry myself with a lot of respect." In Charlie's view, prison was easy because she, unlike the others on her unit, not only eschewed drama but was accepting and helpful to those who were struggling around her. During her interview, Charlie made a point of stating that she was a "good person" despite her participation in gang violence, and her long history of criminal justice involvement. Indeed, throughout her narrative Charlie tended to glaze over the details about the violent behavior in which she engaged and paint herself as a respectable woman.

CONCLUSION

I have always been mindful of my own privileged position in life; however, looking back, I wish I had really taken the time to understand how being white, educated, and growing up middle-class, helped shape my ideological framework, cognitions, and feelings about issues related to marginalization and oppression.

Throughout this research, I experienced moments that forced me to step back and reevaluate my own positionality, and the ways it played a role in my interactions with and interpretations of these women's experiences. For example, many of these women shared details of their lives that they had not previously shared with others for fear of being judged. During the interviews, they talked about engaging in child abuse and neglect, committing violent crimes against others, habitual incarcerations, and how all of these experiences shaped the person sitting in front of me. While it is never a researcher's place to make judgments about participants, I actually found myself downplaying and rationalizing the harms they had caused others and thus troublingly viewing their behaviors as those of victims, rather than a conditioned response to interpersonal and structural victimization. This was challenging to acknowledge, and had I not debriefed with my supervisor and processed my own thoughts daily, my views could have actually harmed the research and these women through the imposition of a "master narrative" that overshadowed the entire purpose of this research: actively listening in order to better understand people's unique experiences (Fine, 1994). I had to reframe my own interpretations and view the participants' stories from their perspectives—as active agents who had made choices in their lives based upon their own constrained positionality. In other words, it was crucial that I understood these women as being shaped by their experiences, but simultaneously shaping their own experiences.

Becker (1996) argues that while participants know their individual and, perhaps, collective (i.e., raced, classed, or gendered) experiences best, researchers who do not identify with the group whom they study can and do bring a nuanced understanding to the research process. For example, through the use of different epistemologies and methodological practices, researchers may expand upon the limits of what we know about a group of people. Thus, while researchers obtain broader information about a particular group of people because they have not shared their lived experiences, they may be able to elicit information that fosters a new perspective or understanding (Becker, 1996).

While Fine (1994) also disagrees that only those who identify as part of the group being researched should be allowed to conduct that research, she does argue that researchers must be mindful of the tendency toward "imperial translation" (p. 80). To avoid this, researchers must be inclusive of everyone's voice within their research, even if certain data do not fit neatly within the context of the other data, something to which Becker (1990) and Palys (2008) refer as acknowledging "messy cases," or rival plausible explanations. Engaging in reflective and reflexive research yields more rigorous methodological practices. Further, in order to promote transformative, social justice-based research, researchers must consistently acknowledge the importance of both context and historicity. In other words, researchers must ground participants' voices in history and their social, political, and economic context.

Becker (1998) encourages researchers to "extend our ideas and images to accommodate more of the 'real world'" (p. 18). Palys and Atchison (2014) add that this is particularly appropriate when entering a social world as an outsider where a primary objective in any phenomenological undertaking, almost by definition, must be to remain open to the views, understandings and priorities of those whose lives one is researching. Consistent with these views, I argue that academics and activists need to work together to develop and incorporate theory and praxis into their respective academic and social milieus. A new theoretical framework needs to be developed, one that encompasses self-definitions and self-valuations and takes account of agentic performances (whether linguistic, behavioral/performative, or through the passage of ideology), by all non-hegemonic groups, and in particular, marginalized women. Critical theory incorporates many strands such as postcolonial thought, certain feminist epistemologies such as Black feminist thought, and Chicana feminism, to name a few.

Diane's opening statement in the beginning of this chapter calls for academics, practitioners, and policy makers alike to listen to the voices of those who have been silenced by society in order to democratize discourse about structural disadvantage, its impact on specific groups of people, and ways to promote change. Through their counternarratives, the participants in this research demonstrated their agency and thus constructed identities that transcended their marginalized positions within the carceral setting, and society at large.

NOTE

1. For further discussion on racialized and gendered relationships among incarcerated women, see Kolb and Palys (2018).

REFERENCES

Becker, H. S. (1998). *Tricks of the trade*. Chicago: University of Chicago Press.

Bruner, J. (1991). "The narrative construction of reality." *Critical Inquiry*, *18*, 1–21.

Byrne, B. (2003). "Reciting the self-narrative representations of the self in qualitative interviews." *Feminist Theory*, *4*(1), 29–49.

Campbell, A. (1984). "The girls in the gang." *New Society*, *69*(1135), 308–311.

Chesney-Lind, M., & Jones, N. (2010). *Fighting for girls: New perspectives on gender and violence*. New York: State University of New York Press.

Collins, P. H. (1991). "Mammies, matriarchs, and other controlling images." In *Black feminist thought: Knowledge, consciousness, and the politics of empowerment*, (pp. 67–89). United States: Taylor & Francis.

Collins, P. H. (1998). "It's all in the family: Intersections of gender, race, and nation." *Hypatia*, *13*(3), 62–82.

Crenshaw, K. (1989). "Demarginalizing the intersection of race and sex: A black feminist critique of antidiscrimination doctrine." *The University of Chicago Legal Forum*, *140*, 139–167.

Hagedorn, J. M. (1996). "The emperor's new clothes: Theory and method in gang field research." *Free Inquiry in Creative Sociology*, *24*, 111–122.

Hesse-Biber, S. J. N., & Leavy, P. L. (2010). *The practice of qualitative research.* Thousand Oaks, CA: Sage Publications.

Kincheloe, J. L., & McLaren, P. (2002). "Rethinking critical theory and qualitative research: Ethnography and schools." *Qualitative Approaches to the Study of Education*, *32*, 87–138.

Kolb, A., & Palys, T. (2012). "Are you down?: Power relation and gender reconstruction among Latina gang members in Los Angeles." *Journal of Gang Research*, *20*(1), 19–32.

Kolb, A. F., & Palys, T. (2016). "Homegirls, hoodrats, and hos: Co-constructing gang status through discourse and performance." *International Journal for Crime, Justice, and Social Democracy*, *5*(4), 29–44. https://doi.org/10.5204/ijcjsd.v5i4.334.

Miller, J. (2001). *One of the guys: Girls, gangs, and gender.* New York: Oxford University Press.
Ochs, E., & Capps, L. (1996). "Narrating the self." *Annual Review of Anthropology, 25*, 19–43.
Palys, T., & Atchison, C. (2013). *Research decisions: Quantitative, qualitative, and mixed method approaches* (5th ed.). Toronto: Nelson.
Riessman, C. K. (1987). "When gender is not enough: Women interviewing women." *Gender & Society, 1*(2), 172–207.
Rymes, B. (1995). "The construction of moral agency in the narratives of high-school drop-outs." *Discourse & Society, 6*(4), 495–516.
Schiffrin, D. (1996). "Narrative as self-portrait: Sociolinguistic constructions of identity." *Language in Society, 25*(2), 167–203.

Part III

BLURRING THE LINES

TALES OF PERSONAL CONNECTION

Chapter 6

Complicity and Compassion

Mediations on Writing and Researching with Incarcerated Women

Tobi Jacobi

What does it mean to be a white, middle-class woman writing and researching the role of literacy with women inside the U.S. prison system? What are the affective impacts of writing with confined women? Is the development of prison writing programming and the study of literacy an adequate response the mass incarceration? How can we manage the inevitable complicities and complacencies that arise when doing activist literacy work inside? These are some of the many questions that influence and complicate my work with writers who are incarcerated and the volunteer teachers who work with them.

This chapter reflects on almost two decades of research on writing behind bars by examining my journey engaging in program design, workshop facilitation, and qualitative interviews with women writers and volunteer teachers. These experiences suggest that scholars who participate in similar research and teaching should develop and rely upon an ethic of care and intentional compassion that can directly contribute to contemporary social justice efforts and sustainable practice. My research with incarcerated women writers began as a late stage doctoral student when a chance to teach a women's life writing course in a state prison eventually developed into a dissertation project focused on the teaching experiences of women leading prison writing workshops. What followed has been fifteen years of program development, teacher training, and engagement with other scholars committed to literacy programming and research behind bars.

Much of this work has taken place in Northern Colorado through the development and evolution of the SpeakOut! Writing Program—a creative and expository literacy program offered through site-specific weekly to confined people in a county jail, community corrections unit, parole, and youth rehabilitation. The program began as a collaboration between university students and faculty and the women's unit at our local community corrections program and expanded over several years to include youth writers and men in the jail and at community corrections. Weekly sessions were held in programming, and multipurpose rooms for groups consists of ten to fifteen "inside" writers and two to four trained university or community volunteer facilitators. Rather than adhering to a strict curriculum, the program grew organically from a set of shared principles informed by feminist and critical literacy practices, intent upon importing some of the social justice values promoted by community-based popular education scholars such as Paolo Freire and Myles Horton. These principles include expectations of shared writing space, collaborative content development, open dialogue, nonhierarchical writing critique as well as a commitment to valuing diverse voices and experiences through the dissemination of writing beyond workshop walls. Each workshop session—sixty to ninety minutes—includes several writing prompts, opportunities to read and respond to local and published writing, and an invitation to submit written and visual work for feedback and potential publication. Thousands of writers have moved through our programs and seen their work circulate globally through the biannual *SpeakOut! Journal* and dozens of volunteers have facilitated hundreds of workshop sessions. Often what begins as a freeform response to a writing prompt emerges a few weeks later (or sometimes fifteen minutes later) as a poem or story or image that reflects life behind bars, life apart of loved ones, and the trials and tribulations of everyday life. *Write about your day. Write a list of things you love. Write a food memory.* It is through such writing prompts that I have come to know and learn from and with women (and men) as they write their lives through the screen of incarceration. What follows, then, is a series of meditations on practice and interactions organized through writing prompts as I reflect upon the messy work of organizing and researching literacy programming in Northern Colorado over the past fifteen years. My experiences suggest that researchers, particularly women, working in carceral contexts can benefit from increased attention to mindfulness practices, self-care, and compassionate activism in order to sustain research trajectories with the potential to affect social change.

WRITING PROMPT 1: Read Some Poems About Collective Identity Together. Choose a Line or Phrase from One of Them to Inspire Our Own Writing and Our Collaborative Poem.

Often, we begin by writing together. We sit in a circle at long tables in room that feels much like a classroom or conference room, white board at one end, chairs neatly spaced at each table. We work with loose lined paper or in composition notebooks and glance up at the clock as we record our ideas on the page, willing time to hurry up or slow down depending upon how inspiration has come. Yet, it is not all familiar. Two-thirds of us wear orange uniforms. We scratch down our ideas with stubby four-inch pencils, shaking out the muscles of our hands every few minutes in an attempt to release the cramping that comes from trying to write big ideas through tiny tools. We are interrupted by loudspeakers, lockdowns, and echoing slammed doors. Still, we write. And we often begin by writing together: *Finish this line "I am from" "we are" "these hands."* We pen words and then each share a line around the room. We listen. We reorganize. This is what emerges:

I AM
The LCDC Women's Group

I am the spark that ignited a great romance.
I am a strong, loving, devoted mother.
I am a stumbling block on my stool, trying to hang onto my spirits.
I am a child of God. I am a respectful, warm-hearted Chicana.
I am not sure who I am anymore.
I am loving, caring, and kind, but to see that side of me, it takes time.
I am a witty, wacky whirlwind!
I am beautiful. I am smart. I am bashful.
I am from a scene called existing.

(*SpeakOut! Journal*, Spring 2012, p. 6)

A Real Woman
a collaborative poem

A real woman is strong
A real woman is herself, but by all means she is not perfect.
She speaks her mind because she is confident, charismatic, and full of character!
A real woman has flaws, but she's beautiful just the way she is.
She knows the meaning of "beauty is only skin deep."
A real woman doesn't need to have her neck elongated
plus her boobs actually bounce!
A real woman fears no man because she loves herself and everybody.
She buys jeans that fit so she eats what she wants. A real woman thinks of
herself as a queen so she doesn't mind living her life to its fullest.
A real woman loves people for their inner beauty so she turns
her back on fashionista magazines. She believes in herself
so when she steps out of bed she shines like a star.

A real woman is a beautiful mother, wife, sister, or friend.
A real woman is a person, and she's sitting right here in this room.

(*SpeakOut! Journal*, Fall 2010, p. 76)

Writing with women inside has been a core experience informing my pedagogical and research interests in understanding literacy and narrative as tools for social change. My experience as a researcher has really been borne out of the building of relationships primarily through program design and facilitation—the research always followed the facilitation of services for and with incarcerated women. This is an important element of reciprocity to lead with and one that reflected my commitment to best practices of service-learning and later community literacy/engagement work. Individual agency and reciprocal gain were intertwined. It is difficult to imagine engaging in carceral research without this element of participatory action and collaboration. These engagements hold me ethically accountable far more effectively than annual institutional review processes and paperwork or the online modules that encourage awareness of power dynamics and representations of the people with whom I work and under whose care bodies of writing reside.

Our program has been circulating women's writing in the *SpeakOut! Journal* under individual and collective authorship for over a decade. The journal is distributed locally and regionally through writers, facilitators, and program administrators, the latter two groups also regularly participating in academic conferences nationally and sometimes internationally. I recognize the power inequities that emerge through persistent questions: *How do we encourage the emergence of voice that does not result in appropriation? How do we navigate the line between complicity—necessary and elective—and complacencies borne out of fear, fatigue, or inadequacies linked to systemic inequities but lived through researcher agendas and bodies?* Much of my time working with writers who are incarcerated, with program design, and in training volunteer teachers to work with incarcerated people has centered on issues of representation, agency, and identity, including writers' and facilitators' perceptions of self and their relationship to power—both beneficial and potentially abusive. My own impulse as a writer committed to buoying and advancing women's confidence in their own abilities to make change and create powerful stories is to forward what veteran community writing teacher Pat Schneider (2003) calls "the conviction that all human beings are artists, and capable of writing in their own voices work that is strong and true" (p. 264). The work featured earlier moves women beyond their initial naming of experience and toward a processing of moments when women press against manhole covers and move through the pain and joy of life toward resilience.

PROMPT 2: Write about a Moment of Surprise, a Moment Where Things Either Came Together or Fell Apart.

I was distracted during the jail reading last night, still thinking about the youth reading the night before, about the kids' words, about the guest poets' performance. I was musing about future programming at the 4:00 pm train crossing, still encouraging the grocery checker to move through my tax-exempt order more quickly. I was juggling event details, and the words—impassioned words—of the SpeakOut! writers braving the podium seemed to bounce off my sweater and mind like tiny balls of sleet, an impenetrable surface. Put out plates. Hide the veggie tray until later. Add official stickers to the blank notebooks. Pause, listen to three poems, check in with volunteers. Remind interns of the timeline. Pour warm soda into ocean-killing plastic vessels. Distribute. Offer cupcakes as apology for a society and culture that insists on physical imprisonment as its primary method of social control of difference, poverty, and the masking of power relations. Wonder if program evaluations were completed. Sigh through realization that IRB renewal remains incomplete, months incomplete.

The SpeakOut! writing workshops are offered in twelve weekly sessions each spring and fall and are facilitated by trained university and community writing facilitators guided by the nonhierarchical community writing practices described earlier. Each series results in a final reading and collaborative issue of the *SpeakOut! Journal*, a print and digital journal distributed regionally (and beyond) without cost to writers. In their collaboratively authored essay, Benjamin Hall, Rhiannon Cates, and Vicki Reitenauer reflect on writing from near and within prison and argue that writing workshops create space and time for post-carceral world-building as notions of "what it means to be human and act humanly are interrogated, revised, and reenacted through and by a circle of narrators and witnesses" (p. 3). One such narrator who confidently took the SpeakOut! stage that night pulled me out of my task list as she introduced herself as "Lil Bit," a name that resonated from previous years. I looked up from food preparation to see an older, but familiar face. She smiled as she read her essay about love, about binaries between desire and rejection about lovers as angels and devils, and about the touch that is longed for, the fear of rejection. She still had long curled hair and I wondered about how that was accomplished in jail, what innovation and human ingenuity made that possible (alongside the crush pencil lead eyeliners, the toothpaste lid shadows). She read her poem, drew in the crowd and then encouraged up the next writer. She rose again a few moments later and preamble her piece with talk about convictions 8, 9, and 10 and the trappings of addiction. Later, over tepid Dr. Pepper, we reminisced about earlier SpeakOut! sessions and how she'd drawn one of the first journal covers for SpeakOut! "It's been fifteen years," I invited. "That makes me feel old," she responded. Me too. Several years of writing alongside women and working with other facilitators revealed an acute need to address the affective components of accumulating difficult stories and the potential for compassion fatigue.

PROMPT 3: Write about Something You Want but Cannot Have.

The "No" List:

You may not distribute the pallet of books on writing that the author wants to donate due to a page misprint.
Pens are dangerous; they can be weapons.
Full size pencils are also dangerous.
No bookmarks printed on card stock. No postcards.
No journals with spiral edges. No journals at all expect composition notebooks, commissary-approved.
No last names.
No jail humor.
No cursing.
Not more than two books.
No peppers on the last-day pizza. No oranges. Orange carrots are okay.
Nothing homemade.
No touching.
No staples, no plastic folders; lined paper is under review.
No publication without gang unit screening.

That literacy is dangerous is a well-worn idea, borne out across centuries of prisoners writing inside. The voicing of divergent experiences, those that challenge the hegemony of dominant culture are often discarded or suppressed. We navigate the rules, bending them when it seems possible to allow different stories to emerge. Doing this work often inspires teachers and researchers. Student interns and community volunteers regularly report on the intensity of their experiences, the gratitude and inspiration they take from each session, the connection they feel to writers through their shared writing communities. Yet, this work is also often overwhelming, debilitating, and depressing. Sometimes the weight of repressive histories and confiscated words presses down hard. This duality is worth putting down on paper. I wonder what exactly our small program can do. Amid decades of racial inequities, protests, and demands for reform, what changes? I try to navigate institutional responsibilities and social justice commitments when volunteers come to me with stories of observed inequities and worries of their own inevitable complicities. We tell ourselves that the spaces we create for free(r) speech matters, but the questions echo: *What can literacy do? What is different today? Anything? What is it that our SpeakOut! Journal might do?*

There are times when the echo of one woman's story reverberates so loudly that it overcomes my ability to bring other people into my life, when my own despondency about holding their narrative close slips over into critique of my own family's needs, wants, and desires. There is Joshua. Years later, I still think of her. Joshua, the name of my nephew, the name of students, literary references, but here the pen name of a woman who participated in both the SpeakOut! workshops and participant in a series of interviews I am still learning from. Joshua who came often and wrote scant words, who had an exigence that I can never fully understand, who makes my white middle-class privilege flash neon. Joshua who asked me directly what I had to offer her as we sat at a small round table in a plexi-glassed room off her housing unit. What resources did I have that could help her she wondered of my tidy notepad and the recorder placed carefully between us? What resources, indeed? As a researcher, I confront this question daily. *When should I speak up? When should I stay silent? When should I not even be present? When is it fair to ask people experiencing incarceration to participate in system change?*

Moments of (white) (academic) privilege recognition:

- In the waiting room while observing people waiting to visit loved ones; being denied, being offered rules/regulations rather than humanity.
- In my own writing. Being able to choose what to reveal about myself.
- In my collaborations. Struggling with how academic to be in the group meetings surrounding the writing of the essay on addiction and mothering inside.
- In my ability to facilitate or not. Choosing to go inside or go home.
- In my academic writings and presentations. In taking writers' words beyond the jail and SpeakOut!
- In designing curricula and imposing my beliefs about social justice upon it.
- In making assumptions about what the writers need/want.

I had to stop going to the jail after about ten years. I could not commit to the regular accumulation of more stories. Writing scholar, Amy Robillard (2014) writes that "when our narratives fall apart, when the stories we tell ourselves collapse in on themselves, we might say that we've come undone. Collapse is caused by a lack of support or intense external pressure" (p. 11). Witnessing and researching the stories that precede and emerge from women's writing about incarceration did not shatter the narrative of a literacy activism that has been a cornerstone of my scholarly identity; it wasn't so dramatic, more like a slow burn, an accumulation, an undermining mirrored by a system determined to reshape a citizenry into an impossible heterogenous white middle-class mold.

PROMPT 4: What Is It Like to Be a Woman Writing Inside?

This isn't so much a prompt as an ever-present contemplation. It was also a standard mid-interview question I asked of both the writers who agreed to writing history interviews and later female volunteers. It was a constant subtext as we all sat writing together, working through the evening's set of activities. It was embedded in my university-sanctioned internship curriculum and in our volunteer trainings. As a woman teaching and researching inside, it has been impossible to avoid gender as a category linked to (unwanted) attention and visible inequity. This became painfully clear when navigating the rules and regulations for moving volunteers or visitors inside (Comfort, 2018; Jacobi, 2018). A few examples:

> *Regressive regulation of volunteer's bodies:* While there certainly is no comparison between the rigid control over dress that prisoners experience and volunteer guidelines, the dress code regulations illustrate gender bias and move to both re-inscribe and enforce Victorian ideals about women's bodies and chastity. When talking with student and community volunteers about how to prepare to come inside the jail, for example, we have frank conversations about the ways that women's clothing and bodies are policed differently than men's: no shorts, no short skirts, no sandals, no sleeveless or low cut shirts, no headscarves, scarves, or necklaces. Training warns against touch and anticipates manipulation of volunteers by prisoners (e.g., the weak feminine mind).
>
> *Unnecessary Attention and Embodied Empathy*: When I was heavily pregnant with my son, a guard chose to direct repeated sharp and infantilizing verbal commands at me as I went through the usual process of encouraging workshop participants. The women circled me, protective of both me and the SpeakOut! program. Later (and often) as we marched single file along the corridors between the women's housing units and our workshop room, we passed the men's outdoor recreation courts, windows with hands pressed to the glass, catcalls filling our passage. Both were instances of particular vulnerability which made me more sensitive to how people, particularly women, were being treated inside, an embodied moment of learning and empathy.
>
> *Unnecessary Regulation of Visiting Bodies*: As I sat with SpeakOut! volunteers in the jail lobby for half an hour, back when physical visits still

happened in the adjacent room, a woman came in with an infant and a toddler boy. She was on time for her visit. She had driven for hours. They wouldn't let the infant in because she didn't have the right paperwork. Somehow a copy of the birth certificate wasn't enough. Her work to keep it together—baby, toddler, long drive to a jail for a brief visit—all started to crack apart as they called us to line up and head into the jail. *What difference does it make, I wondered, if the birth certificate is a photocopy or original in this modern era? What possible difference could it make in the twenty minutes that woman would spend looking through plexiglass at a loved one? Hold the baby up to the glass, juggling toddler, infant, and well-worn phone?*

The emotional labor of conducting volunteer work and research inside spaces of confinement and women's researcher bodies is seldom discussed, seldom inquired about or acknowledged in grant funding applications, research surveys, or final reports. Yet we experience secondary traumas in our movements, our interactions, and in the silences, we witness and contribute to.

BEYOND WRITING PROMPTS

When I couldn't hold any more women's narratives, I turned away from teaching inside toward other forms of writing: poetry, creative nonfiction, storytelling, and overt research on self-care for people who work in carceral settings. The latter emerged as a very real need that was emerging for program volunteers who experienced shorter commitments (a semester or two usually) to the program, but who still experienced secondary trauma and compassion fatigue as stories of loss, addiction, and confinement mounted and as they also had to confront the privilege of being free to move in the world in ways the writers they worked with could not. As a Community Literacy Center, we recognized this reality and conducted qualitative research among our volunteers, developed and implemented training materials, and published several articles (Tuthill & Jacobi, forthcoming; Yenne et al., 2015; Jacobi & Roberts, 2016). These are efforts I am proud of, though the ongoing risk of fatigue and trauma persists, since it is impossible to avoid the collision of worlds, times when tidy articulations of engagement and wholeness as a scholar-human come crashing together in unexpected ways. In responding directly to the usual and unusual traumas that come with working in correctional spaces, we contribute to and draw upon a rich literature of writing through trauma (Pennebaker & Chung, 2011; MacCurdy, 2007; DeSalvo, 1999).

Those collisions happen all the time. Last spring I went into the office on a normal day, a teaching day, a day with a full to-do slate that was swiped partially away when a new colleague called my name as I unlocked my office door, asked me if I knew Chandara. I flipped through my mental rolodex. Chandara, Chandara, a student we shared? Someone from the jail? Someone from the community? My colleague was interested in prison work and writing, a shared interest. I placed Chandara in the jail, in SpeakOut! from a few years back and then in a special writing collaboration focused on mothers, addiction, and incarceration (see Von Weller et al., 2018). I turned back across the hall and grabbed the book that our essay had appeared in and peppered my colleague with questions: Do you know her? Do you know how to find her? I've been trying to figure out how to find her to give her a copy of this book that has our collaborative essay? And that was when my colleague stopped me: "She died." Swipe the rest of the mental to-do list away. Oh. She died. I'm holding the book in my hands, the book with the essay on addition and mothering, the essay with the letter she wrote to her adult son, so full of hope and promise. She died. And then my colleague filled in some bits and pieces. She didn't know her well. She had been struggling some. She didn't know how she died, but she did know that Chandara had lost her son in the last year. The son in the letter in the essay in the book I could never deliver. And so falls apart all the good intentions, the promise of reciprocity and hope of research and programming to shift the trajectory of the lives of people recovering from life traumas that include incarceration.

I am saying her name. She wanted her real name on the essay, and as an adult, she has every right to make that decision. I don't know how she died. My colleague found out on Facebook, a bland and sorrowful post by a barely acquaintance. I asked her to let me know if she was able to find out more or any way to contact relatives who I could send the book to. I sat with my disappointment for the days that followed guilt and disappointment that I hadn't made a stronger effort to reach out to Chandara and the other four women who coauthored the text, some students, some writers in the jail. It feels like a failure. I'm glad her words live on in print. I'm glad the letter to her son is there. She kept a copy. I hope it made its way to his hearing before his own young death. This episode does little to bolster my own questioning of when and where we find success in the prison research and literacy work we do, though it does motivate my desire to do right ethically and methodologically by the people I work with, dead or alive.

What does it mean to do this research? Always searching across disciplines to find others invested in the work. Always navigating the line between activism and academics and feeling confusion about academics who suggest that it is possible to be objective, who aim to conduct research and gather data without acknowledging the historical atrocities that precede them and the fear of research that most carceral institutions operate from. For me, it is impossible to do research inside without bearing the burden of the wrongs researchers have done, the wrongs that continue to be done as stories are collected and exploited, as narratives are circulated with the hope of demonstrating evidence-based knowledge, but that often ignore or at least hold at bay the emotional and affective dynamics that influence research practices, that renew and deepen the sense of mistrust that exists between those who lock up and those who live locked up (or watch friends and family living that way).

TOWARD REFLECTIVE INTENTIONAL RESEARCH PRACTICES BEHIND BARS

How to Avoid Being in the Way: Notes to Self on Decolonial Aspirations:

I am not in the way when I make materials available to women and men in jail, the tools of literacy such as texts, paper, space for writing, and prompts to inspire new ways to approach writing.
I am not in the way when I teach university courses on prison literacy and writing. This works to introduce students to texts that they rarely have the opportunity to engage. It raises awareness about the often invisible world of prison as well as questions of justice for young adults who have the potential to influence workplaces and curricula in future spaces.
I am not in the way when I offer students and community members opportunities to learn how to work with incarcerated people. They need to direct access in order to understand how systems of oppression work.
I am not in the way when I make space to read diverse books on prison systems.
I am not in the way when I make intentional choices about where to seek philosophical and economic support for research and programming inside.
I am not in the way when I work with students (inside and outside) on projects that articulate inequity and move toward decolonial practice.
I am not in the way when I engage with the national and international community of prison/jail writing teachers.
I am not in the way when I decenter research traditions and writing practices by writing together in ways that dismantle academic and mainstream hierarchies.
(At least this is the hope)

Reflecting upon two decades of work in carceral spaces illuminates the need for intentional and regular reflective practice, particularly for women engaged in research within the U.S. justice system. These two questions remain at the forefront of my mind: *How do researchers navigate the potential hoops designed and maintained by the system? What kinds of emotional labor are frontloaded onto women scholars engaging in this work?* In reflecting across the research and programming I have initiated within carceral spaces, I note that the invocation of stories about two SpeakOut! women writers who died under only vaguely visible conditions after their release from the jail. One perhaps a death from cold, homelessness, the other perhaps from a life shackled by addictions. The constant might be loss itself: Joshua lost her husband to a heart attack that created an avalanche through her life; Chandara wrote about the pain of separation while in jail and then I can imagine the horror of losing her young adult son in the past year. I cannot know what it feels like, but I can imagine the return to the numbness of substance abuse in the face of that kind of loss. A turn toward self-care and compassion fatigue research demonstrated the direction that I could feel myself moving—both as an observed need for my students/volunteers but also as a reality for my own lived experience as a writing workshop facilitator, a researcher, and a keeper of stories.

When Eric Garner lost his life on a New York City sidewalk in 2014, we listened and responded to public outcry by continuing to make space for open dialogue and writing as both an outlet for and response to injustice. Several SpeakOut! writers produced social justice-inspired poetry and prose for submission in the journal and then organized a peaceful protest at our fall reading by holding up signs that read "We can't breathe." Even as this essay emerges, urgency remains as we navigate endemic and persistent racisms. Masked and unmasked people—myself among them—struggle to understand the global pandemics that rage on, both physical and philosophical. The expectations and tensions that exist between social justice activists and academics remain palpable. The past fifteen years of my life have been spent cultivating and facilitating a program that is built upon principles of social justice, access to literacy and language as tools for understanding how we engage and come to know one another. I worry that I have been trained out of effectiveness by those who are also academics, that we are forever preaching to the choir, a choir that can use language well but that doesn't always create meaningful change for those beyond its boundaries. While some find opportunity for justice work inside higher education; others leave academics, choosing to pivot commitments to writing studies away from the oppression of increasingly corporatized universities and toward a community-based model of elective engagement in web-based writing retreats focused on intentional practice. I have chosen to remain committed as a literacy researcher and project leader, though I am primarily behind the scenes. When I do visit the jail workshops, I am comfortable and often see writers who recognize me from past sessions or events, even as we head toward our fifteen-year anniversary. Current practices of incarcerated children and separating families is dismaying, disgusting, and dehumanizing and must inspire and invigorate efforts to create strong connections between carefully rendered qualitative and quantitative research and outcomes that support social justice. Women scholars can lead these efforts by frontloading ethics of compassion-based activism through the research methodologies we practice. As I imagine the next five years and the research questions that will inform and shape our practice, I am hopeful that compassionate, mindful, and decolonial practices will be at the center of our collaborative efforts. I am hopeful that the mentoring I can offer to rising scholars, writers, and returning citizens will be gracious, patient, and reciprocal. I am hopeful that we will continue to think and think and think with the people who remain behind bars about a more promising way forward.

REFERENCES

Comfort, M. (2003). "In the tube at San Quentin: The 'secondary prisonization' of women visiting inmates." *Journal of Contemporary Ethnography*, *32*(1), 77–107. https://doi.org/10.1177/0891241602238939.

DeSalvo, L. (1999). *Writing as a way of healing: How telling our stories transforms our lives*. Boston, MA: Beacon Press.

Hall, B., Cates, R., & Reitenauer, V. (2019). "Out of time: Accomplices in post-carceral world-building." *Humanities*, *8*(64), 1–11.

Jacobi, T. (2018). "Institutional mothering: Middling between university, home, and jail." In K. Mantas & L. Peterson (Eds.), *Mothering and/in/through mid-life* (pp. 82–91). Ontario: Demeter Press.

Jacobi, T., & Roberts, L. (2016). "Developing self-care strategies for volunteers in a jail writing program." In L. Abrams & E. Hughes (Eds.), *The voluntary sector in prisons: Encouraging institutional and personal change* (pp. 331–361). New York: Palgrave MacMillan.

LCDC Women's Writing Group. (2012). "I am." *SpeakOut! Journal* (Spring), p. 6. Available at: https://speakoutclc.wordpress.com/journals/.

MacCurdy, M. (2007). *The mind's eye: Image and memory in writing about trauma*. Amherst: University of Massachusetts Press.

Pennebaker, J., & Chung, C. (2011). "Expressive writing: Connections to physical and mental health." In H. S. Friedman (Ed.), *The Oxford handbook of health psychology*. New York: Oxford University Press.

Robillard, A. (2014). "On narrative collapse: Dementia, depression, and the significance of narrative resources." *Survive & Thrive: A Journal for Medical Humanities and Narrative as Medicine 1.1*. Available at: https://repository.stcloudstate.edu/survive_thrive/vol1/iss1/8.

Robillard, A., & Combs, D. S. (2019). *How stories teach us: Composition, life writing, and blended scholarship*. New York: Peter Lang.

Schneider, P. (2003). *Writing alone and with others*. New York: Oxford University Press.

SpeakOut! Women Writers. (2010). "A real woman." *SpeakOut! Journal* (Fall), p. 76. Available at: https://speakoutclc.wordpress.com/journals/.

Tuthill, S., & Jacobi, T. (forthcoming). "Self-care as ethical practice for teachers and volunteers working behind bars." In P. Alexander & S. Smith-McKoy (Eds.), *Teaching literature and writing in prison.* New York: MLA Press.

Von Weller, C., Joplin, J., Pecchio, S.,Willkomm, L., Miller, K., & Jacobi, T. (2018). "Mothering through addiction and jail." In W. Peterson, L. Armstrong, & M. Foulkes (Eds.), *Mothers, addiction and recovery: Finding meaning through the journey* (pp. 49–66). Bradford, ON: Demeter Press.

Yenne, E., Alessi, L., & Jacobi, T. (2015). "Lockstep trauma: The challenge of social justice literacy work behind bars." In L. Finley & K. Concannon (Eds.), *Peace and social justice education on campus: Faculty and student perspectives* (pp. 133–152). Cambridge: Cambridge Scholars Publishing.

Chapter 7

Empathy and Identity

Mothers Researching (Incarcerated) Mothers

Beth Easterling

MULTIPLE IDENTITIES: RESEARCHER AND MOTHER

"My name is Beth and I am a graduate student studying sociology and criminology. I am doing a project on how incarceration affects families. . . . I am interested in the mother-child relationship and finding out things that families experience and types of services that they think might be helpful to them. I am a mom myself, so I know the strong bond that mothers share with their children. My goal is to finish my degree and have a career where I continue to study families experiencing incarceration. Hopefully I will have the opportunity to go beyond this type of research and be involved in programs and services to help families with relationships and personal needs."

Those are the exact words I wrote, practiced, and spoke to incarcerated mothers nearly ten years ago when I first began research for my dissertation, which focused on how mothers in prison navigate the challenges of parenting on the inside, with special attention paid to the experiences of ambiguous loss (see Boss, 1999) and the negotiation of mother identities and roles while incarcerated (see Easterling, 2012, 2014; Easterling & Johnson, 2015; Easterling & Feldmeyer, 2017; Easterling et al., 2018). Nearly a decade later, and thankfully no longer a graduate student, I am still pursuing those professional goals as a professor. One of the biggest challenges of my research agenda has been the emotional work involved in being a mother while studying mothers and their children who have been impacted by incarceration.

All of the lessons and practice in graduate school did not prepare me for the *emotional* negotiation of *my* identity as a mother throughout my dissertation research and future projects. What began with many tears from those I was interviewing evolved into my own emotional turmoil and years of reflective work of defining myself not only as a researcher but also as a mother, who is active in research involving other mothers, who happen to be incarcerated. Other researchers have noted the huge responsibility and sense of privilege that come with doing sensitive research. Studying researchers who had performed sensitive research on health-related topics, Dickson-Swift (2007) and colleagues note:

> They often felt that they had been afforded a privilege by being allowed to listen to stories that were often private and intimate. . . . The privilege of being allowed to access and initiate story also meant that many researchers in the current study felt a sense of responsibility to do something with that story. For some, the responsibility of being given the story weighed heavily on their conscience, leaving them with the feeling that failing to do something to help that person's situation would be letting those people down. (Dickson-Swift et al., 2007, p. 340)

These words ring true in my own experiences, despite the fact that the researchers involved in Dickson-Swift and colleagues' study were exploring different topics. In my own situation, the shared mother identity with participants in my study intensified the anxiety that revolves around my own professional expectations for my research. In exploring the mother identity further, I discuss my senses of privilege and responsibility, and the emotional responses that resulted. The dichotomy of a shared identity with my participants coupled with very different experiences with mothering was challenging for me.

According to Greer (2002), who explored the emotional negotiation that occurs for women who are incarcerated, "walking an emotional tightrope" involves using strategies (including diversions, self-reflections, and humor) in order to cope with the variety of often conflicting emotions that women face while incarcerated. Such contemporary research has begun to recognize these gendered struggles for those who are living in prison, but it still largely ignores the "emotional tightrope" of women who are doing research in prisons. In particular, performing qualitative research inside prison walls can be a very emotional experience. When researching sensitive topics as qualitative researchers, "We go into other people's lives, sometimes at a time of crises and stress and we ask them to talk in detail about their experiences" (Disckson-Swift et al., 2007, p. 327). I argue that the gendered experience for women doing research in women's prisons creates additional and unique emotional challenges. Those challenges are magnified when it is a *mother* researching *mothers* who are incarcerated, creating conflicting emotions between the researcher and the mother identities. As qualitative research is typically a collaborative process, concerns of power and equality as well as the experience of empathy can potentially hinder the research process, but it does not have to be that way.

In this chapter, I reflect on the experiences of my journey doing qualitative work inside prison (and beyond prison walls with children who have had parents who have been incarcerated), with a focus on the challenges of negotiating my identity as a mother, while managing the deep emotions that come with that identity. My goal is to broaden the discussion surrounding experiences and challenges of mothers doing research on mothers who are incarcerated. I include the lessons I have learned to help mitigate my own emotional challenges in order to fulfill my roles as a researcher, while taking on the huge professional responsibility and emotional task of retelling and analyzing the stories of my research participants—all while holding the master status of mother. I describe some tools and tips I have used through a phenomenologically informed approach (see Easterling & Johnson, 2015) and the biographical-interpretive method (see Hollway & Jefferson, 2000), inspired by feminist epistemology (see Ramazanoglu & Holland, 2002), to help navigate this "emotional tightrope" of sorts.

EXPLORING THE MOTHER IDENTITY

The concept of "motherhood" is embedded within our culture, with the idea of mothering ("a historically and culturally variable relationship in which one individual nurtures and cares for another," see Glenn, 1994, p. 3) as natural and universal for women. In the 1900s, the concept of the "ideal mother" emerged and motherhood evolved from a biological classification to a "noble calling" (Morash & Schram, 2002, p. 73). Glenn (1994) notes that "agency is central to an understanding of mothering as a social, rather than biological, construct" (p. 3). Prior research suggests that becoming a mother can have a strong influence on how the mother perceives herself (Laney et al., 2015). This phenomenon is evident in my own life and seemed apparent for the women I interviewed while they were in prison. Personally, becoming a mother fundamentally changed my identity and, thus, the way I see myself as well as the way I interact in society. My social identity as a mother and the agency I embody as a free woman were in stark contrast to mothers I spoke with who were behind bars, where society strips individuals of identity and attempts to limit agency on multiple levels. As such, the mothers who volunteered to take part in my research study had lost the ability to actively mother in any traditional sense due to incarceration. This resulted in feelings of grief and ambiguous loss (see Boss, 1999 and further discussion below) for those mothers because they were unable to fulfill traditional duties related to mothering.

Incarcerated mothers challenge societal norms and expectations. Glenn (1994) suggests, "For most of the twentieth century an idealized model of motherhood, derived from the situation of the white, American, middle class, has been projected as universal. In this model, responsibility for mothering rests almost exclusively on one woman (the biological mother)" (p. 3). Enos broadens this discussion in her work on mothers in prison, suggesting that a hegemonic perception of mothering consists in the following ideas:

1. Mothers are completely engaged with their priceless children and totally absorbed by this work;
2. Mothering takes priority over all other work and is the ultimate fulfillment for women;
3. Mothers are all-powerful and direct the development and future of their children, and a failure here will replace the future of children at risk;
4. Only certain caretakers—namely, biological or adoptive mothers—can "mother";
5. Mothers face motherhood with adequate time and resources;
6. Mothers perform the emotional work necessary to maintain "happy" families;
7. With respect to mothering, race and class account for little (Enos, 2001, p. 23).

These generalizations of mothers are clearly more attainable for some women than others, even in free society based upon socioeconomic status and family structure, for example. Mothers in prison are unable to adequately fulfill mothering roles and perform mothering duties by societal standards. Nonetheless, incarcerated mothers are *still mothers* and motherhood is often a central and important identity for these women, serving as a master status (Easterling, 2012).

In my research, mothers who were incarcerated shared that being a mother was integral to their ability and motivation to survive the incarceration period. They stressed the importance of holding on to motherhood to maintain self-esteem and purpose in their lives, despite the sadness of being separated from their children within the confines of prison. During one group interview in 2011, I asked mothers if they still felt like mothers. One woman responded: "It's about the only thing they can't take away from us." Such a simple reply suggests the deep meaning "motherhood" holds for mothers experiencing incarceration (Easterling, 2012). And it was these types of conversations that triggered my emotions, realizing that the deep love

I feel for my own child and my self-identification as a mother are also felt by women who do not have the ability to be part of their children's daily lives. While my mothering abilities are not often criticized (other than the fact that I am a working mother with an only child, which violates many mothering expectations, but that is a subject for another book), I quickly realized that the women who were sharing their stories with me did not enjoy such luxuries despite our shared mother identity and love for our children. My initial emotional response was difficult and intense, inhibiting my ability to complete some of my earlier interviews, as I shut down. It spilled over into my personal life, making me feel sad. I struggled with the responsibility of having to retell these mothers' stories, realizing I connected so deeply with the experiences of motherhood, but so little with the realities of life behind bars.

Regardless of the objective circumstances and mothering roles before prison, mothers still hold on to the ideal of motherhood while incarcerated (Easterling, 2012; Enos, 2001; Morash & Schram, 2002; Owen, 1998). The identification with oneself as a mother is central to the personal identity of many incarcerated mothers and, regardless of the objective nature of pre-prison relationships between mother and child, incarcerated mothers tend to idealize relationships with their children and focus on the happy memories they shared. Once incarcerated, women are faced with a significant amount of time to reflect on the consequences of their behaviors, their situations, and the effects on their children. Those objective circumstances prior to incarceration coupled with the unavoidable separation during incarceration encourage compounded feelings of loss and failure, including the loss of motherhood (Easterling, 2012). Incarcerated mothers may continue to "hold themselves to the standard set by ideal constructions of motherhood and feel inadequate in comparison" and are likely to be consumed by a significant amount of guilt from the loss of their children (Morash & Schram, 2002, p. 75). Losing the role as (and having to renegotiate the identity of) mother can be one of the most difficult elements of adjustment to incarceration (Hardesty et al., 1993).

Within criminology, studies of identity have largely been framed around labeling theory and specifically to clarify and predict how labeling affects identity, which affects recidivism. My research referenced in this chapter examines the (re)construction of motherhood as mothers navigate prison life, focusing on how mothers fulfill and perform the mother role in pursuit of holding on to the mother identity (see Easterling, 2012). I am considering identity construction as an active process; the women I interviewed are agents in self-definition of a widely held societal expectation. As someone who has also constructed my own identity as a mother (both personally and in relation to hegemonic standards), my empathetic and emotional reactions to the data I was collecting were in response to the identity I shared with my participants.

EMPATHY WHEN RESEARCHING (INCARCERATED) MOTHERS

Empathy can be defined as the ability to understand another person's emotions or the ability to take a perspective that can understand another person's position (Guo et al., 2019). On an individual level, one may "put herself in someone else's shoes," so to speak. While sociological research is limited on gendered empathetic responses, some evidence suggests that women bear a disproportionate amount of empathy when compared with other groups in society (Davis, 1993) and that mothers, in particular, may at least share the perception/feeling of empathy toward other mothers, even if they are not able to accurately guess other mothers' feelings (see Hodges et al., 2010). In my own situation, I certainly *felt* empathy toward the mothers I was interviewing, even if I did not fully understand or have personal experience with their unique situations regarding mothering, or even life in general.

Salice and Taipale (2015) have developed the concept of group-directed empathy, which may be more fitting for the mother conducting research on mothers in prison. In short, they "suggest that it is possible to have an empathetic act when the target is not an individual or even individual members of a group, but rather *the group itself*" (Szanto & Krueger, 2019, emphasis in original). I would argue this is the "type" of empathy I experienced so intensely during my time researching other mothers, who were in prison. While their individual stories invoked strong emotions, it was the *overall* connection I felt with these women *as mothers* where my empathy ran the deepest. The shared experience of motherhood and the mother identity helped me relate to my participants, but also invoked a strong empathetic response that resulted in personal emotional turmoil. By being able to "put myself in the shoes" (on some subjective level) of the mothers who were in prison, in some sense I thought I felt a version of their pain and I grieved for their losses, not because I had shared their experiences, but because I shared a categorical or group identity with deeply embedded societal definitions and expectations. Imagining the losses they felt through the stories they shared with me, which included rich descriptions of their pain as mothers, struck a personal chord with me.

As I began my many hours in a women's prison researching mothers, I was overwhelmed by my constant inner dialogue of: "I'm a mother. She's a mother. But we are living two VERY different lives." I came to do my work every morning, left every afternoon and returned after lunch, and then left to spend the evening with my own child. I found myself almost ashamed to admit my freedom to the mothers I was interviewing, fully recognizing the differences between us were already known and obvious. My field notes from my first round of interviews reflect this internal conflict: "I felt a strange feeling—not guilt but similar—and I did not want to tell her [my first participant of the afternoon] that I went to Subway, etc. I was very aware of our different statuses at this point." The pull between mother and researcher identities were competing and strong.

Part of my method for gathering sensitive information was to connect with the women I was interviewing—connect *as mothers*. Rapport is key for gathering qualitative data, and the process of building rapport can encourage the researcher to share information about their own lives, which is not always accepted in other methods of research (Disckson-Swift, 2007). I naively went into the project excited to connect on my similarities with my participants—we were all mothers, so we could easily talk about motherhood, right? Not necessarily. While we were all mothers, our experiences were not similar at all—at least not at the time I was conducting the interviews and, through those interviews, it was apparent that our experiences were not very similar even before the participants' incarcerations. My research interviews, and literature reviews to accompany, put these dissimilarities into context. My field notes reflect some of the ways I grappled with this information at the time: "I am also blown away by the issues with family backgrounds of abuse and neglect. So many of these women volunteer information on terrible childhoods. This solidifies my goals in helping CHILDREN of these [incarcerated] women, in hopes of breaking the unfortunate cycle." Reading between the lines and relying on my recollections from that time, this speaks to my pull as a mother permeating my researcher identity. In my own life, I am constantly focused on the well-being of my child. Even in my professional life, it would seem like I am searching for ways to assist other mothers in helping their children, albeit indirectly. The nature of my own motherhood provokes emotions (including some level of empathy) that spill into my professional work whether it be taking more a parental role with my students or trying to find ways to help fellow mothers who are part of my research studies.

Beyond the connection with motherhood in general, my emotions in some ways mirrored the emotions my participants showed during our time together. When a researcher is confronted by strong emotional reactions of her participants that she can connect with on a very personal level, it "may compel researchers to reflect on aspects of their own lives, which can be an emotional experience" (Dickson-Swift, 2009, p. 70). From the start of my research project, I felt a connection with the mothers I was talking to, but I simultaneously struggled to come to terms with the differences in power and experience between my participants and me. While I was fulfilling my mothering roles on a daily basis, this aspect of their lives (along with many others) was a loss for the mothers in my study. My evenings away from the prison and the weeks that followed the conclusion of my interviews were filled with my own feelings of guilt and sadness when reflecting on the stories of the mothers I interviewed. I find solace in knowing that other researchers have experienced similar responses, though it is not often discussed openly in academic circles. When researching sensitive topics, researchers have "reported occasions when they were emotionally overwhelmed during the research, stating that this was often directly attributable to the participants becoming emotional" (Dickson-Swift et al., 2009). Our hesitancy to more widely discuss emotions is also noted by Dickson-Swift et al. (2009): "As students, researchers and professionals, we are products of a long process of socialization into academic life, often heavily reliant on the value of science and objectivity above all else. The difficulties that researchers have in speaking about their own emotions may be borne from this" (p. 66). I certainly experienced such difficulties. I hope that the topic of this chapter, and indeed this entire anthology, helps to open this discussion.

Over time, I was able to negotiate my own emotions to better complete my research interviews in the moment and analyze my data after the interviews were over. Perhaps that ability came from a combination of desensitization (a reaction also felt by the researcher-participants in Dickson-Swift and colleagues' work), gaining experience, and the drive to complete my research project. Still, new challenges emerged. I felt a connection with the mothers who graciously agreed to share their stories to be a part of my project. So terminating that relationship, which is always part of the researcher-participant dynamic, also came with an emotional response. I had learned so much about these women's lives and their love for their children. As much as I tried to be only an objective observer, in reality, I was a participant in my own research project (see Presser, 2008) even after the conclusion of the interviews and I evolved as an individual through the entire process. Perhaps the shared mother identity with my participants even deepened my involvement in my project. But once my data collection was complete, I walked out of the prison indefinitely. What would happen to the mothers in my study? I had to be comfortable not knowing the answer to this question. What was my responsibility to these mothers? What was my job? These two questions had more concrete answers. And those answers helped me to overcome the hardest parts of the emotional hurdles I was facing. I held a huge responsibility to the mothers who volunteered for my study. I had to tell their stories, accurately and respectfully. Further, it was my job to finish my dissertation and later disseminate my findings to a wider audience in honor of and respect for those who shared their stories with me.

Liebling (2014) notes, "The appropriate master status of all in social science research is 'personhood,' with all the equal claims to privacy, dignity, and respect that this term implies" (p. 482). When we are conducting social science research within a prison, issues such as privacy, respect, and claims to dignity become problematic (see Liebling, 2014). When a researcher-mother is attempting to "level" the master status with her participants, the master status is even more precise—not only personhood, but motherhood, both of which are difficult to level when one participant is free and the other is confined. This has the potential to create internal/emotional struggles during the research process. Inherently, while doing research within a prison setting, "Experience is intensified. . . . Evaluations of one's circumstances are often performed below the level of consciousness—at the level of emotion. So prisoners' evaluations, and also our own as researchers in the field, are shaped by their experience of feelings. Emotion is a source of evaluation of circumstances" (Liebling, 2014, p. 483). Prison walls can magnify social problems and injustices that are present in free society—experiences for all who are confined by those walls can be extreme. These experiences and emotions are felt by both those living in the prison and, though very differently, also by those doing research in prison. Adding the connection with the mother identity between researcher and subject, I believe, intensified my emotional reactions to the research I was conducting and the struggles I encountered in grappling with our vastly different social locations and the varying power dynamics of our lived mothering experiences.

Other scholars have explored the idea that conducting research on sensitive topics can engage researchers in a high level of empathy and caring as a result of their research and the qualitative methodologies they employ (Dickson-Swift et al., 2007). As such, the idea of "emotion work" comes into play. First coined by Arlie Hochschild (1979), emotion work refers to work that involves other people's emotions (James, 1989; Dickson-Swift et al., 2007). Sensitive research topics can involve displays of emotion from participants, which can create difficulties for some researchers (Dickson-Swift et al., 2007). "If we acknowledge that qualitative research is an embodied experience that requires some level of emotion work then we need to think about how we actually do emotion work and what that might mean" (Dickson-Swift et al., 2009). For me, it meant personal struggles in completing my interviews and in handling my own emotional responses, particularly when reflecting on the stratification in mothering abilities between the mothers in my study and my own personal life. The dual identity of mother and researcher was at the root of this struggle. In exploring others' work, I find that it is imperative that I not focus so much on binary identities that are competing, but rather explore and try to embrace the idea of having a fluid identity (see Thomson & Gunter, 2011), allowing myself to flow between the identities of mother and researcher as well as to redefine myself due to my experiences. As such, I turn now to a discussion on tools and tips that can help to deal with seemingly competing identities and the emotional responses that occur as a mother researching incarcerated mothers.

TOOLS AND TIPS

The challenges of reconciling empathy, identity, and all of the emotions that come with those aspects of being a mother researching (incarcerated) mothers can be daunting. Dickson-Swift et al. (2009) note that it is imperative that researchers doing sensitive work learn to accept the emotions of their participants and manage their own emotions that emerge as a result; if not, emotional exhaustion is a very real risk for the researcher. Still, there are still ways to be successful in navigating the prison research at hand, with the emotions that go along with that research. A reliance on and deeper understanding of the method we are using can go a long way in pushing past the emotional challenges of researching vulnerable populations, particularly those we empathize with on such a deep level. In my own experience, having a vocabulary to adequately discuss our experiences as well as the experiences of those we study has been key. Looking toward theoretical traditions to contextualize results can be helpful in overcoming difficult emotions during research, by allowing a framework within which to describe results.

Understanding ourselves as part of the collaborative process of qualitative research in the unique position as prison researchers is imperative to grappling with the emotion work of this research. Presser (who I was lucky enough to have as a dissertation chair and mentor), in her work evaluating the narratives of violent men, views the qualitative interview process as a social transaction. She notes, "I am myself a contributor to or 'co-producer' of the narrative data. As they spoke, the men in my study were already incorporating the interview—all that it involved and signified—into their narratives. The fact of the interview and specifics of the interview exchange were significant experience for them. The interview shaped their life stories" (Presser, 2008, p. 8). In a similar fashion, my interviews and discussions with the incarcerated mothers who volunteered to participate in my study signify a social exchange. Though I was seeking to gain information from my participants, *I*, too was part of the interactions. Thus, the social transactions of the interviews (including my roles in them) also shaped the stories the mothers shared and became part of their stories and their journeys. Being able to define and articulate these experiences has been key for me as a researcher. It also helps to contextualize the social exchange as an important part of research.

Throughout the research process, a focus on method is also key to overcoming the obstacles including but not limited to the emotional difficulties involved in mothers researching mothers who are incarcerated. A focus on method goes beyond the actual tools and techniques used in data collection and analysis. You can also find strength and overcome obstacles by building on the work of others who have come before you. Of course, literature reviews are key in designing a study. But you can also find support from colleagues (see Dickson-Swift, 2007) and mentors who have faced similar challenges. My dissertation committee was invaluable in providing support and ideas to move my research study forward. Friends and colleagues who had completed similar research were also helpful—to the point that I was able to quickly establish a relationship with prison administration thanks to a fellow graduate student (who had recently completed her studies, see Benedict, 2009) who had done research in that prison previously. These professional connections are helpful in moving forward in studying a protected population who is often difficult to reach.

Vocabulary for research is also key in pushing through research difficulties, including the emotional ones. As mothers, we learn that it is important to attach words to experiences and emotions for our children; as sociologists, we learn the importance of such words as symbols in society; as mothers/sociologists doing research in prison, we must develop a vocabulary to explore our "subjects'" experiences and answer our research questions. We must then use established vocabulary and understanding of our place as a co-contributor in our own research, along with our academic training, to try and better understand the experiences of those we study. As mentioned, one of the challenges of studying protected populations and addressing sensitive subjects, particularly when we somehow identify closely with our participants, is the huge responsibility that comes with taking stories from people's lives and turning those into meaningful research findings while doing justice to the human beings behind the story.

Theory can be especially helpful in utilizing vocabulary to explore your data while being mindful of the human element of research. For me, ambiguous loss theory has been crucial in this process. This theory (see Boss, 1999) describes the uncertain loss someone feels when they are psychologically present but physically absent (such as in the case of parental divorce or a family move) or physically present but psychologically absent (such as in the case of Alzheimer's disease). Boss explores ways ambiguous loss is different from a typical loss or death. For example, in ambiguous loss, there is no formal ceremony (like a funeral) for closure or widely held societal understanding of how to manage the loss. Using the theory of ambiguous loss has helped put my findings into a theoretical framework for research purposes. My findings suggest that incarcerated mothers experience ambiguous loss in multiple ways—the physical loss of their children and the psychological loss of the mother identity (Easterling, 2012). Further, without any formal intervention, mothers utilize the agency they have even while incarcerated to renegotiate mother roles and the mother identity to help deal with that ambiguous loss (Easterling, 2014).

Using the theory of ambiguous loss has also helped me on a personal level. It gives me a vocabulary and context within which to better understand the experiences of incarcerated mothers and also provides a sense of hope. I see that the mothers in my study were not helpless—they regained their agency (that the prison system serves to destroy) through active (re)negotiation of the mother role and, thus, of the mother identity (Easterling, 2012). Having such a productive way to explore these findings helps me better deal with my emotional and empathetic responses. It helps me see the mothers in my study not only as victims of a system (and perhaps life circumstances in addition to potentially making what society would label as "bad" decisions to "get" them to prison). It helps me view the women as active agents in their own lives, with strength and perseverance and eyes toward better futures, with happier lives for themselves and their families, despite their prison confinement at the time of our interviews. Through the reliance on theory, I have a vocabulary with which to better articulate my findings, which is beneficial in disseminating information as well as dealing with my own emotional turmoil.

Over time I also came to recognize my responsibility to those who will do future research. While I was able to get some fabulous assistance through formal and informal networks, I know not every researcher has the same relationships with people doing similar studies. I would have loved a "how to" guide that not only explored the steps one would take when completing such a project but also something more formal that also explored the human side of this research—the emotions and personal struggles. As a woman in academia, I often feel like I have to put on a hard game face to compete in my field. I think discussions and topics such as those that are included in this anthology are much needed and would have been helpful to me as a graduate student new to this type of research.

Always remembering the responsibility the researcher holds to the participants in her studies is helpful in the process of overcoming obstacles, challenges, and to keep pushing forward. The mothers I interviewed shared their lives with me. Though I was not incarcerated myself, we occupied the same space within the prison walls to discuss one of our most intimate and coveted relationships—the one with our children. We shared this experience through dialogue and often emotion, even if it was only for a short time. While my own emotions were sometimes overwhelming, I kept pushing forward because it was my duty to use the data that was collected from the women for my study in pursuit of better knowledge and understanding of their experiences in order to help them and other families impacted by incarceration.

I spent a lot of time writing personal thank you notes to the women who shared so much of themselves with me. As no gifts were allowed (I asked about sending stationary or stamps to help the mothers better communicate with their loved ones), the only way I could "give back" immediately was to thank the women and hopefully brighten one of their days with some mail. My hope was also that I would "give back" with my work—that I could help tell these mothers' stories to a larger audience, hopefully spreading more understanding toward them and their situations. Even now, I hope, I am giving back by helping other researchers anticipate and better deal with the challenges of this kind of emotion work to help themselves and the participants in their studies. I do this in honor of the women who helped me complete my project, who challenged and changed my perceptions of what it means to be not only an incarcerated mother but a mother in general, and who continue to motivate me to do the hard work of researching families and incarceration.

ADVICE TO MY FORMER SELF

In both the personal and the professional realms of my life, I often ponder what things would be like if I could go back and do it all over again knowing what I know now. I assume that this is a common thought project we share as human beings, and women researchers in particular. These kinds of explorations can potentially be of help to others. As I mentioned, I do feel a responsibility to help others who are embarking on similar professional journeys as I did. And I am hopeful in some small way I can assist others in moving forward through the challenges successfully.

If I could go back in time and give my former self some advice, first and foremost I would remind myself that it is okay to feel whatever I may be feeling and to acknowledge those feelings and use them for good instead of somehow seeing them as being weak as a scholar. "In acknowledging the importance of emotions in the research process, we must also challenge the dominance of the western philosophical tradition that judges emotions to be the anathema to academic research" (Dickson-Swift et al., 2009, p. 63). I reiterate, we must acknowledge the importance of emotions when doing research. Starting out on this journey, I would shut down when the mothers I was interviewing would cry, ending interviews early and being apprehensive to ask emotional questions during later interviews. It was hard for me to handle their emotions because it invoked such a strong emotional response on my end—and I tried to ignore, versus acknowledge, those emotions. But, I learned to deal with it. After the first day, I started to bring tissues to my interviews. Some of the women I was interviewing were definitely going to cry. And that is okay—for them and for me. I owed it to my participants not to shut down, but rather to move forward and allow them the opportunity to tell their stories. Having tissues in hand was a way I could show compassion and help them even if it was in a very small way. And it gave us both a moment to pause and connect on a real human level before we moved forward to complete our collaborative work for the project.

I would also encourage my former self to engage in more in-depth self-reflection than I did at the time. I am still a work in progress in accepting my dual identities as a mother and researcher. I should recognize the challenges (including the emotional ones), accept them, and build in "tools and tips" to keep moving forward through such self-reflective practices. My phenomenologically *informed* approach did not include the element of bracketing (see Chan et al., 2013) that pure phenomenology utilizes. In hindsight, this tool may have been very helpful in my own work. My comments regarding a focus on the method should include using such tactics in a conversation with my former self. I would also more heavily use field notes. I did take field notes, but wish I would have written down and reflected even more. It is helpful to look back and put things into context. You can never have enough personal reflection. Looking back, it is odd that I did not write more about my experiences. I remember holding back tears while reflecting on my days at my hotel in the evenings after my interviews. I think I threw myself into focusing on the work to be done to deal with the emotional difficulties I was having. I tried to ignore my emotional response, but in hindsight perhaps this is something that should be embraced. My own emotional work and reflection *is part* of the research process.

I cannot say this enough: never forget *why* you are doing the work. This is a privilege, which comes with responsibility. Through dealing with my own emotional turmoil, I began the journey of putting my mission first and knowing I *had* to get the work done, not only for myself, but because I owed it to the women in my study. For them, I am forever grateful. Because of them, I will keep moving forward with my research agenda. Thanks to them, I have learned a great deal about myself. In honor of them, I will keep pushing forward and work to improve myself—as someone who is constantly working on my shared identity as a researcher and a mother.

REFERENCES

Benedict, R. W. (2009). *Giving back not giving up: Generativity among older female inmates.* Unpublished doctoral dissertation, University of Tennessee, Knoxville.

Boss, P. (1999). *Ambiguous loss: Learning to live with unresolved grief.* Cambridge, MA: Harvard University Press.

Chan, Z. C., Fung, Y., & Chien, W. (2013). "Bracketing in phenomenology: Only undertaken in the data collection and analysis process." *The Qualitative Report, 18*(30), 1–9. Retrieved from https://nsuworks.nova.edu/tqr/vol18/iss30/1.

Davis, P. H. (1993). "Women and the burden of empathy." *Journal of Pastoral Theology, 3*(1), 29–38.

Dickson-Swift, V., James, E. L., Kippen, S., & Liamputtong, P. (2007). "Doing sensitive research: What challenges do qualitative researchers face?" *Qualitative Research, 7*(3), 327–353.

Dickson-Swift, V., James, E. L., Kippen, S., & Liamputtong, P. (2009). "Researching sensitive topics: Qualitative research as emotion work." *Qualitative Research*, *9*(1), 61–79.

Easterling, B. A. (2012). *Parenting behind bars: A qualitative study of incarcerated mothers.* Unpublished doctoral dissertation, University of Tennessee, Knoxville.

Easterling, B. A. (2014). "Ambiguous loss, concrete hope: Examining the prison experience for mothers from an ambiguous loss framework." In D. Polizzi & M. Braswell (Eds.), *Transforming corrections: Humanistic approaches to corrections and offender treatment* (2nd ed.). Durham, NC: Carolina University Press.

Easterling, B. A., & Feldmeyer, B. (2017). "Race, incarceration, and motherhood: Spoiled identity among rural white mothers." *The Prison Journal*, *97*(2), 143–165.

Easterling, B. A., Feldmeyer, B., & Presser, L. (2018). "Narrating mother identities from prison." *Feminist Criminology*, *14*(5), 519–539.

Easterling, B. A., &. Johnson, E. I. (2015). "Methodological challenges of qualitative research with vulnerable families." *The Qualitative Report*, *20*(10), 1568–1575.

Enos, S. (2001). *Mothering from the inside: Parenting in a women's prison.* New York: State University of New York Press.

Glenn, E. N. (1994). "Social constructions of mothering: A thematic overview." In G. Chang, E. N. Glenn, & L. R. Forcey (Eds.), *Mothering: Ideology, experience, and agency* (pp. 1–32). New York, NY: Routledge.

Greer, K. (2002). "Walking an emotional tightrope: Managing emotions in a women's prison." *Symbolic Interaction*, *25*(1), 117–139.

Guo, Q., Peng, S., Cai, M., Zhang, X., & Song, K. (2019). "Why are smarter individuals more prosocial? A study on the mediating roles of empathy and moral identity." *Intelligence*, *75*, 1–8.

Hardesty, C., Hardwick, P. G., & Thompson, R. J. (1993). "Self-esteem and the woman prisoner." In B. R. Fletcher, L. D. Shaver, & D. G. Moon (Eds.), *Women prisoners: A forgotten population.* Westport, CT: Praeger.

Hochschild, A. (1979). "Emotion work, feeling rules, and social structure." *American Journal of Sociology*, *85*(3), 551–575.

Hodges, S. D., Kiel, K. J., Kramer, A. D., Veach, D., & Villanueva, B. R. (2010). "Giving birth to empathy: The effects of similar experience on empathetic accuracy, empathic concern, and perceived empathy." *Personality and Social Psychology Bulletin*, *36*(3), 398–409.

Hollway, W., & Jefferson, T. (2000). *Doing qualitative research differently.* London: Sage.

Laney, E. K., Lewis Hall, E. M., Anderson, T. L., & Willingham, M. M. (2015). "Becoming a mother: The enfluence of motherhood on women's identity development." *Identity*, *15*(2), 126–145.

Liebling, A. (2014). "Postscript: Integrity and emotion in prisons research." *Qualitative Inquiry*, *20*(4), 481–486.

Morash, M., & Schram, P. J. (2002). *The prison experience: Special issues of women in prison.* Prospect Heights, IL: Waveland Press.

Owen, B. (1998). *In the mix: Struggle and survival in a women's prison.* Albany, NY: State University of New York Press.

Presser, L. (2008). *Been a heavy life: Stories of violent men.* Urbana, IL and Chicago: University of Illinois Press.

Ramazanoglu, C., & Holland, J. (2002). *Feminist methodology: Challenges and choices.* London: Sage.

Salice, A., & Tiapale, J. (2015). "Group-directed empathy: A phenomenological account." *Journal of Phenomenological Psychology*, *4*, 163–184.

Szanto, T., & Krueger, J. (2019). "Introduction: Empathy, shared emotions, and social identity." *Topoi*, *38*, 153–162.

Thomson, P., & Gunter, H. (2011). "Inside, outside, upside down: The fluidity of academic researcher 'identity' in working with/in school." *International Journal of Research and Method in Education*, *34*(1), 17–30.

Chapter 8

On the Possibilities of Emotional Praxis for Feminist Prison Research

Lindsey Raisa Feldman

PRISON RESEARCH AS BEARING WITNESS

I begin with a statement of my positionality—a white woman, a person who has never been incarcerated, an anthropologist turned (briefly) wildland firefighter—not simply as a performative declaration of the researcher self, but because who I am frames the narrative of this chapter, and more importantly, who I am framed the shifting epistemological approach of my research, studying the daily experiences of incarcerated men fighting wildfires in Arizona. A major aim of this chapter is to understand positionality as beneficial not just for more ethical research methods, but to increase the possibility of criminological research that simultaneously produce new modes of knowledge, action, and being.

This chapter draws on my work with the Arizona Department of Corrections' Inmate Wildfire Program (IWP), in which incarcerated people are contracted by the state to fight wildfires. I became a certified wildland firefighter and spent fifteen months fighting fires alongside incarcerated crews. I found that this labor program presents an experiential paradox for its participants. It is at once exploitative—with little pay for risky work, and little material support upon release from prison—while simultaneously transformative for those who fight fires. By "transformative," I mean that certain aspects of wildfire fighting provide individuals with more complex and powerful notions of selfhood than are typically obtainable on the prison yard.

Over the course of my research, I identified three major aspects of incarcerated peoples' self-identities that were positively impacted by the IWP: (1) a physical and symbolic movement away from the social categorization that occurs in the carceral system; (2) a construction of alternative masculine identities based on tenets of vulnerability, intimacy, and racial inclusion; and (3) an expression of complex working identities that offers a sense of self that is antithetical to the obedient and routinized modes of being on the yard. Even as this labor program operates within the strictures of an inherently punitive regime, it provides space for participants to reject certain aspects of modern incarceration's subjugating effects.

The above findings were not expected when I wrote the various grants and research proposals at the outset of the project. My initial approach was a more straightforward critique of prison labor, with a lack of theoretical insight into the complexity of everyday life, and an ignorance of the creativity of self-making by those behind bars. My research questions and findings shifted as I immersed myself in the field, changing into my fire gear each day and conducting interviews outside under the stars. The very location of the research—beyond prison walls—and the role I embodied as a woman, and particularly as a woman drawing on a feminist research ethos in a seemingly hypermasculine space, resulted in me changing the questions I asked, and thus changed the arguments I eventually made.

As a brief first example, based on what I was witnessing on the ground and against my presuppositions going into the field, I began asking crewmembers about the emotionally intimate relationships that they formed with each other and listened attentively to how they described these relationships as a space of healing against the pains of incarceration. Eventually, my arguments and theories shifted to address these more complex realities of interpersonal intimacy to which I had borne witness. During the physically and emotionally intensive year and a half of fieldwork, I developed an emergent approach to the questions I chose to ask, and I did not ignore the emotional weight of these questions. Embarking on research using this reflexive feminist approach (Kirsch, 2005) also came with the recognition of my own positionality and my fleeting role as researcher in this fraught space.

As I began grappling with the role of power and privilege in my own act of *being* in the field, I simultaneously began asking questions about the resistance to power within the prison, and the reclamation of complex selfhood for those with whom I worked each day on the fireline. Once again my project expanded to incorporate another layer of complexity; instead of a straightforward account of the inherent injustices of a carceral labor program, I began writing about the daily, intimate resistance against dehumanization these firefighters engaged in—by the work of fighting fires itself, and through the emotional space this work, surprisingly, afforded. As such, I found that conducting research with a dedication to reflexivity and what I will describe as an emotional praxis resulted in an emergent benefit: bearing witness to the daily acts of dignity made by incarcerated people in an overwhelmingly oppressive space.

This chapter describes how prison researchers can explore the potentials of such acts of bearing witness in their own projects. First, I will detail the gendered dynamics of this particular ethnographic space, and I will argue that challenging the assumptions of both femininity and masculinity in the prison can be a fruitful first step toward destabilizing reified stereotypes of prison more broadly. Next, I will describe the pains and possibilities of engaging emotionally in one's work. Finally, I will argue that feminist prison research should be conducted in non-normative carceral spaces like that of the fire-line, in order to push knowledge production forward in more nuanced ways, through understanding how individuals behind bars are able to uphold hope and dignity each day.

NAVIGATING THE GENDERED DIMENSIONS OF "MASCULINE" RESEARCH SITES

Of the hundreds of pages of field notes I wrote during my time with prison fire crews in the open spaces of Arizona, one slightly ribald entry best summarizes the peculiar gendered dynamics I faced as a woman fighting fires alongside incarcerated men. This excerpt is short, and in its original form was scrawled across the pages of a small notebook I carried in my pants pocket on fires. In massive, shaky block letters, signifying both my adrenaline and my stifled laughter, I scribbled, "OMG I JUST SQUATTED TO PEE AND I LOOKED DOWN AND I WAS PEEING ON A RATTLESNAKE BUT I COULDN'T YELL BECAUSE THEN 20 DUDES IN PRISON WOULD COME RUN TO HELP ME AND THAT WOULD BE AWKWARD WOULDN'T IT???"

I choose to include this relatively personal set of field notes here in part because it's an apt description of some of the bewildering predicaments I found myself in, given the relatively extreme nature of my project. But I also include it because it isolates one of many moments of intimacy in the course of fighting a wildfire. Many things are stripped bare when out on the fireline for weeks, at times including actual bodies. In moments like the one given earlier, when I found myself hovering rather vulnerably over a startled rattle-snake, I was reminded of my positionality not just as a researcher, but as a woman deeply immersed in a masculine cultural landscape.

There has been a range of scholarship on the way women precariously enter into, or are barred from, normatively masculine workspaces like fire-fighting (Ainsworth et al., 2014). Research has similarly been conducted that describes the challenges women face when working inside of prisons (Farnworth, 1992). These researchers conclude that masculinity operates to exclude both women and non-hegemonically masculine men from partici-pating in certain arenas through key strategies, like questioning a person's physical strength or their ability to participate in "locker room" discourse, or through outright harassment or assault.

In recent years, and as evidenced by this volume, researchers have turned their attention inwards, examining not just how women are treated in workplaces like those mentioned earlier, but how women researchers themselves navigate field sites, notably the prison, that have long upheld the hegemony of the masculine for incarcerated people, staff, and researchers attempting to do work inside. And although feminist criminologists in particular have begun to shine a light on these challenges (Doucet & Mauthner, 2014), given my project's unique intersection of prison and firefighting cultures, there were few blueprints for navigating any specific gendered challenges I would face.

One guiding principal I took into my research came from Maleta (2009) who described meritocracy as a key tenet in firefighting culture. According to Maleta, appealing to the cultural tenet of "just do it" is one of the ways a woman can enter into normatively male spaces and, over time, even shift structural norms (like hiring practices) in those spaces. Engaging in meritocracy, that is, showing that she is capable putting in the work, allows men to rethink who, generally, is capable of supposedly "masculine" performance. I tested this hypothesis and found it to be true during my fieldwork. The fact that I chose to actually fight wildfires alongside incarcerated crews showed two things to these individuals (relayed as confessions to me over the course of my research): (1) that I was not afraid to take on the challenge of hard, risky work, and (2) that I was interested enough in their lives to spend days and weeks with them, as opposed to just going in and out of the prison yard for interviews.

On the very first wildfire I fought, which happened to be my first day of research, I hiked up the spiny, crumbling ridge of a mountain in 105-degree heat. My nerves, the exertion, and the heat got to me—I threw up the powdered eggs I had for breakfast within thirty minutes of hiking. Because the blaze was active, the crew and all but one correctional officer hiked on to fight the fire. The remaining officer and I sat on a rock while I drank Gatorade and recovered. As soon as I felt ready, we got up and slowly climbed the mountain, the officer matching my sluggish pace. When I eventually stumbled up to the top of the ridge a few miles later, I was greeted with outright glee, jokes, and jabs, and warmth by the crew. On my first day, I had passed a test I didn't know existed: I pushed myself hard, too hard, and that is what this crew expected of every single one of their fellow members. From that point forward, I was "in."

This is not to say that vomiting should be a requisite act for conducting fieldwork in normatively masculine spaces. I was mortified at the time. But upon reflection, I realized what a boon this bodily function was on my very first day of fieldwork. It immediately shifted the conversation away from my gendered presence and toward the casually intimate presence of a laboring body trying its best. Gender was, for a moment, usurped by the nature of the field site and the shared experience of the group, and it is this moment that set the course forward for my research. In the months that followed, not once did I feel excluded from working with this group of men because of my gender (to be clear, I fully understand that decisions may have been made without my knowledge by the prison staff and firefighters to shape my experience of certain tasks or fire events).

Instead, over fifteen months of fieldwork, I felt that my "othered" position was not based on my gender as I had initially presumed, but due to my outsider status—the crew reminded me often that I wasn't in prison, less so that I wasn't going to be a career firefighter based on my femaleness (I think my scars, burnt pony tails, and hospital bills for kidney stones made this abundantly clear to us all). That isn't to say that these crews operated with a non-biased approach to gender writ large. Elsewhere (Feldman, 2018) I describe how the IWP is an atypical carceral space in that it offers individuals the ability to engaged with more complex and inclusive masculine identities. Yet it is still a patriarchal space, with individuals engaging in hegemonic masculine performances and holding biases against, for example, the only all-women prison fire crew operating in the state. But from my vantage as a researcher, lack of access to my field site due to my gender was not a major concern.

If not access to the field, what was inherently impacted by my gender was the data I collected. As has been noted by several female scholars conducting research inside prison, both informal and formal interviews are guided by implicit gendered biases on the part of both researcher and informant (see: Kilty, 2014). For example, although I will argue that participation in the IWP helped individuals to enact alternate forms of masculinity based on emotional intimacy and vulnerability, a fraught topic that prisoners never chose to discuss with me was sexual assault and coerced sexual acts inside prison. I heard allusions to crewmembers' experiences with it here and there, but they refused to speak about it directly with me.

As one crewmember told me bluntly, in a conversation that was the closest I got to the subject, "We aren't gonna tell a girl about that, it's nasty business." In response, I wanted to point out what might be considered my "feminine" credentials, as a former crisis counselor for survivors of sexual assault, or as someone who has experienced gendered harassment myself, in order to get access to this critically under-discussed aspect of imprisonment. But when my informants a priori excluded me from this discussion, I chose not to push the issue, because of my fear of "forcing" incarcerated people to discuss something so potentially traumatic. Yet, though I was excluded from that specific conversation, once our interviews ended a few informants told me that they hadn't shared particular experiences of incarceration with anyone else, but chose to share them with me because they felt a level of comfort with me as a woman, particularly a woman representing a non-carceral regime. Thus was the give-and-take of my gendered fieldwork experience; on the one hand surprisingly open and on the other entirely closed off.

There were other gendered concerns that arose during my research. Importantly, for me, these did not include my safety, although my life being in danger was a concern for most people I talked to when I embarked on this project. The idea of a woman hiking miles out into a forest with a group of all-male incarcerated people and prison guards, and camping there for days, presented a shocking, almost taboo research context. However, I was not afraid, nor was I ever given a reason to feel afraid. The concerns that arose for me were less overt, and again had to do with the power differentials between the crew and me. In short, and in retrospect what I realize was problematic, I was afraid to exert femininity lest I create a distraction or temptation for IWP crewmembers. Based partially on directives from the department, but also from this fear, I felt a compulsion to perform masculinity in as many ways as I could to avoid any awkward encounters with crewmembers. As a person who in daily life often has painted nails, wears makeup, and wears dresses, I made every attempt possible to avoid these cultural markers of femininity.

This body policing is true for all non-prisoners entering the prison space. Wives and girlfriends of incarcerated people will be sent away from visitation without seeing their loved ones if their shirts are too low cut or their pants too tight (Comfort, 2003). As broader societal gendered norms are put under a magnifying glass in the carceral context, there is a maligning of women's sexuality, coupled with the inherent assumption of the uncontrollable sexual nature of men. It took time for me to approach these tropes critically in my own field site. Based on the strong suggestion from the guards of the IWP to wear only my fire clothes around the prison crews, I wore the same baggy, beige fieldwork uniform each day. I was also told, and followed, the directive to not physically touch any crewmember. Of course, sometimes on the fireline this would be impossible. One crewmember helped put my burning pants-leg out by bear-hugging my leg, another caught me under the arms when I took a tumble down a rocky hillside. But even as I came to know the crew, I was impeded by typical physical displays of intimacy—slaps on the back, high-fives, or hugs—that crewmembers showed each other.

Over time, I was able to reflect on my own initial assumptions about my presence as a distraction, and my militant obeisance of shielding my femininity. I came to understand these choices as my attempt to maneuver through—and therefore uncritically uphold—a patriarchal social system. As an anthropologist, I admit that it took me some time to remember that my own interactions with research participants are beholden to the same social structures that are so easily deconstructed in others.

Moreover, I note here that we as researchers are capable of thinking critically about how we choose to move through our field sites, and further, to use this reflexivity to lay bare structures of power and push our research ethics and praxis forward. In my case, I challenged myself to move past my initial assumptions about what disturbances my presence would cause, and more broadly about masculinity—not just as it affected me, but as it affected the men with whom I worked. As I more fully understood the role that hegemonic masculinity played in the prison, I also began noting the ways in which the fire crews asserted a fundamentally different way of practicing masculinity for themselves and with others. My research questions changed, moving toward a project that didn't assume what the prison and broader society often assumes about men. Instead I began seeing—and writing about—emotional intimacy, inclusive masculinity, and the various ways the panoptic power of the prison temporarily waned as crewmembers asserted their personhood on the line.

Although I never directly challenged any of ADC's orders about physical contact or dress code, after months fighting fires with these individuals, I certainly presented a fuller version of myself to them, and shared in the vulnerable, funny, and inherently corporeal nature of firefighting alongside them. The first thing I did after quickly disengaging from my snake encounter was to run and tell them the funny story, and they howled in laughter. As our relationship grew more familiar, I slowly began incorporating the emotional intimacies of human interaction into my research. I did this because I was led to it by what I saw and what I heard. Similarly, I chose to face the gendered power dynamic of conducting fieldwork as a woman within a deeply masculine space. The push and pull of this dynamic—having a certain power as a researcher, yet also the institutionally designed lack of power as a woman in a patriarchal bureaucracy—led me to think critically about this dynamic, challenge it in my daily interactions and shared intimacies with the crew, and eventually incorporate more nuanced reflections on gender overall into my ethnographic reflections.

THE EMOTIONAL FLUX OF RESEARCHING IN PRISON, WHILE NOT IN A PRISON

As I left the field for the very last time, one crewmember succinctly stated what he had hoped to see in my research. After we shared our goodbyes, he added, "Make sure you get them to see us as people." In this moment, he provided not only a call to me as an anthropologist embarking on the dissemination phase of my project, but also offered a reaffirmation of the dignity of personhood that he and every other crewmember upheld while incarcerated. As a non-incarcerated researcher who, over the course of many months, began engaging with concepts of emotion, hope, and dignity in my analysis, I was simultaneously engaging with the emotionally fraught flux of this fieldwork: to move in and out of the lives of these individuals, and what it meant to do fieldwork in a space that was at once firmly situated in the prison regime, but also taking place far beyond prison walls.

To help explain the realities of researching in a fluctuating field site, I turn to my early days of field notes. This entry serves as an example of two interrelated ethnographic moments: the movement of the crew from the prison yard to the fireline, and in that movement, the tension I held as an ethnographer doing research in two spaces that seemed so antithetical to one another.

> *Fieldnotes. Early June, 2015.* At the beginning of regular workdays, the crew files into the sallyport of their prison yard. This is a small square open-air antechamber tacked on to the corner of the yard, made up of barbed wire, that serves as the entry and exit for inmates and staff. Starting around 5 or 6 in the morning, every Monday-Thursday, work crew after work crew file into the sallyport and are counted, given their lunches, and shuttled on to white vans to pick up trash off the side of the highway, or prune flowers at the courthouse of the local town. The wildfire crew goes through the same motions as these other crews, but I noticed during my observation of the sallyport that there occurs a subtle transition that differentiates the fire crew from the others: a transition of bodily posture, camaraderie, and a general sense of selfhood.
>
> I joined the crew in the sallyport today. Rex and Chief, two of the crew officers driving the wildfire buggies, picked me up and we drove on complex to the yard where the crew was. The crew was called out of their sleeping quarters, ready to go, and filed into the small caged space. The exit process takes about five to ten minutes, depending how fast or motivated the guard is. While we waited, the crewmembers who identify as Christian passed around scripture chosen by Teddy, the de facto pastor of the group. Reading from a small scrap of paper with a bible verse scribbled down in pencil, Teddy recited today's affirmation of grace and recovery. While that occurred, other guys start stretching, prepping their muscles for the physical exertion of today's project. Rex and Chief chatted with the guard manning the sallyport, figuring out logistics, seeing if anyone called out sick (not today).
>
> The personal jokes between crewmembers got going at this point. Just yesterday, a new crewmember had started, and today the sallyport served as a space of sly initiation. Donald had almost quit on his first day, when one of the correctional officers did the obligatory first day death hike with him, strapping ninety pounds on both their backs and hiking straight up the ridge of a mountain that was on the land where they were doing a project. But he made it, barely. He smoked, he had no teeth so it was hard to eat, he was in his sixties, he was

> homeless for years before going to prison. His body was not attuned. But he showed up again today, his second day, to some good-natured ribbing from other crewmembers. "Hey old man, yeah! You made it, you're standing up!" One guy joked, slapping him hard on his back, causing him to waver on his feet a bit. Donald smiled a gummy smile and said, "I'm stronger than I look, fellas," and raised his bicep like Popeye the Sailor. Everyone laughed. [Over the months, he would become known for his uncanny ability to hike ten or fifteen miles without stopping, cigarette in his mouth. But that day, his assertion was just a promise of strength.]
>
> The most surreal part of my morning in the sallyport was how distinct a space it is (both literally and metaphorically—it means leaving), but also how in view it is to the rest of the prison yard. If leaving the prison is a daily rite of passage, then the sallyport is the "separation from the main group" stage, but not really: this yard is flat and dry and made up mostly of dirt, which means that this small square fenced off area was in full view to all the other inmates who weren't leaving that day: either because they were sick, or didn't have the proper clearance to leave the complex and thus had to work on the yard itself. It felt almost cruel to keep glancing at the groups of men wearing orange sweatpants and white shoes, sitting on the picnic table or standing under the singular mesquite tree on the yard, all who were staring at the crew as they started to joke and nudge and pray. No one on the crew looked back toward them, but I did, several times.

As I wrote these field notes during the first few weeks of my research, I became aware of the dual nature of my field site—the prison and the fireline—and the tension therein. The prison yard is one of the few places in the world where daily life is nearly as routinized and restrictive as it is made out to be. This is not to say that prisoners simply fall in line or become automatons, but the prison as an institution is designed to create a space of total control (Goffman, 1961). On higher security yards, the sallyport doesn't represent much of anything except maybe the way to get to the medical clinic, because leaving the prison isn't an option. But in lower-level yards, the sallyport becomes a portal to something else, somewhere else.

I would talk to newly minted incarcerated firefighters on the day they had left the prison for the first time in three, or five, or twenty years, and they would explain the profound effect of leaving on every single one of their senses, as well as their psyches. The concept of coming and going—of *movement*—is one we as free people may not think twice about, but I sensed its power after that day in the sallyport when I could not stop glancing behind me to look at the individuals who would not get a chance to leave that day, and then turning back to watch the fire crew gently push their way out of the holding cage, pile into the big wildfire buggies, and emerge just a few minutes down the road in their firefighting clothes, laughing, all physical markers of their incarceration gone.

There were myriad moments throughout my fieldwork where I had to confront my positionality as a researcher who is not and has never been incarcerated, and with that the inherent privilege in my own movement in and out of the lives of the crew. At the end of each workday, the sallyport appeared in view again, but this time it meant that men had to "pop and squat," or be subject to an anal cavity search, before entering into the main space of the yard and going about the rest of their afternoons. Unlike the mornings I spent observing the crew leaving the yard for the day, I did not witness this invasive and dehumanizing reverse process, instead waving goodbye to them as they pulled up to the sallyport, their temporary movement stilled. As I drove away into town and my rented casita, I was wrenched with an observer's—an interloper's—guilt. Other prison researchers have similarly explored what feels like a sense of voyeurism into the inner workings of the carceral system (Beyens et al., 2013; Hannem, 2014), particularly because of our ability to write comfortably about it after the fact, in a space of our own choosing.

This is, of course, an established concern in anthropology and the social sciences more broadly, the intricate dance between obtaining access to oppressed groups while taking care to conduct research (and later, analysis and writing) ethically and reflexively. There is a clear need for ethnographers to be transparent about their role—often emotionally charged—through the data collection, analysis, and writing process, in order to most rigorously explore the questions they set out to answer. I recognized that my positionality as a non-incarcerated person directly affected my research, and therefore my conclusions. In the previous section, I wrote that crewmembers wouldn't discuss sexual assault with me; this is one of several aspects of prison life I do not understand, and I therefore had to acknowledge as a limit to my understanding. Lorna Rhodes, one of anthropology's foremost prison researchers, approaches this issue,

> Fundamentally, no outsider/observer can "participate" in the situation of the prisoner . . . the ethnographer may get past the tour to an extent, but prisons are pervaded by an interpersonal opacity that thwarts even those who govern, manage, or live in them. To forget one's position as an outsider is to be in danger, not only from interpersonal trouble of various kinds but, more enduringly, from alarming emotional and intellectual identifications. Here the ethnographic desire for alignment with one's subject(s) must be relinquished or at least bracketed. (Rhodes, 2001, p. 76)

I only partially agree with Rhodes's assessment of non-prisoners doing prison ethnography. While I agree that it is necessary to confront the distance, opacity, and possible elements of coercion that may arise in doing research, I do not think this results in needing to bracket or "relinquish" one's emotional alignment with prisoners. Instead, I believe the honest, reflexive accounting of the emotional nature of prison research can be incorporated into the ethnography to further the project's goals and to establish a research praxis that challenges hegemonic ways of thinking about the prison and incarcerated people.

As such it is necessary to confront the emotional toll of our research, with its competing challenge of humanizing a dehumanized population while addressing the hurt they caused others (Smith & Wincup, 2002). This requires emotional labor (Kirsch, 2005) both from the researcher and research participants. I write about my own emotional labor at occasional points in my ethnography, not in order to myopically over-state my role in the project (Crewe, 2007), but to highlight how moments of confusion, or pain, or disgust I felt led me to ask more interesting ethnographic questions. My initial research question was straightforward, but I was quickly thrown down more emotional rabbit holes like those raised in my first visit to the sallyport: What does freedom come to mean for men who leave the yard for the day, only to return? What feelings emerge for crewmembers when they change out of their prison clothes for weeks on end, and is this ultimately meaningful when they eventually have to put that orange garb back on again? How do I theorize the raw emotion I hear time and time again in my interviews, when crewmembers state that facing a wall of flames feels safer than being on the prison yard, because on the fireline, they have family who will fight for their lives?

These emotionally resonant questions emerged because I abandoned the goal of proving an a priori theory of subjugation during my time with the IWP. Instead, I developed what I call an emotional praxis, or as Ingold (2014) describes it, a commitment to "correspondence." Ingold defines this as "the forward movement of one's own perception and action with the movements of others" (p. 389). By attending to the "multistranded and inherently intertwined nature" of myself as the researcher and the crewmembers as research participants, I engaged in a project where my questions and answers changed based on what I heard and also what we felt. I took up Ingold's call to allow for the complex lives I was immersed in to fundamentally shape my project. He writes of this precarious but powerful research ethic, "It is like pushing the boat out into an as yet unformed world—a world in which things are not ready made but always incipient, on the cusp of continual emergence" (p. 389).

What emerged in my daily participant observation in atypical carceral spaces like the sallyport, the fireline, and the infinite darkness of a remote mountaintop were the emotions of my informants, and my own emotional responses to our unfolding closeness. As such, the emotional benefits of the IWP—and how these benefits acted as a form of daily resistance to the dehumanization of incarceration—began to emerge front and center as a critical epistemological approach to my project.

Over the past few decades, the field of anthropology has begun to acknowledge the benefit of incorporating emotional and attentive aspects of ethnography into one's analyses, perhaps indicating a final move away from the age-old dichotomy between rational/emotional, objective/subjective (Doucet & Mauthner, 2007). The field of criminology is similarly acknowledging such a need. Liebling (1999), in her foundational piece on the need for emotionally engaged prison research, states that the "art of research" is a "deeply satisfying undertaking. Its joys and its pains are part of what makes it meaningful. Without some account of its real nature, we misrepresent the nature of knowledge. The very term 'empiricism' (the Greek word *emperia* means 'experience') refers to the view that all knowledge comes from experience, from perception and from sense-data" (Liebling, 1999, p. 165).

Liebling has been joined by an increased number of researchers (Jewkes, 2012; Reiter, 2014) who argue that approaching prison with emotional depth does not negate the ability to approach it empirically, all while retaining rigorous data collection methods and the acknowledgment of one's positionality as a researcher (Mason & Stubbs, 2010). Yet there is a concern, as Jewkes (2012) states, that "if we disclose the emotions that underpin and inform our work, our colleagues will question its 'validity' and perhaps even our suitability to engage effectively" (p. 63) in this type of research. Over the course of disseminating my data, both to scholarly and non-scholarly audiences, I have been asked if my research methods are fully valid given that I have an obvious passion for maintaining the dignity of incarcerated people. In response to these questions, I have a clear response: I flatly reject that prison researchers must maintain emotional distance to be theoretically or methodologically sound. I was able to achieve my data measurements while accepting the emotional nature of my fieldwork.

Importantly, I also used the emotional connection to my work as a call to action to engage in applied dimensions of the project—such as writing a policy brief with recommendations to improve the material conditions of the crews that I presented to ADC leadership, or publishing photo essays in popular magazines to challenge public narratives of incarcerated men. All ethnography is inherently relational, and thus emotionally engaging, and this is what I consider the emotional praxis we as ethnographers can use. We are capable of placing ourselves within our texts responsibly, stating our inherent biases, our limitations, our unique vantages, and our personal connections, all which serve to increase the political and public resonance of our work.

POSSIBILITIES FOR RESEARCHING DAILY CARCERAL RESISTANCE

The renowned historian G. Sykes is known for the phrase "the pains of imprisonment" (1958). He describes these pains as a series of deprivations—of liberty, autonomy, and relationships, to name a few. These pains are a common trope in the criminological literature, particularly because they have only become truer throughout the twentieth and twenty-first centuries. With the reflexive turn in the social sciences, prison scholars have begun writing about the pains of *doing* criminological research. Observing the deprivations and inhumanity of incarceration, often with a limited ability to enact structural change, can be challenging (Beyens et al., 2013). A connective thread across reflexive literature on prison research almost always positions emotion as synonymous with pain for researchers and incarcerated people alike, because of how pain is so directly confronted in the carceral field site.

This leads me to some concluding remarks that serve as a set of possibilities for anyone taking up emotional praxis in prison research. There was no question that I encountered pain during my fieldwork. In interviews and informal conversations, incarcerated people shared stories with me about the trauma of imprisonment, or the trauma that occurred in their lives that partially led to their presence on the prison yard. I was confronted with correctional policies and ideologies that shocked me in their degradation. But in the open spaces of the IWP, where I spent the majority of my time, the inhumanity of imprisonment was challenged through emotional connection and the reclamation of a complex sense of self. A final reflection from my fieldwork serves as an example of this point.

I sat alongside a group of incarcerated firefighters on a ridge of a remote mountain peak, in a pine forested wilderness that had become a second home for the fire crew and me over a summer of Forest Service contract work. There was no cell phone service for miles; the guards had to take turns driving thirty minutes down a pitted, narrow timber road to call the prison complex and check in. It was the height of summer and the air was so saturated with monsoon moisture that when you looked around, the trees and grass looked painted in oil. I had joined a small group who had decided to take a post-dinner walk to the edge of the campsite to watch the sunset from a vantage that spilled out down the mountain, far beyond to the east, into the flat plains of New Mexico. We found a spot to sit that was next to a blackberry bramble and we ate them until our fingers turned purple. Two crewmembers walked up to the bend in the trail and saw a mama black bear and her cub on the far side of the ridge, they turned quickly around to rejoin us, eyes wide and laughing in awe. We sat and watched the sun dip golden over the horizon of another state. As we each nestled into our patch of grass, the older toothless crewmember from the sallyport, Donald, sighed. I asked him what the sigh was for.

"Do you think this might be what freedom is?" Donald replied. I laughed, and so did another crewmember, Stevie, who was standing and mindlessly playing with a long blade of sawgrass next to him.

"What do you mean? We're in prison, remember?" Stevie replied.

Donald thought for a minute, and then tried again. "What I mean is . . . even before I was locked up, I didn't know about this view. I didn't feel this peace I feel right now. I'm not free, but I *feel* free, just in this moment, you get what I'm saying?" Stevie stood silent. A third crewmember reached for a blackberry and squished it between his fingers. The juice dripped on the forest floor.

After a long pause, Stevie replied. "Yeah, I get that. I actually feel pretty fucking good right now too. Maybe, you know, that's all that freedom means?"

His voice upticked into a question, and the moment stretched into silence and eventual twilight. We walked back to camp. It was a moment that profoundly affected me as a researcher, grappling with the very question that Donald and Stevie considered. The daily moments of the IWP were so inherently different than the moments I spent on the prison yard, and this tension was held for me as a researcher and for participants of the program as well. Over the course of conducting fieldwork and writing about it, I struggled with addressing the duality of my project: the pains and joys, the deprivation and fulfillment, the prison yard and the wildfire.

In many ways, I have had to leave this tension as a question, like we did on that mountain ridge. I continue to ask myself how moments of peace or feelings of freedom can help to challenge the overwhelming pains of incarceration. But just as I discovered the need to enact an emotional praxis in my work, so too did I eventually see this paradox of the IWP as an emergent path forward for my work and potentially for the work of others. I believe it is necessary to conduct research in anomalous carceral spaces where incarcerated individuals can more readily push back against the pains of imprisonment, if not structurally, then just as importantly at the daily level. Prison researchers can and should pay attention to the nuanced ways incarcerated people resist dehumanization, even if this is simply feeling a moment of peace or questioning the definition of freedom, and conduct research in spaces where this is more likely to occur.

In the IWP, challenging dehumanization took the form of incarcerated wildland firefighters finding and maintaining a sense of self-identity that is not subjugated by the carceral regime. Individuals in prison are categorized and made into less-than-people, which results in their treatment as "criminals" as opposed to full, complex human beings. This has obvious deleterious effects both psychologically and physically and can severely alter the way prisoners construct their own identities even upon release (LeBel, 2012). This social cauterization (Simmons, 2011) impacts people's personhoods so deeply that it might be easy for scholars to ignore the possibility for incarcerated individuals to be agential, to operate in a way not wholly determined by the prison. The question that emerged in my work, that I now put forth for others, is how we look for this agency, for this intimate resistance against imprisoned subjectivity.

Increasingly, people are looking to agential forms of identity construction in prison (Opsal, 2011; Rowe, 2011). Toyoki and Brown (2013), for example, describe the "identity work" or "the mutually constitutive processes whereby people strive to shape a relatively coherent and distinctive notion of personal self-identity" (p. 717), of Polish prisoners through their daily discourses of selfhood. They argue that people in prison are capable of continually shaping and reshaping who they think they are and *could* be, which therefore allows them to "engage in micro-processes of resistance" (p. 718) against the limits of dignity in prison. Jewkes (2005) describes this ability of individuals to creatively adapt to their circumstances, saying, "Individuals are not mere bearers of structure; they are complex amalgams of several influences, responding to their life experiences with greater or lesser degrees of compliance and confrontation, defining their own individuality in terms of both cultural conformity and resistance" (Jewkes, 2005, p. 61). The prison system in the United States is designed and operated to uphold the criminal social category, but this does not mean each individual in prison will blindly accept this categorization. Incarcerated individuals, even when utterly degraded and maximally confined, continue to resist punitive penal regimes determining their right to personhood (Rhodes, 2005; Taylor, 2016).

To fully explore these acts of self-affirmation, I argue that it is important to conduct research in carceral spaces where identity work and other forms of emotional resistance might occur. These might be spaces like peer mentoring groups, creative writing classes, or animal therapy, to name a few. In sites like these, researchers can pay close attention to the continual negotiation of identity, dignity, and hope within institutional structures like the prison, as rigid as they may outwardly seem. As Rowe (2011) states, "Identities are imported into prison, shift in response to the experience and are negotiated—projected and defended—in social encounters" (p. 574). Accepting the idea that individuals in prison can craft their own self-narratives, and do not necessarily submit to their own subjectification as "criminals" but have potentials for other senses of self, allows us to see identity a site of negotiation and even resistance to apparatuses of power. It is also the attendant result of engaging in emotional praxis in one's research.

But as I call for other researchers to examine acts of daily resistance using an emotional praxis for research, I also acknowledge that applying the concept of resistance is difficult in a context of confinement because it risks romanticizing individuals' efforts to navigate their life in prison (Bosworth & Carrabine, 2001). Some other scholars argue that "resistance" is not even the appropriate term when discussing individual acts of adjustment or self-affirmation (Rubin, 2015). Perhaps, then, resistance as I am defining it as a research aim could also be called "challenges to dehumanization," or what Labotka (2014) refers to as "claims to dignity." The fact that a member of the IWP, who might establish an identity of firefighter rather than be subjugated as a criminal, might be making a claim to dignity. Ignatieff (2001) argues,

> Ironically, it is often those who are deprived of their liberty, slaves and prisoners, who remind us of the connection between dignity and freedom. They refuse to surrender the tiny margin of autonomy that is left them, and they use it to assert their unvanquished sense of self. Thus there is a chain of association that connects together the idea of dignity with the idea of freedom, and both in turn with the capability to maintain and express personal identity. (pp. 165–166)

On the ridge of the mountain that day during my fieldwork, Donald and Stevie spoke aloud what Ignatieff outlines mentioned earlier: to feel a sense of peace can also be seen as the maintenance of dignity, because it allows for one's possibility for freedom. This is intimately linked to what it means to exist in the world as fully human (Appiah, 2001).

In my work with the IWP, I examined the processes by which incarcerated men construct emergent, non-subjugated identities, and I suggest that these processes of identity work are continual daily challenges to the dehumanizing effects of incarceration. This analysis emerged only after I began my fieldwork, upholding the "revolutionary" potential of participant observation (Shah, 2017). I argue that acknowledging both the limitations and possibilities of one's own gendered positionality, along with a commitment to emotional methodological engagement, allowed this work to emerge. Although this project is unique in its cultural context, I urge prison researchers to examine similarly anomalous carceral spaces and to begin centering concepts of dignity, hope, and personhood in both their theories and actions, in order for transformative conversations about the future of a non-carceral world to emerge.

REFERENCES

Ainsworth, S, Batty, A., & Burchielli, R. (2014). "Women constructing masculinity in voluntary firefighting." *Gender, Work & Organization*, *21*(1), 37–56.

Appiah, A. K. (2001). “Grounding human rights.” In A. Gutmann (Ed.), *Human rights as politics and idolatry* (pp. 101–116). Princeton: Princeton University Press.

Beyens, K., Christiaens, J., Claes, B., De Ridder, S., & Tubex, H. (2013). *The pains of doing criminological research.* Brussels: VUB Press.

Bosworth, M., & Carrabine, E. (2001). “Reassessing resistance: Race, gender, and sexuality in prison.” *Punishment and Society*, *3*, 501–515.

Comfort, M. L. (2003). “In the tube at San Quentin: The ‘secondary prisonization’ of women visiting inmates.” *Journal of Contemporary Ethnography*, *32*(1), 77–107.

Crewe, B. (2007). “Power, adaptation, and resistance in a late-modern prison.” *British Journal of Criminology*, *47*, 256–275.

Doucet, A., & Mauthner, N. (2007). “Feminist methodologies and epistemologies.” In C. D. Bryant & D. L. Peck (Eds.), *The handbook of 21st century sociology* (pp. II-36–II-42). Thousand Oaks, CA: Sage Publications.

Farnworth, L. (1992). “Women doing a man’s job: Female prison officers working in a male prison.” *Australian & New Zealand Journal of Criminology*, *25*(3), 278–296.

Feldman, L. R. (2018). “Forging selfhood: Social categorisation and identity in Arizona’s prison wildfire programme.” *Howard Journal of Crime and Justice*, *57*(1), 21–36.

Goffman, E. (1961). *Asylums: Essays on the social situation of mental patients and other inmates.* Garden City, NY: Anchor Books.

Hannem, S. (2014). “Grappling with reflexivity and the role of emotion in criminological analysis.” In J. Kilty, S. Fabian, & M. Felices-Luna (Eds.), *Demarginalizing voices: Commitment, emotion, and action in qualitative research.* Vancouver: UBC Press.

Ignatieff, M. (2001). “Dignity and agency.” In A. Gutmann (Ed.), *Human rights as politics and idolatry* (pp. 161–173). Princeton: Princeton University Press.

Jewkes, Y. (2005). “Men behind bars: ‘Doing’ masculinity as an adaptation to imprisonment.” *Men and Masculinities*, *8*(1), 44–63.

Jewkes, Y. (2012). “Autoethnography and emotion as intellectual resources: Doing prison research differently.” *Qualitative Inquiry*, *18*, 63–75.

Kilty, J. (2014). “The evolution of feminist research in the criminological enterprise.” In J. Kilty, S. Fabian, & M. Felices-Luna (Eds.), *Demarginalizing voices: Commitment, emotion, and action in qualitative research.* Vancouver: UBC Press.

Kirsch, G. E. (2005). “Friendship, friendliness, and feminist fieldwork.” *Signs*, *30*(4), 2163–2172.

Labotka, L. (2014). *Healthy, beautiful hair: Cultivating the self in a women’s prison.* Doctoral Dissertation, School of Anthropology, University of Arizona.

LeBel, T. (2012). “If one doesn’t get you another one will: Formerly incarcerated persons’ perceptions of discrimination.” *The Prison Journal*, *92*, 63–87.

Leeder, A., & Wimmer, C. (2007). “Voices of pride: Drama therapy with incarcerated women.” *Women & Therapy*, *29*(3–4), 195–213.

Liebling, A. (1999). “Doing research in prison: Breaking the silence?” *Theoretical Criminology*, *3*(2), 147–173.

Maleta, Y. (2009). “Playing with fire: Gender at work and the Australian female cultural experience within rural fire fighting.” *Journal of Sociology*, *45*(3), 291–306.

Mason, G., & Stubbs, J. (2010). "Feminist approaches to criminological research." *Law School Research Paper No. 10/36.* Available at SSRN: https://ssrn.com/abstract=1597469.

Opsal, T. (2011). "Women disrupting a marginalized identity: Subverting the parolee identity through narrative." *Journal of Contemporary Ethnography, 40*, 135–167.

Reiter, K. (2014). "Making windows into walls: Strategies for prison research." *Qualitative Inquiry, 20*(4), 417–428.

Rhodes, L. (2001). "Toward an anthropology of prisons." *Annual Review of Anthropology, 30*, 65–83.

Rhodes, L. (2005). "Changing the subject: Conversation in supermax." *Cultural Anthropology, 20*(3), 388–411.

Rowe, A. (2011). "Narratives of self and identity in women's prisons: Stigma and the struggle for self-definition in penal regimes." *Punishment & Society, 13*(5), 571–591.

Rubin, A. (2015). "Resistance or friction: Understanding the significance of prisoners' secondary adjustments." *Theoretical Criminology, 19*(1), 23–42.

Shah, A. (2017). "Ethnography? Participant observation, a potentially revolutionary praxis." *Hau: Journal of Ethnographic Theory, 7*(1), 45–59.

Simmons, W. (2011). *Human rights law and the marginalized other.* Cambridge: Cambridge University Press.

Smith, C., & Wincup, E. (2002). "Reflections on fieldwork in criminal justice institutions." In T. Welland & L. Pugsley (Eds.), *Ethical dilemmas in qualitative research.* United Kingdom: Ashgate.

Sykes, G. (1958). *The society of captives: A study of a maximum security prison.* Princeton: Princeton University Press.

Taylor, D. (2016). "Between discipline and caregiving: Changing prison population demographics and possibilities for self-transformation." In P. Zurn & A. Dilts (Eds.), *Active intolerance: Michel Foucault, the prisons information group, and the future of abolition.* New York: Palgrave Macmillan.

Toyoki, S., & Brown, A. (2013). "Stigma, identity, and power: Managing stigmatized identities through discourse." *Human Relations, 67*(6), 715–737.

Part IV

WHAT WE KNOW NOW

CAREER REFLECTIONS AND LOOKING AHEAD

Chapter 9

From *Captive Audience* to Cultural Penology

Reflections on a Career in Prison Research[1]

Yvonne Jewkes

INTRODUCTION

> Prisons can be "stimulating, exhilarating, and curiously life-affirming environments in which to do qualitative research, and . . . a positive and powerful stimulus in the formulation of knowledge." (Jewkes, 2012, p. 69)

This chapter tells part of the story of my career as a prison researcher. My understanding of the editor Jenny Schlosser's aspiration for this volume is that it will humanize some of the most prominent female researchers working in the field of prison studies, and inspire future generations, not only to pursue their career ambitions but also to be unafraid of acknowledging their apprehensions, appraising the obstacles that face them, and applauding the mentors that have inspired and assisted them. With that in mind, the chapter will recount a little of how I ended up becoming an academic criminologist and prison researcher, the people who mentored and motivated me, the challenges I faced, the ongoing joys and pitfalls of doing fieldwork in prisons and what I think I've learned from the experience.

Many of the contributions in this volume will answer the call in the editor's brief to bring to light the "uniquely gendered experiences of women researchers in the male-dominated area of prison and corrections research . . . so that new scholars just entering the field will have some insight into the challenges we faced and how we overcame them." While this might be an accurate summation of prison research in the United States, it has not been my experience in the UK and I had to confess to Jenny that I neither felt that being a woman has negatively impacted on my research career, nor that I had faced particular hurdles in what is actually no longer a male-dominated field in the UK or in the European jurisdictions in which I have worked. In fact, in the two decades since I conducted my first piece of prison research, the field has grown rapidly and one only need attend a prisons conference, workshop, or panel in the UK or in most parts of Europe to realize that prison research is in good health and is heavily dominated by female scholars. Why this should be the case is a mystery, but it reflects a wider gender imbalance within criminology and related fields, including sociology, psychology, and carceral geography.

I suspect that my relatively straightforward path in prison research is quite common in jurisdictions where issues of gendered identity are bound up with professionalism and presentation of self, including dress, confidence, and curiosity, but not hindered by hegemonic assumptions about women's abilities to conduct research in "tough" environments. However, it must be acknowledged not only that considerations of the relatively unproblematic impacts of gender become more complicated when they intersect with other factors, including ethnicity and age (Phillips & Earle, 2010), but also that my good fortune in studying for my doctoral thesis at the University of Cambridge and being introduced to prison research by one of its most experienced and esteemed exponents, Professor Alison Liebling, undoubtedly greatly eased my early career path.

When I first met Alison in 1997, she was a senior researcher at the University of Cambridge. As my supervisor, she was crucial in my development as a prison scholar. I had absolutely no experience of prisons; I knew nothing about criminology. My degrees were in English and mass communications research. But I was confident in my abilities as a writer (I had recently published a textbook) and I was adaptable. I had started degree programs in politics and sociology at Leicester Polytechnic (now De Montfort University), as well as contributing to the launch of a new Centre for the Study of Public Order at the University of Leicester where, as a twenty-three-year-old, I taught senior police and criminal justice personnel. I was excited by the possibilities that the expansion of higher education seemed to promise and keen to grasp the many opportunities that were being presented to me. The idea of registering for a PhD at the University of Cambridge was daunting, ridiculous even. My parents were not university educated and I had not been expected to do a degree, let alone go on to do an MA and a PhD at the University of Cambridge—it all seemed rather surreal. But with the help of Loraine Gelsthorpe, who was then director of PhD Studies (and is currently director of the Institute of Criminology), who assisted in finding me funding, and Alison, who recognized in me a kindred spirit and instinctively knew how to unlock my potential, my doctoral studies quickly and rather easily fell into place.

That is not to say that my training at Cambridge didn't involve a constant—and indeed still ongoing—negotiation of the complexities of insider and outsider identities. But it would be dishonest if I did not point out that I have benefited enormously from being associated with the Prisons Research Centre that Alison founded, or that I have shamelessly name-dropped her at several points in my career in order to gain access to custodial environments around the world! It would be equally disingenuous to imply by omission that I have not also benefited greatly from the example, supervision, mentoring, inspiration, thinking, writing, and friendship of male colleagues and antecedents, as this chapter will acknowledge.

BECOMING A PRISON SCHOLAR

When asked why they do prison research, many academic scholars will cite reasons that center on their strong sense of justice and injustice, or on wanting to make a difference to the lives of others. I must confess that my own decision to conduct research in prison was a great deal less noble. No, my interest (as a PhD scholar coming from a background in media studies) was in prisoners as a captive *audience*. I say at the beginning of the work that was published under that title (Jewkes, 2002) that my aim was to "explore the importance of media forms and content within a unique context: the prison" (p. ix) but, actually, when I started out, I don't think I had any idea whatsoever of the uniqueness of prisons. I believed that researching an audience who were confined spatially, temporally, and sensorially would tell me something about how important media are in the organization of social reality and the multiple ways in which we navigate everyday life. Researching in conditions of confinement, I thought, would reveal why media matter to *all* of us in the ways that they do. So, my focus really wasn't on the prison—I might easily have chosen another type of institution or restricted space—a boarding school, a convent, or (much less likely, I admit) a submarine.

I can't remember how I ended up applying to do my PhD at the Institute of Criminology at the University of Cambridge. It was 1997, I was working as a full-time lecturer in media studies at De Montfort University, having completed a masters at the Centre for Mass Communications Research at the University of Leicester. Yes, these were the days when you didn't need a PhD to gain an academic post—though the lack of a doctorate and, undoubtedly my gender and age, were reflected in my lowly starting salary. This was long before the term "gender pay gap" had been coined, though we did spend a lot of our time talking about the "glass ceiling." And I soon realized that, while lack of a PhD had not prevented me from securing full-time employment, it would be a barrier to career progression.

The ideas for my thesis had come from long conversations with friends and colleagues, notably Rinella Cere (now at Sheffield Hallam University) and Tim O'Sullivan (Emeritus Professor at DMU). I had sent my proposal to several media/cultural studies departments but hadn't yet found the right supervisor, when someone—I wish I could remember who—suggested I try Cambridge. Initially hesitant because I really didn't consider myself an Oxbridge sort of person, far less a criminologist, I was somewhat persuaded by John B. Thompson who was (and is) professor of Sociology at Cambridge and was external examiner at my own institution. His book *The Media and Modernity* (1995) influenced my developing thinking that individuals select from the intense and infinite mediascape to make sense of their lives, to form relationships, to transport them to imagined worlds, to give them a sense of ontological security and, as Thompson puts it, "to inform and refashion the project of the self" (1995, p. 233). I could see how this might be pertinent within a "total institution." John was also a thoroughly nice man.

In the early 1990s, a type of audience research called "reception analysis" was popularized by David Morley in *Family Television: Culture, Power and Domestic Leisure* (1986) and *Television, Audiences and Cultural Studies* (1992). Like Thompson, Morley reconceptualized media influence, seeing it not as a force beyond an individual's control that inflicts negative effects on susceptible audiences, but as a resource that is consciously and selectively used, or indeed rejected, by people. In the deregulated and burgeoning media marketplace of the early 1990s, with its sudden proliferation of forms, outlets, channels, and titles, the omniscience of any single medium diminished, and it was recognized that audience members will seek out images, messages, and meanings that relate to their sense of self-identity, status, and often niche preferences. In short, by the mid-1990s, researchers had dismissed concerns about what the media do to people and turned the question around, asking instead, "What do people do *with* the media?"

I was particularly fascinated by the finding that television viewing was strongly gendered and that through the operation of power over this media technology, the dominant social group—men, or when they are not present, male children—restrict the range of material and symbolic options open to the less powerful members of the household; women and girls. On the whole, according to Morley, men enjoy uninterrupted access to the kinds of television they designate as important and have no qualms about using it as a primary means of relaxation in what they regard as their leisure time. The male "head of the household" would usually watch television from a favorite armchair, with the remote control to hand and would determine the conditions in which programs were watched (e.g., in silence or permitting critique or enthusiastic participation). Women tend to watch in a much more haphazard and distracted fashion, frequently combining the viewing of their favorite programs with attending to the needs of other family members. In contrast to their male partners, women are still to be seen at work within the domestic sphere, even if they have paid employment outside the home as well, and consequently their viewing preferences are frequently overlooked. What would happen in an all-male environment, I wondered? Would some lower-status men effectively be "feminised," their viewing preferences quashed by the more "alpha" males in the group?

I had heard anecdotally and through stories in the press that the communal TV rooms in custodial settings were frequently "flashpoints" that could become violent when men in prison disagreed over which channel would be watched. By the time my fieldwork commenced, collective television viewing was becoming less common in prisons, precisely because it could ignite tensions. "In-cell TV" was gradually rolled out across the prison estate, though not before I observed that communal TV viewing in prison replicated many of Morley's findings concerning media consumption within the family: "We discuss what we want to watch and the biggest wins. That's me. I'm the biggest," was a typical comment from a male respondent in Morley's 1986 study that had resonance in the prison context. However, in my study, it was mostly solitary, in-cell viewing (and reading and listening) that revealed a range of motivations and identity constructions, some of which were familiar to all media consumers (passing time, becoming informed, chilling out) and some of which had a particular salience (enhancing one's credentials as a violent man, "tuning out" of the aggressive prison culture), or poignancy (escapism, evoking memories of loved ones) in the context of the prison.

And, while in-cell TV undoubtedly made prisons calmer and more orderly environments because they were introduced as a vital component of the Incentives and Earned Privileges scheme, whereby noncompliant prisoners could find their television sets confiscated for bad behavior, my PhD findings bore out Morley and Thompson's belief that media consumption was a dynamic, reflexive, and fluid dimension of identity formation and social structure. In-cell television precipitated longer lockup periods, but it was never simply going to be an "electronic babysitter" or "multicolored narcotic," as several governors described it, with all the connotations of soporific passivity that those terms imply (see Jewkes, 2002). Nonetheless, for all its acknowledged advantages to prisoners, it's advantages to prison managers were at least equally great, and I concluded that personal television sets were being used as a "sweetener" intended to mask, or compensate for, the situational control measures that were creeping back into the logic of imprisonment. For the prison service, the media's capacity to "normalize" everyday life inside prisons ensured that the embedded practices of imprisonment—however undemocratic, unpopular or unpleasant—are accepted as natural to prison inmates over time.

Reading the final paragraph of *Captive Audience*, I am struck by how "Cambridge" it sounds! In the space of three years, I had well and truly metamorphosed from media studies lecturer to prison studies scholar:

> One of this study's key findings is that power is not uni-directional, but flows in and through prisons in multifarious and complex ways. Media—in their role as both a resource and a constraint—have altered the delicate balance of power within prisons and continue to subtly change and shift relations of dominance and subordination. An understanding of this paradox—that media are used both as a source of empowerment by prison inmates and, at the same time, as a means of control over them—enables us to begin to address some important questions that remain at the heart of much prison literature; namely, why is it that when prisoners apparently enjoy greater standards of living than formerly, are more integrated into the world beyond the prison walls than ever before, and are enjoying greater civil and legal rights than their predecessors, do their personal testimonies indicate that they may be experiencing a greater depth and weight of imprisonment than at any time previously? How is it that prisons seem—on the surface at least—more humane and yet at the same time are more punitive? It is these paradoxical questions that future prison research might usefully address in order to extend our understanding of the complexities of the social world of prisons. (Jewkes, 2002, p. 190)

And, indeed, Ben Crewe (now professor at Cambridge and Deputy Director of the Prisons Research Centre and a collaborator on many projects) did just that, extending the depth/weight metaphor to "tightness" to give a sense of the way that power in prison is experienced as "both firm and soft, oppressive, yet also somehow light" (Crewe, 2011, p. 522). Interestingly, Ben came from a cultural studies background and had written about contemporary masculinities, their cultural representations and men's lived experience (Crewe, 2003). And, as an aside, before he became a renowned penologist and professor of criminology at the University of Edinburgh, Richard Sparks also wrote about media, culture, and masculinity (e.g., Sparks, 1992, 1996). I think it is probably no coincidence that, of my peers, it is Ben and Richard whose writing I most admire and have falteringly sought to emulate. They each have a way with words, an elegant, yet surprising, turn of phrase, which has on many occasions had me mentally genuflecting in admiration.

As I said, the PhD was intended to be primarily a piece of audience research, not a contribution to prison scholarship and I sometimes reflect on how different the thesis would have been had I been based within a media/cultural studies department. It became a study of social and structural power that owed a debt to the likes of Thompson and Morley, but I now understood the context to be one of pain, resistance and social-psychological survival.

This was entirely Alison Liebling's influence. The first books she recommended I read were Gresham Sykes (1958) *The Society of Captives* and Stan Cohen and Laurie Taylor's (1972) *Psychological Survival.* I have so far omitted to mention that previously I had been registered as a PhD candidate at another university (where I worked, so my fees were waived, but where there were no prisons experts). My supervisor had offered me little advice beyond "Go and read Foucault."

What a relief, then, to pore over the rich and highly accessible descriptions of prison societies written by Sykes and Cohen and Taylor. Ironically, Alison was not (and still isn't) in the least bit interested in television and I was only her second PhD student (Mary Bosworth paved the way). But Alison is a voracious reader and she intuitively understood what would unlock the field for me. She was, and is, deeply embedded in prisons, often in the high-security estate, to very probably a unique degree, which meant that she had an unrivalled amount of wisdom and experience about prisons to pass on to someone who had none. In fact, there are relatively few scholars who spend the whole of their careers doing prison research "in the field" because the psychological, emotional, and physical demands on one's self are simply too great. But Alison has a rare drive and has devoted her career to getting deep inside the prison. Her research has had an incalculable impact on prison policy and legislation in the UK and elsewhere, and her influence on sociologically informed prison scholarship has been inestimable. More than all of that, though, she is motivated by compassion and empathy and she imparted to me the importance of finding humanity in inhumane environments, which is something I have taken through my career.

FINDING HUMANITY IN INHUMANE ENVIRONMENTS

> The appropriate master status of all in social science research is "personhood," with all the equal claims to privacy, dignity and respect that this term implies. (Liebling, 2014, p. 482)

> "Thank you for sharing your story. No one has spoken to me like that for a very long time." (prisoner)

This quote is from a prisoner, who I interviewed in a high-security prison in Norway, who was thanking me for simply sharing with him a personal experience from my life. It was an attempt to connect on a human level—a commonality of personal experience that transcended the fact that I was an academic researcher interviewing him for a research study. The conversation that precipitated his gratitude was as follows:

> [Him] I remember when I was being driven to the prison. It was an ordinary car. They just use police cars or even civilian cars to take us to prison here. And I was looking out of the windows thinking, this is going to be the last time I see grass and fields and sheep and all that stuff for a very long time. And I started to cry a little bit, just at the thought of losing all of that, you know? Losing touch with nature and life and the outside world. Seeing sheep and cows brought it home to me, the loss. I'll never forget that feeling. Sorry. I'm sorry, that must sound really stupid.

> [Me] Not at all. I once was very ill. . . . A doctor told me that if I didn't get to hospital immediately, I could be dead or brain dead by the end of the day. But they didn't have an ambulance, so my partner had to drive me to hospital. And I remember that feeling, being driven through the countryside to the hospital . . . sheep and trees and green fields. And I had that exact same feeling. This could be the last time I ever see all this.

We had gone slightly off-piste in terms of what we were meant to be discussing, as often happens in semi-structured, one-to-one interviews. As we exchanged our experiences, while sitting on opposite sides of a picnic-style table in a yard outside the man's accommodation block in a high-security Norwegian prison, while an officer stared at us with some bemusement from inside the building, we both found our eyes welling with tears. It was only for a few moments; we quickly regained our composure and returned to our roles as researcher and interviewee, though with a slightly changed atmosphere. About ten minutes later, the officer came to return the man to his cell but, before he entered the building, he made very direct eye contact with me and thanked me for sharing my story.

The revelation that no one had spoken to him like that for a very long time underlines a point that Alison immediately instilled in me with when I took my first tentative steps as a criminology PhD candidate at the University of Cambridge in 1997; which is that one of the reasons many of us end up spending much of our professional careers inside prisons is to "puncture the myths" about people who are incarcerated in them (Christie, 2000, p. 12); and this seems an opposite point—in the chapter but also, more broadly, at this historical moment in time—to reflect on the political context of what we do. Another of Alison's PhD students was Deborah Drake (currently head of Social Policy and Criminology at the Open University) whose doctoral research aimed to shine a light on the very "deepest" end of the penal estate at a time when security had risen to a level of prominence that eclipsed every other consideration, including what it means to be human. In her 2012 book *Prisons, Punishment and the Pursuit of Security*, she dissects politically invoked notions of "evil" and argues that we must separate the action from the perpetrator and avoid essentialist explanations that overlook the social origins of violence and cruelty. The transformations in penal security that she charts can be traced back to escapes from the high-security estate in 1994 and 1995, which ushered in a new regime of fortified perimeters, increased use of CCTV internally as well as externally, strict volumetric control of prisoners' property and a dramatic reversal of policy on all privileges that could be presented by the media as inappropriately conceived indulgences to an antisocial population. More significant even than these, however, were the changes made to countless everyday procedures, practices, and activities that combined to form insidious and pervasive erosions of humanity. For Drake, the high-profile escapes that precipitated these measures were viewed politically as a fortuitous catalyst for change.

Since Deb published her book, a further hardening of penal sensibilities has coalesced around new antiterrorism legislation (and new offences that have widened the carceral net, such as "joint enterprise"), brought in following several attacks involving multiple victims in London and Manchester. As I write in December 2019 in the UK, a Conservative landslide election result has seen a politician who has promised to deliver 10,000 more prison beds and increase sentences for serious offenders, elected as prime minister. His depressingly predictable response to events two weeks earlier, when a man convicted of terrorist offences killed two young people at a Learning Together event organized by colleagues from the Cambridge Institute of Criminology, before being fatally shot by police, tapped into dominant political-cultural discourses of vengeance and punitive punishment and sidestepped the inconvenient truth that two of the "heroes" who tackled the offender on London Bridge and undoubtedly prevented further fatalities were (ex)offenders convicted of serious crimes. The media's reporting of the events that took place on 29th November 2019 contained many typical themes (among them "ideal" victims, a perpetrator whose ethnicity and prior convictions lent themselves to journalistic stereotypes of "otherness," the "enemy within" and so forth, the discovery that the offender had served only half of his sentence, which was characterized as evidence of a broken criminal justice system, his attendance at what was reductively reported in all the mainstream media as a "rehabilitation conference," which provided ironic "proof" for the right-wing press of the limits of rehabilitation, etc.). All these familiar tropes were seized upon by politicians on the campaign trail, demonstrating that the political doctrine that the "wilful exclusion, segregation or exile of certain members of society is an appropriate response when particular, socially censured acts are committed" (Drake, 2012, p. 24) has no less purchase in 2019 as it had a decade earlier.

However, on this occasion, there was a powerful counternarrative in the form of the father of one of the victims who was fatally stabbed. David Merritt was given a platform by national newspaper *The Guardian* (and his words were immediately reported across all press, broadcast and social media) to write about how "livid" Jack would be if he saw the political capital that was being made of his death. By all accounts, Jack Merritt and Saskia Jones were drawn to the potential power of education in prisons out of a strong personal sense of (in)justice, and a healthily conflicted relationship with power and authority:

> He would be seething at his death, and his life, being used to perpetuate an agenda of hate that he gave his everything fighting against . . . [he would want] a world where we do not lock up and throw away the key. Where we do not give indeterminate sentences, or convict people on joint enterprise. Where we do not slash prison budgets, and where we focus on rehabilitation not revenge. Where we do not consistently undermine our public services, the lifeline of our nation. Jack believed in the inherent goodness of humanity and felt a deep social responsibility to protect that. (*Guardian*, December 2, 2019)

My reason for discussing this here is to underline that there is always a political context to what we do, and isolated events like the one described inevitably have some fall-out for many of us (one being that our universities suddenly start subjecting our research to greater scrutiny—not, I would surmise out of any particular concern for our welfare, but more to ensure they are safeguarding their reputations). Further, though, not only was David Merritt's tribute to his son a scathing attack on the UK's most senior politicians, and an implicit acknowledgment of the importance of initiatives that bring together academics and people serving prison sentences, but also it was above all testament to the passions and motivations of young academics who are drawn to the Institute of Criminology. It seems to me that there is a particular, shared characteristic that unites people who learn their craft within the Cambridge Institute and Prisons Research Centre; a knowledge that the research is conducted in, and is about, difficult and sometimes risky places, but it is done with a humane, person-centered, emotionally intelligent sensibility.

GENDER, EMPATHY, AND EMOTION: STAYING THE RIGHT SIDE OF THE LINE

Of course, I am not suggesting that rigorous, important prison research is not occurring outside of Cambridge—far from it. But the annual two-day conference hosted by the Prison Research Centre (PRC) remains a catalyst that brings together an ever-wider group of senior researchers and practitioners with newer entrants to the academic study of incarceration. Meanwhile, it is difficult to say what the impact of female dominance has been on the field of prison research on this side of the Atlantic. Keramet Reiter (2014) has noted that American social science research has embraced a heavily quantitative approach to mass incarceration, in contrast to the reflexive, interpretive perspectives more commonly found in European scholarship, and I am tempted to very unscientifically suggest that the quant/qual divide broadly reflects gendered skills, interests, and opportunities. As reductive as that may sound, I suspect it is the case; indeed, it might be the impetus behind this edited volume and Jennifer Schlosser's ambition to bring together, celebrate, and inspire female researchers who conduct qualitative research in prisons. And, as I said at the start of this chapter, I do not feel that being a woman in prison research has hindered me, although I have written about the differences in the way that men and women conduct themselves and are perceived in the field (Jewkes, 2012, 2014; Jewkes & Wright, 2016). In general, I think that female ethnographers are more likely to be assigned different identities or "labels" by research participants and gatekeepers based on marital status, physical appearance and sexual dynamics, as well as notions of professional status, social power, ethnicity, class, gender, and age; although see Crewe (2014) and Ugelvik (2014), for critiques arguing that men are not immune to similar treatment, being more likely to be assessed on the basis of physicality, class and certain cultural knowledge and competences. And, while I have surmised that it may be that women are more likely to acknowledge the emotional content of prison research, I think both Ben and Thomas would dispute that.

In any case, and whatever their gender, academic scholars rarely wrote in any detail about these issues until fairly recently. There are exceptions: my article in *Qualitative Inquiry (QI)* was inspired by an earlier contribution to that journal, by Bosworth et al. (2005) who chastise researchers for presenting their analyses in the form of inhuman data, resulting in prison studies becoming "cold, calculated, surgical . . . no blood—no humanity" (2005, p. 259). They accuse criminologists of losing the capacity to care: "Keep it statistical, inhuman, no compassion" (ibid). This is not an accusation that could be leveled at Alison Liebling, who has written (at least) four articles that candidly convey the emotional texture of prison research, blending compassion, integrity and "humanness"—and together they reveal much about her character and "personhood" (see Liebling, 1999, 2001, 2014, 2016). *The Pains of Doing Criminological Research*, a collection edited by Beyens et al. (2013), tells many stories about the ways in which gender shapes interactions with research participants and reveals the prison researcher as a person who may be prone to empathy, unease, apathy, or even disgust. Coretta Phillips and Rod Earle were other important exceptions to the general rule about not revealing anything of one's self; for example in their coauthored article published in 2010, Coretta discusses her dual insider/outsider as a mixed race woman in prisons and notes that aspects of shared identity based on ethnicity were cancelled out by a male respondent who positioned her as a sexualized gender subject and regarded their interview as "more of a date" (Phillips & Earle, 2010, p. 367). This can be relatively common in environments whose métier is deprivation (Jewkes & Wright, 2016, offer further examples), and where "rapport" can sometimes be mistaken for a deeper personal connection. It can occur on both "sides"; respondent and researcher. A prison governor once said to me that many people whose professional life takes them into prisons, whether as scholars or practitioners, "get the prison bug," finding the melee of all human life strangely addictive; an attachment that can run risks of the ethnographer "going native" or over-romanticizing prisoners.

So, while we can hypothesize about some of the attributes that make a "good" prison researcher, as I have done throughout this chapter, it must be remembered that conducting fieldwork in secure settings is an intensely personal and highly individualized enterprise, and I have also witnessed some colleagues who enter the field with naivety, who simply do not take to research in prisons, or who make the research about themselves, not about their research participants. This is a tricky line to keep on the right side of, as I discussed in the *QI* article. In that paper, I argued that the accounts of others can aid our understanding of the processes, pleasures, and pitfalls of QI, particularly if they reveal something of the self. I quoted Carolyn Ellis, who has done much to popularize, and make acceptable, autoethnography—"a social project that helps us understand a larger relational, communal and political world of which we are a part and that moves us to critical engagement, social action, and social change" (Ellis, 2009, p. 229). Good autoethnography, she says, "works toward a communitas, where we might speak together of our experiences, find commonality of spirit, companionship . . . and solace" (ibid.). I imagine this perfectly sums up Jenny Schlosser's ambition for this edited collection.

My objective in *QI* was to encourage reflexivity and honesty, but without losing sight of the bigger picture. As Abi Rowe intimates (incidentally, another excellent prison researcher who was supervised by me and Deb Drake—one of the great things about the career we have chosen is being able to pass on the baton), "ethnography proper" has the capacity to examine what can be learned from reflecting on our presence in the field that "we could not otherwise have access to" (2014, p. 406). My aim was to explore how acknowledgment of the ethnographer's biography, motivations, and emotions can uniquely enrich data, analysis and writing up. The article received quite a lot of attention and led to an invitation to guest edit a special issue of *Qualitative Inquiry* two years later on "Doing Prison Research Differently." It also encouraged others to reflect on their biographies and interrogate the significance of self in their ethnographies (see, for example, the excellent special issue of *British Journal of Community Justice* 14(2), guest edited by Jaime Waters in 2016 and Steve Wakeman's brave and brilliant article published in the *British Journal of Criminology* in 2014). On the whole, then, these contributions enriched prison studies and I was gratified that I had played a small part in this new reflexivity among prison researchers. In a few cases, I felt it unfortunate that some contributions lacked epistemological and theoretical rigor, and in a very small number of instances, self-reflection tipped over into self-absorption. My emphasis was intended very much to be on the "emotional investment required of ethnographic field-workers studying *stigmatized and/or vulnerable 'others'* in settings where differential indices of power, authority, vulnerability and despair are felt more keenly than most" (2012, p. 63) and to encourage researchers to own up to "*empathetic* feelings of anger, frustration, fear and outrage" (2012, p. 72; emphasis added). Here, I was addressing Bosworth et al.'s criticism that criminologists' failure to discuss the extent to which "most prisoners conceal a tumult of unplumbed anger, frustration, fear, and outrage at their imprisonment" undermines our ability to effectively critique the penal system (2005, p. 259). My call was for empathetic connection, not introspection, and my intention was certainly not to distract from what the research is "really about" (Crewe, 2009).

As Liebling intimates in her statement that our master status when conducting research should be "personhood," with equal claims to privacy, dignity, and respect, I believe that empathic connection requires an orientation of "equality." When any of us conduct social science research in criminal justice settings, we enter a world in which power flows overtly, and become infused with, as well as subject to it. Sometimes, with or without awareness, we wield it. We might operate "upward," "downward," or across less obvious and shifting configurations of power or levels of authority, involving gender, age, ethnicity, and nationality, class, professional, and other personal characteristics, all with hidden or explicit implications for status and positioning. But in order to build trust, solicit authenticity, know the culture (custodial and academic), and overcome not only power differences between researchers and research participants but also differences and difficulties within research teams (something, incidentally that is not widely written about, despite it being anecdotally widespread), we both claim and respect status. Working in a field that involves constant negotiation and use of power requires emotional intelligence. That and a bedrock of data and analysis to offer as evidence are essential.

COMING FULL CIRCLE: SOME CONCLUDING THOUGHTS

I have felt fortunate to be able to pay tribute in this chapter to some of the people who have inspired me, mentored me, befriended me, and collaborated with me in my formative years. I count myself as very lucky to be around in an era of prison scholarship that has meant I could learn from and know some of those who shaped knowledge about imprisonment in the UK and Europe in its formative (1970s–1990s) years, while also being able to collaborate with some of those who are conducting prison research today and taking the field in a multitude of new and important directions. I have further benefited from working with people not just in criminology, but from a wide range of other disciplines and fields, as well as those who work as professionals within the criminal justice system. But, as will be clear by now, no one has influenced my career more than Alison Liebling. I still remember our first meeting. Alison took me for tea in Cambridge. I wore a dress. I was terrified. She took me in, believed in me, was generous with her time and ideas, made me know I could do this. In the early days, she inspired me with her knowledge, experience, humanity, and enthusiasm. She was interested in me, but only as a result of getting to know me through my ideas and my work. And over the intervening two decades, she has become one of my closest friends and allies.

Jennifer Schlosser's final question to the contributors to this volume was, "knowing what you know now, what advice would you give your former self as you were just starting your prison research journey?" Truthfully, this is a tricky question to answer; I'm not sure I would have done anything very differently. Not a natural risk-taker (in life), I was always quite brave in the decisions I took in my research, and in my career more widely; for example, when struggling to place my early interdisciplinary work in a journal, because it very often fell between fields of inquiry, I decided to found my own journal—*Crime, Media, Culture*, which launched in 2005, five years after I completed my PhD. I'd advice new scholars to never think "I'm not the kind of person who . . . ," or "I hope to publish in that journal one day in the (distant) future." Confidence will take you a long way in an academic career, as will be getting along with people and building a network of like-minded and similarly ambitious academic friends. They will be lifelong allies, collaborators, facilitators, gatekeepers, sounding boards, confidantes, and conference buddies.

It is also important to research and write about issues that you genuinely, passionately care about or have an intellectual interest in. In very recent years I have returned to my academic roots and written about prisons using literature and ideas from the arts and cultural studies. I reread Dante's *Inferno* as inspiration for a couple of pieces on retributive policy-making and penal hell-holes (Jewkes, 2014, 2015), I have cofounded a new book series (with

Sarah Moore, Travis Linnemann and Jules Willan), called *Emerald Studies in Culture, Criminal Justice and the Arts*, as well as the new Sage journal *Incarceration*, which my fellow editors Ben Crewe and Thomas Ugelvik and I hope will, among other things, develop and promote a new subfield of "cultural penology." And after several years researching the rehabilitative potential of prison design, I am now writing and reading about architectural theory, aesthetics and atmospheres, and finding myself not only encountering new research opportunities, but able to write about them in a way that connects me with the cultural studies literature that inspired me to become an academic in the first place (Jewkes & Young, 2020).

So, as a final epithet, I will reflect on the fact that I have been inspired by the thinking, and tried to emulate the writing style, of a small group of like-minded (and, actually, not so like-minded) scholars during my career, but I have always stayed true to the ideas that made me want to carve out a career as an academic thirty years ago. My greatest inspirations come from work outside "criminology." I am motivated by writings from a broad and eclectic range of fields, which, inevitably, I read through a lens of incarceration. For example, in recent weeks, I have read Bachelard's *The Poetics of Space*, Pallasmaa's *The Eyes of the Skin: Architecture and the Senses*, Kazda and Caves's *Airport Design and Operation*, and Wohlleben's *The Hidden Life of Trees*, all of which now have scribbled notes in their margins pertaining to my experiences in prisons. I can't claim to read a fraction of what Alison does, but I have learned from her that reading around a subject—or just reading for pleasure—enriches our criminological insight and produces more interesting work.

NOTE

1. Sincere thanks to Ben Crewe for reading and commenting on an early draft of this chapter.

REFERENCES

Beyens, K., Christiaens, J., Claes, B., De Ridder, S., Tournel, H., & Tubex, H. (Eds.). (2013). *The pains of criminological research*. Brussels, Belgium: VUB Press.

Bosworth, M., Campbell, D., Demby, B., Ferranti, S. M., & Santos, M. (2005). "Dong prison research: Views from inside." *Qualitative Inquiry*, *11*, 249–264.

Cohen, S., & Taylor, L. (1972). *Psychological survival: The experience of long-term imprisonment*. Harmondsworth: Penguin.

Crewe, B. (2003). *Representing men: Cultural production and producers in the men's magazine market*. London: Bloomsbury Press.

Crewe, B. (2009). *The prisoner society: Power, adaptation, and social life in an English prison.* Oxford: Oxford University Press.

Crewe, B. (2011). "Depth, weight, tightness: Revisiting the pains of imprisonment." *Punishment & Society*, *13*(5), 509–529.

Crewe, B. (2014). "Not looking hard enough: Masculinity, emotion and prison research." *Qualitative Inquiry*, *20*(4), 392–403.

Drake, D. (2012). *Prisons, punishment and the pursuit of security.* Basingstoke: Palgrave.

Ellis, C. (2009). *Revision: Autoethnographic reflections on life and work.* Walnut Creek, CA: Left Coast Press.

Jewkes, Y. (2002). *Captive audience: Media, masculinity and power in prisons.* Cullompton: Willan.

Jewkes, Y. (2012). "Autoethnography and emotion as intellectual resources: Doing prison research differently." *Qualitative Inquiry*, *18*(1), 63–75.

Jewkes, Y. (2014a). "An introduction to 'doing prison research differently.'" *Qualitative Inquiry*, *20*(4), 387–391.

Jewkes, Y. (2014b). "Punishment in black and white: Penal 'hell-holes,' popular media and mass incarceration." *Atlantic Journal of Communication* special issue on "Reframing Race and Justice in the Age of Mass Incarceration," *22*(1), 42–60.

Jewkes, Y. (2015). "Fear-suffused hell-holes: The architecture of extreme punishment." In K. Reiter & A. Koenig (Eds.), *Extreme punishment: Comparatives Studies in detention, incarceration and solitary confinement.* London: Palgrave.

Jewkes, Y., & Wright, S. (2016). "Researching the prison." In Y. Jewkes, J. Bennett, & B. Crewe (Eds.), *Handbook on prisons* (2nd ed.). Abingdon: Routledge.

Jewkes, Y., & Young, A. (2020). "Sensory reflections on a Japanese prison." In K. Herrity, B. Schmidt, & J. Warr (Eds.), *Sensory penalties: Exploring the senses in spaces of punishment and social control.* Bingley: Emerald.

Liebling, A. (1999). "Doing research in prison: Breaking the silence?" *Theoretical Criminology*, *3*(2), 147–173.

Liebling, A. (2001). "Whose side are we on? Theory, practice and allegiances in prisons research." *British Journal of Criminology*, *41*, 472–484.

Liebling, A. (2014). "Postscript: Integrity and emotion in prisons research." *Qualitative Inquiry*, *20*(4), 481–486.

Liebling, A. (2016). "The Dalai Lama, prisons, and prisons research: A call for trust, a 'proper sense of fear,' dialogue, curiosity and love." *Prison Service Journal*, *225*, 58–63.

Morley, D. (1986). *Family television: Culture, power and domestic leisure.* London: Comedia.

Morley, D. (1992). *Television, audiences and cultural studies.* London: Routledge.

Phillips, C., & Earle, R. (2010). "Reading difference differently? Identity, epistemology and prison ethnography." *British Journal of Criminology*, *50*(2), 360–378.

Reiter, K. (2014). "Making windows in walls: Strategies for prison research." *Qualitative Inquiry*, *20*(4), 417–428.

Rowe, A. (2014). "Situating the self in prison research: Power, identity and epistemology." *Qualitative Inquiry*, *20*(4), 404–416.

Sykes, G. (1958). *The society of captives: A study of a maximum security prison.* Princeton, NJ: Princeton University Press.

Thompson, J. B. (1995). *The media and modernity: A social theory of the media.* Cambridge: Polity Press.

Ugelvik, T. (2014). "Prison ethnography as lived experience: Notes from the diaries of a beginner let loose in Oslo prison." *Qualitative Inquiry*, *20*(4), 471–480.

Wakeman, S. (2014). "Fieldwork, biography and emotion: Doing criminological auto ethnography." *British Journal of Criminology*, *5*(5), 705–721.

Chapter 10

Women in Our Own Right or "Honorary Men"?

Reflections on a Professional Life in Prisons Research

Alison Liebling[1]

INTRODUCTION: "MOTHER-SISTER POWER" IN PRISONS RESEARCH

OK, I'll talk. But I want to be interviewed by the Professor!

—(Prisoner, to the research team, Liebling et al., 2011)

You don't look like a Professor!

—(Cambridge Taxi Driver, 2008)

In prisons, where I have ended up engaged in continuous research for more than thirty years, being a (competent, approachable) woman has been mainly a positive experience, despite some of my anecdotes to come. I can't say whether being a woman has been "an advantage," since many of the men I do research with do just as well. When I think about how power and gender intersect in the world of prison research, I recall the powerful, likeable prisoner above who was making a claim: if he was to be heard, he wanted to be heard by the most experienced, influential member of the team. It was certainly also relevant that I was a woman. We had engaged in many long, informal conversations over a period of several months in a detailed study of the prison he was in. He knew that he was a "key informant": someone who knew his complex and intense environment well and who was highly articulate about it. All three members of the research team were women in that project, as it happened. Several prisoners in this long-term prison for men commented playfully, and typically in this culture, that this was "an advantage" since they were "short of female company." There was no doubt in this case that power and gender blended instrumental with emotional appeal. I was, by this time, a known female figure who "got listened to," but who would be sympathetic, patient, and engaged. This was, he felt, worth the effort, and the emotional as well as social risk of engaging in a long interview.

Many prisoners in this project made observations about my professional status. They were admiring ("you've worked hard"), reassured ("she knows what she's doing") and leveling ("Greetings to you and your Firm") as well as apparently unthreatened and willing to be genuinely personable (many asked about my well-being, working life, or thoughts about recent policy and political developments and their implications for me). Long-term prisoners are both well disposed toward higher education (and therefore to representatives of it) and so steeped and experienced in the flow of power that they detect its shape, and potential, in a moment—even at a distance. There are forms of female power they dislike (sexual power, sometimes used by women officers, and narrow, risk-oriented psychological power, deployed by a distinctly female psychological profession; see Warr, 2020). Unusually, perhaps, prisoners revere, and welcome, educated or privileged "mother-sister" power, if I can call it that, because they feel it is on their side. It *is*, if what we mean by "their side" is taking their experience and personhood seriously, finding ways of making sense of life with them, in a context, showing what is "morally at stake," and "speaking truth to power" in ways that might change the future. I refer here to my own approach, as I have learned to characterize it, and do it, over the years, but this kind of work is certainly not unique to me. I think of Barbara Owen, Keramet Reiter, Elaine Genders and Elaine Player—there are very many others—all of whom have devoted substantial portions of their lives to this style of prisons research.

The project I am referring to above is recent, of course. It hasn't always been like this. Surviving "gender," and learning to navigate others' expectations of us, or the constraints they place on us, is a lifelong task, in our professional work and out of it. In this chapter, I will try to tell my "gender" story more narratively, or in some kind of order. I raise many questions and answer some. Is there a distinctly "female" version of the activity of doing prisons research? Does the term *mother-sister power* capture something of how we do it (I like the term). Is our theorizing different from the theorizing of men (see Howe, 1999)? Or our data collection? Are our motives, and our academic lives, distinctive?

I would like to start with an extract from a recent blog because these remarks, written recently and without the self-consciousness involved in formally "writing a chapter," communicate something important about my research style and values:

Mary Bosworth invited me to reflect on my long-term prisons research experience for her Border Criminologies blog: What changes? What stays the same? How does the long-term nature of our engagement in prisons influence how we think, feel, act, and write? There is such a lot to say. . . . I have a few friends (and colleagues) who were once participants in my various studies, and who are now out; or they were staff or Governors, and I befriended them. Some left the Prison Service in traumatic circumstances. I have to be careful to keep my current interests in their former world to myself. I feel like I belong to a cohort (united by something like the "liberal consensus" that existed around me then). There are not many of us left.

I have thought about this question most in relation to my two (now three) studies of HMP Whitemoor, each about ten years apart. The experience of dramatic change—a marked reduction in safety and trust, and in staff professional confidence—between the first and the second studies haunts me still. I was thrown by the challenges of having to work out whether I had changed—was I more sensitive to violence? Did I see better, with trained eyes? Had life events, or the aging process, interfered with my capacity to make connections with new groups of prisoners? Or was the prison simply radically different? How was I to be sure? This study was the first to make me doubt my ability to diagnose a prison, as well as my motivation to continue in prisons research. I recovered, in due course, but it took some strategic realignments, a return to Appreciative Inquiry, and a search for "better" prisons, with trust flowing, to achieve that. I have had similar qualms in more recent years, watching prisons disintegrate in the wake of staffing cuts and shortages. I still look for "better" prisons, only to be mostly disappointed. Some really are exceptional—even now—and I am always happier and more at home in these places. "Good" prisons are bad enough to supply plenty of material for critical and theoretical analysis. The contrast between the best and the "others," including the worst, has always been where the most interesting questions lie (for me).

I was in an interesting prison last week and, as usual, was happiest in a long conversation with an individual prisoner who was showing me his novel in the library, and some poetry he had submitted to the Koestler competition. We went off-piste pretty quickly. His mate made me a mug of tea, and I was confident that this long, unstructured chat was both a good way of understanding this prison, and a way of showing respect for his personhood. I learned a few things about Caribbean cooking, and I left feeling what I have so often felt in prisons research: what a mixture of humanity and tragedy, hope and injustice, curiosity and sadness, human tenacity and defeat . . . the whole world is here, magnified. I have only ever had one style, and I stick doggedly to it despite the proliferation of constraints and the shortening of time: friendly. Why shouldn't I be open, interested, flexible, in this world of human beings? The increasing pressure to nail down every question, avoid "talking to the men about their backgrounds," and limit the "research transaction" to a formality makes me want to be Cohen and Taylor, Tony Parker, and Kirsty Young (yes, Desert Island Discs) all rolled into one. Sticking to this style has caused me untold problems in the rest of my (mainly working) life—strain and frustration, absences from other and competing commitments, ridiculous working hours, an office full of notebooks I have never digested, the feeling that I need to stop, at some point, and write about it all. But it is all in there somewhere, and (I think) has made my teaching lively and heartfelt. It means I really do know what has gone on in prisons over the last thirty-three (eek) years. But there is so much unfinished business . . .

Moving up the academic chain (something I still feel was kind of accidental or unplanned) has the advantage that I can now take other people with me, rely on their skills when I can't be there, get interested in their projects, and watch interesting research questions take on a different shape in a different person. But, like Mary, I also feel the burdens of multiple and unending commitments. Let's face it, modern academic life is pretty gruelling at times, especially once you come eye to eye with the rapidly alienating nature of neoliberal higher education. I sometimes go to prison for a rest. And for humanity.

(Liebling, Still in the Field:—Oxford University Border Criminologies Blog, November 1, 2019)[2]

This piece was about the distinctiveness of doing prison research for a long time rather than specifically about being a woman in the field, but it is hard to separate my continuity in the field from any other aspect of my experience. One of the questions I have had to think about in writing this chapter is whether the relevance of our gender in prisons research changes over time. It does. On the one hand, seniority "takes over," and adds power, so whatever we feel inside, we become regarded by prisoners, staff, and senior managers, as influential, as possessing authority, as "Alpha," as I illustrated earlier. Long-term prisoners read the published results of research closely. I have had several experiences of being introduced to high-profile prisoners in small and special units who have said, "I've read all your work." Some give me insightful (and usually affirming) feedback on specific reports. There is a feedback loop. At these moments, I feel a satisfying sense of competence and recognition: "You know I know your world, and that I care about it"; so we can start the conversation from there. I love the feeling of research as a continuing dialogue: a never-ending search for a better grasp of "the real" (a reference to my great guide, George Eliot; see Liebling, 2020). On the other hand, returning to some fieldwork notebooks from my early research life made me realize, for the first time, how vulnerable I once was, how unable to "speak out" or even properly register what I now recognize as abuse. This was abuse of prisoners, and sometimes of me.

I wrote the first draft of this chapter from memory and imagination: my current feeling, taking the "whole" of my research experience into account. Once the draft was complete, I found myself searching for old fieldwork notebooks one evening at home, curious to retrieve memories. I found a relevant notebook (I keep everything and made thorough notes). The front portion of each A4 notebook (1 for each prison) was for detailed notes on all activities and observations: what I did, what I saw, what was said, and so on (with illustrations of cell or disciplinary adjudications layout!). The back was for personal reflections, books I was reading, and more general thoughts. I was alarmed to find that I had edited and simplified my account of thirty-four years ago. Forgotten frustrations, ethical dilemmas, and mistakes were all there. There were notes about prison officer Christmas parties, finding three red roses at the gate, officers using body belts and other violence "unofficially," and some anxieties about my boundaries being threatened, as well as accounts of long and meaningful interviews, and outstanding work being carried out by all kinds of staff. The notes were "gold dust" (I felt, when I rediscovered them). They challenged some of the "smoothing over" of my research life I had unknowingly introduced. So, as this is the final draft, I will include here some personal observations (edited a little, to protect individuals), from another time and place, perhaps still familiar to many novice prison researchers, and (for me) worth remembering and reflecting upon as I revisit the rest of the chapter. These notes were from a former Young Person's prison. It had changed role, to become a (theoretically more helpful) Youth Custody Centre:

Northbridge fieldwork notes, 1986.

Northbridge is certainly a "big nick"—the whole set up is different to either Littletown (a former Borstal) or Midwood (a Detention Centre). The staff are more "macho" and serious and, having worked with adults, a bit tougher and more cynical. The staff are very "protective" toward me—they lock me in offices, don't let me stand around in corridors—and this afternoon, when all the officers went running to the call of an alarm bell, I found myself locked in the Education department! That was quite an experience—the first time I've seen or felt any tension or fear in a prison. Nothing happened, but I am now aware of the risks, especially after my "hostage" talk with the Security Officer.

My Assistant Governor (AG) minder organized an officer into showing me the tea room—a portacabin that used to be the officer's mess but has been "demoted" to a tea room on the orders of the medical officer here. It got a bit dirty and unhygienic over the years. So I was shown in . . . gasp . . . to a smoke filled room, with a table, full of super-macho officers playing cards and smoking. Nude pin-ups on the walls and a look of horror on their faces as a "young lady" was announced. Help! I thought. I quickly discovered that if I stay in my office and phone xxx, the orderly (a trusted prisoner) will bring me tea and I will automatically be included in the tea boat. What a relief. I don't think I'll be spending much time in there . . .

My guide talked about the dispute last year—it peaked for about a week in April, when trainees were smashing up their cells and sending burning furniture out of the windows. One Principal Officer was injured—in some way it was "fortunate" for him to be able to "go sick" because he was coming in for some fire from trainees for aligning himself with management. He told me to always let the Senior Officer know when I am in the AG's office on A Wing, just in case I get barricaded in!

. . . I'm stuck! I can't do a thing. The Chaplain is not here (only 1 hour late), no probation officers, I can't get over to any files without pleading, and I don't feel like doing files anyway. During a conversation with (Senior Probation Officer) I suddenly realized why working here is so difficult. It is the restriction of movement, and the air of general secrecy, and the ambivalence of staff feeling toward (female) "outsiders." It has finally driven me to despair. I would feel better if there were some moral support here, but there isn't. This is simply a difficult prison to work in. I'm not surprised that (senior probation officer) has crumbled under the weight. Imagine if he were female as well as being a probation officer!

. . . So I end up lodging with the softest, leftyist Assistant Governor imaginable, who moved here from his communal house in Liverpool. He reads the Guardian and has a theory about "sharing" in relationships. . . . His is a co-counsellor and has also been a social worker. He doesn't want to be seen too much in that light here—the two roles are largely incompatible at his grade. . . . He was only living in a conventional family because the commune had broken up. He said I was a great listener—and that I'd be good at living in that way. He certainly "goes deep" very quickly. This morning I'd offered to drive him to the station at 7:30 a.m. There was a mug of tea outside my bedroom door. I'd needed it, getting up at that hour. He gave me a hug when he left. That was a fast friendship!

There were other notebooks—one documenting violence and demeaning treatment of terrified young men. I "ranted" in the back of the notebook, which I shared with my then supervisor on his occasional visits to my fieldwork outpost. His response to my emotional outbursts by letter, at first and then over time, on car journeys to prisons, started off a deep and lasting intellectual relationship, as he shared his own emotional experiences of fieldwork, in the days of the movement to abolish the death penalty in the UK.

Writing this chapter has made me reflect on the role that gender once played, and continues to play, in my professional life, which is also 'my life' with more inquisitive openness than I have attempted before. I have asked myself many questions, often for the first time. Are we as women always subject to male "entitlement" (Frances-White, 2019)? Is my way of understanding prison life and culture gendered? Are my emotional responses in prison distinctly "feminine"? Are my fears, on the rare occasions when they have been evoked, grounded in my gender? Why was I so drawn to appreciative inquiry as a method? Is the "critical, competitive mood" in academic life (see Felski, 2015) inherently masculine? Writing this chapter has been a process of discovery as well as description, so I am grateful for the invitation to do it. To address these kinds of questions authentically, I found I had to go back to the beginning and retrace the steps: how and where does gender "show up" in our research lives? There were some surprises and challenges along the way.

BECOMING A PROFESSOR

As I suggest in the account earlier, I am still a bit surprised that I have ended up as a professor (and in Cambridge). I am not always sure that I want to tell people-in-general in case it alienates them or makes them too curious or deferential. I am, of course, both pleased and proud—what an amazing and privileged job—but this was not "the plan." The plan (I thought) was to stay as free and lowly as possible, working on other people's research projects, or—at my most ambitious—to return to York, where I studied politics for my first degree, and start up a Department of Criminology there. I also had some vague sense that I would like to work part-time. I had done my master's degree part-time, and the lifestyle (working in a pub at weekends, volunteering for victim support once a week, and still having enough time to get to the end of my reading lists) suited me very well. My mother had worked part-time. I never took my own financial "role" very seriously, younger generations may be horrified to learn, until this became a necessity. I still fantasize about going part-time, eventually (now as part of a retirement plan!) I like life. In ways I can only see now, I benefited from both the "freedom" women of an older generation had to see work as optional, and the opening of professional doors to women. My working life developed organically, and was driven by interest, or compulsive curiosity, rather than by design or ambition.

I was strongly encouraged (by my then male and American head of department) to apply for a professorship, at a time when the University also sent letters of invitation to its female staff, to begin to address their stark under-representation at senior levels. When I arrived at Cambridge University in 1987, 4 percent of its Professors were women. It is now 18.3 percent. The "Russell Group average" is 20.9 percent.[3] More attention is paid to these figures now, and there is action to both understand and improve them. There is a widely criticized gender pay gap, among other inequalities, so still much work to be done. I would not have dared apply, at that point, without his explicit support. He pointed out that I had the right profile, had just published a major book, and he argued that I had a strong case. I spent three weeks filling in the application form—with the typical conscientiousness and perfectionism of women in academic life. I learned that my male colleagues who had been promoted before me had been far less conscientious and had a more blasé and efficient attitude to form filling. But I remember thinking, only when I got to the end of the form filling process, that actually I did meet all the criteria. I had to see the evidence in writing, and organized under headings, before I believed it.

Those who celebrated my promotion to professor with the most feeling and enthusiasm were the women librarians and administrators in the Institute of Criminology, and the Porters at Trinity Hall, who had all known me since I was a PhD student. The symbolism was recognized, in other words, by those with the least power. Once I became a professor, I was frustrated by the number of University Committees I was invited on to ("we need a woman"), and by the exposure to some taken-for-granted ways of doing business that just seemed archaic. Being a woman professor (who disappears off to prison much of the time) is both a privilege and a challenge. My model of working—engaged, determined to be in the field with my colleagues, pursuing an intellectual life, and leading a research group—sometimes conflicts with broader assumptions about what "being a woman" in a university setting might mean to others ("great, a welfare tutor!").

In general, I feel fortunate to "have been" a woman at this time and in this place. I still find some aspects of holding and using power tricky and (scarily like my mother) I like to think that I am "friends with," as well as responsible for, my PhD students and younger colleagues. I got that wrong now and again, especially in my early days, but I am very proud of the fact that a number of my very best friends are my former women PhD students (including Mary Bosworth and Yvonne Jewkes, now both Professors themselves). What a delight it is (as my MA supervisor said) when former students become colleagues and friends. I have grown my own mutual support network. This has been one of the many satisfactions of my professional life.

This collection is intended to include personal reflections and experiences, so I will venture in that direction, despite some lingering anxieties about exposing aspects of my life I often hold in reserve. My work is all about how we survive and flourish, and what kinds of environments make that possible, or not, in prison (but also more generally). Most of my work focuses on the use of authority—its changing shape, and its effects, and the differences between good or "right" and bad versions of it. I didn't choose to study suicides in prison; it chose me. I was so puzzled and moved by the thoughtless and often cruel institutional response to the vulnerability I witnessed in my first encounters with prison life that I just had to understand more. I didn't connect my choice of topic with my personal experience at the time, but I was aware that I found some of the reading around the subject too painful to bear, and so I avoided it. At some point in the PhD a young prisoner told me about his mother's suicide attempt. I was asking questions about "anyone else in the family" who had attempted suicide when I asked about their own attempts. He remembered an ambulance arriving at his house when he was about ten years old; his mother's absence while she was in hospital. The aftermath. It dawned on me, undramatically, that I remembered that too. My home life had been, for various reasons, chaotic. A largely absent father (who was very "present" in my heart), and a vulnerable mother made me "the stable parent"; a sort of "moral perfectionist," with some quite serious consequences for my development. So, the enduring themes of my working life—good order, authority, safety, freedom or agency, vulnerability and survival—had deep origins.[4]

Women friends occasionally told me, in late night chats, that I was "seriously feminist": that is, I didn't really recognize male power. But male friends often told me that I was "very feminine." This is curious. I had somehow skirted the gender-power question in my professional life by a kind of blindness to its significance (until more recently—see further). I definitely wanted to be "one of the boys" at school because I wanted their skills and freedoms, their "self-actualizing life," from an early age. Later, I still wanted what the boys had—to be read and taken seriously by men, as well as by women, and to acquire all the relevant skills for doing research as well as I could. I made some deliberate choices (against others' assumptions or suggestions) not to specialize in the study of women in prison (although I don't leave women out) and to master (or know how to use, at least) quantitative methods. This was the same as wanting to do woodwork or play tennis instead of netball. At many points in my life I have been included in "boys' clubs" without really noticing (or realizing, to my shame, that other women were being excluded). I vividly recall realizing that one of my closest friends and role models was "male" only when his wife, also a scholar-in-the-making, gave birth to their first child. Ah, I thought. He's got a wife. Maybe that was the slow beginnings of a broader realization that being a woman was professionally significant and brought with it several dilemmas and disadvantages that I had overlooked.

For example, in 2008, I was invited to give a keynote lecture on the moral quality of prisons—my specialist area—at an international conference in Prague. I was greeted warmly afterward by a Norwegian director of the training academy for prison staff, who congratulated me on my "very fine lecture." His first words to me were, "I've read your book." He meant my book on prison officers, which explores what their work consists of, at its best (Liebling & Price, 2001). It describes the "right use of authority": a variety that is professional, humane, helpful and organized, and extremely difficult to accomplish. It is very highly skilled work. He had liked the book very much and had used it often in the training of staff. His next words were, "I thought you were a man."

A few years before this, one of my then PhD students returned from a trip to America to meet various academics relevant to his research, which was a kind of development of my work on suicides in prison. He was very excited by the trip and met several interesting and helpful scholars. One of them knew of my work in this area, and so congratulated him on having me as his supervisor. I don't know how the conversation proceeded after that but reporting back, Joel, my PhD student, said to me, "He thought you were a seventy-year-old man!" My "voice" (i.e., my writing, or my work) is well regarded, I am told. But it is constructed as masculine. Aged masculine. Why is that, I wonder? I often find myself encouraging my women students to "speak more authoritatively" and to eliminate "the tentative" ("perhaps," "maybe") from their writing; to be bold. It saddens me that I still encounter "the tentative" in the writing of many of my women students. I hope I support them appropriately, by being a mentor, example, and admirer of their potential. Their smartness shows up in so many ways, but they still so often seriously underestimate themselves. I found a writing voice early on in my life, and it was always stronger, clearer, and more confident than my speaking voice. I don't know why. I still write to think, and find my way.

The huge advantage of being a bright, eager-to-learn woman (for me) was male patronage, which I have to admit, I sometimes welcomed, despite its dangers, especially when it came in the form of intellectual encouragement and companionship (how I wished I could meet a George Henry Lewes!).[5] I probably lacked the confidence and ambition to take what have turned out to be the most important steps in my career without their support. Sometimes, of course, being made welcome in a man's world goes wrong, and we lose ourselves. I have had to learn that accepting support is a very different thing from succeeding on terms set by men; and that there are women "mentors" out there, if we look hard enough, or wait long enough (or grow our own). More experienced men who helped me significantly (with intellectual questions, self-doubt, professional interest and support, or pressure to apply for posts) in my early academic life occasionally revealed expectations—at the time or much later—of help back (research assistance, management of their legacy), or of sexual or romantic engagement (domestic slavery!). I value reciprocity but, obviously, I prefer this to take place naturally and was shocked, as well as wrong footed, by one or two of these requests. While these demands have by no means been frequent, the very few women mentors I have found over time have been endlessly generous and have never asked for anything in return. There are male and female significant others in my field who I treat "almost as family." But even in families, we sometimes have to navigate power relations. This is an ongoing process. It is the case, now that I reflect on it, that in my professional life so far, I have only had to negotiate power with the male members of my academic "family." I discovered later in life that talking to others is a very important step in seeing what is happening to us, individually and collectively, and in formulating appropriate strategies.

When I first started out as a student, and then research assistant, doing fieldwork in mainly male prisons, I did experience sexual harassment (not just in prisons), and inappropriate questions about "what my boyfriend thought about me doing a job like this." In my first project, before I started my PhD, I worked as a research assistant on the project I draw on earlier on *Young Offender Throughcare* led by a male professor (Keith Bottomley) at Hull University who became a lifelong friend. The post involved fieldwork in three prisons, for about eight weeks in each. In each prison, there was a settling in period, finding an office, getting to know the staff, starting to carry out interviews. Usually, I was nervous, but curious enough to also feel excited. In my second prison, Northfield, I thought I was starting to get the hang of prisons research. Not so. This prison, which was closed in 2013, was ancient and traditional. It had originally opened in 1788, and its buildings had been added throughout the eighteenth and nineteenth centuries. It had at one time the largest treadmill in the world. My office was a cell, and I couldn't see the face of the orderly (a trusted prisoner) who occasionally made me tea from a cabin outside in the grounds. He pushed the mug through the open grille at my window. One day, there was a knock at the door. A large principal officer opened it and stood in the doorway looking at me. Outside the door were the radial wings of a traditional prison. "Hello," he said, and paused. "I just want you to know that I don't approve of women working in my prison," and with that he shut the door. "Oh," I thought. "Better find some allies."

My ally in those days was a "hippyish" male AG with good social work skills. Partly organized through my supervisor, I had accepted paid lodgings with him, and his family, in his large prison quarters next to the prison (I did this often throughout my research life, with men and women, a practice some of my colleagues found boundary-breaching; I could write a book about just that!). I found the blending of professional with personal knowledge and friendship irresistible, in certain cases, provided it was understood on both sides that I would (and could) continue to be "ruthlessly honest" about how I understood their world. I wanted to know everything, about everyone in the field, so I could sympathetically understand even practices I disapproved of. I had forgotten about the detail, now included earlier in the text, of feeling horrified by the officer's tea room, and a bit nervous about whether my boundaries were understood. Interestingly, these original fieldwork notes challenge the account I am constructing today of a "me" who was sure footed and asserting her right to be ruthlessly honest. Actually, I was winging it.

Later, in my research life, I found ways of building trust with skeptical prison officers, using appreciative inquiry, but that too is another story (see Liebling et al., 1999). I have had to practice very demanding and complex diplomacy and self-management skills to "get this right," most of the time. I still remember, painfully, my two mistakes. Saying too much, at the wrong moment, to the wrong person. Being "too honest," and unguarded or impulsive. Both scenarios ended in tears (but equally, were resolved).

Mostly, I have found prison officers helpful to me, after some initial skepticism, or occasional harassment, and once they understand that I am interested in their professional lives. Sometimes their accepting or favorable attitude toward me comes alongside an expressed disdain for prisoners, which is tricky, but important, to handle appropriately (see Drake, 2014). I increasingly try hard never to "collude" with, and occasionally to challenge, disrespectful treatment, while keeping the dialogue open. This is definitely something I learned on the job and did not get right in those early days. Sometimes an officer's switch from skeptical to "desperate" is rapid, and a basic research question unleashes hours of disturbing testimony about the strains, pressures, and traumas of prison officer (or related specialist) work. This, I suppose, might be gendered: we become understanding providers of sympathy and comfort, suspending judgment and offering support. This is about simultaneously "taking" while "not taking" sides (see Liebling, 2001). Now and again I have had to exchange looks with a prisoner which says, "I am sorry he said/did that; I hope you know," and, "OK, I know." We might even get to talk about it later. Observation is so important in prisons research: being there (e.g., at an adjudication, or when something happens on a wing) so often leads the way to the building of a shared account. But it can be challenging, especially when we see or experience things we wish we hadn't, on all sides. This has been my life.

My casual attitude toward work (no longer possible for new generations in a different economic climate) meant I had "the luxury" of thirteen years on medium term postdoctoral contracts (two and three years each). This kind of lifestyle is now regarded as an insult, and as exploitation, a position I now largely support. It was easier to make do on low pay when you were without debt and higher education was expanding. I worked for free between contracts, wanting to complete reports or coauthor books, with or without pay, and I flourished, with the freedom to devote myself to fieldwork tasks, well-defined projects, and immersion in what became a cumulative intellectual trajectory.

Through commissioned or sought projects on (for example) suicides in prison (there were four different projects on this subject), small units for difficult prisoners, incentives and earned privileges, staff-prisoner relationships, values, practices, and outcomes in public and private sector corrections, the changing nature of staff-prisoner and prisoner-prisoner relationships in high-security prisons, conceptualizing and measuring the moral quality of prison life, and the changing role of trust and forms of order in prison, and I have come to learn, with increasing clarity and confidence, that *how people feel treated* is fundamental to the survivability of prison life. Human beings need *recognition*—that is, a "real meeting" in which their whole being or personhood is acknowledged. In the very best prisons, being treated as a person with a complex inner life and with potential (a *Thou,* or experiencing subject) can lead to transformative experiences. In the worst prisons, where sentences become extreme, and prisoners feel treated as an *It* (an experienced object) prisoners become despairing, angry and alienated or violent, and they may turn into the dangerous "other" they are treated as. Cynicism and distrust are destructive (yet "intelligent trust" is such a challenge). A tragic perspective among staff—non-perfectionist, psychologically informed, discerning, and supportive—can save and change lives. Prisoners evaluate their circumstances and treatment *morally*: their experiences are morally oriented. They are often very willing to engage in moral reflection about their lives and relationships but this is more likely in "morally intelligible prisons." These findings (my conclusions from many different projects and attempts at writing, ongoing; see, e.g., Liebling, 2015; Liebling et al., 2019; Auty & Liebling, 2019) are relevant to all of our lives. Every moment of my precarious, hazardous, and often overwhelmingly demanding working life has been worth it to tread this path.

When I ended up getting a permanent job, I was (rightly) nervous. My voluntary, highly appreciated, teaching quadrupled and became taken for granted. I struggled to do (enough) fieldwork, manage projects from an uncomfortable distance, and deal with unfathomable administration. I was part of the team developing an entirely new masters course for senior managers in criminal justice, to be delivered in the so-called vacation periods. It took many years and several crises before I was back "in the field" (the research income was still there, as I had lived this way for so long), somehow working out how to balance teaching, research, writing, and administration, and still stay alive. My professional and other friends all know that this is an ongoing struggle, but the luxury of tenure came like a warm blanket after a cold wind: I had not understood what I had missed, except during those precarious moments where someone (e.g., in the Prison Service organization) wanted to pull my creatively sourced funding (usually over Christmas). It was a surprise to me how satisfying it was when "today's work" also feels like an investment in the future. To belong and be part of something enduring.

I still find doing the research I do "wildly exhilarating" even if I sometimes have to stand back from the field or look in prisons abroad—in Norway and the Netherlands—to easily find the kinds of values and practices I get excited about. It has been difficult to watch, and know so much about, the deterioration of order and stability in prisons in England and Wales since the reductions in staffing levels in 2013, and the lengthening of sentences. But I have to say that I have chosen a career path that has enabled me to flourish, and find freedom, paradoxically, in prisons research.

These days, I am very aware of my "privileged" role on the edge of the Prison Service, and the fact that what I say seems to get listened to (almost beyond my comfort zone). I have mainly escaped the "gender trap" in the prisons world and, once I grew some confidence, have felt treated gracefully in it.[6] I have long felt accepted or, less straight-forwardly, constructed as an Honorary man, in my department, in terms of my status (which feels "equal") and freedoms. I can't complain about feeling discriminated against in my academic life, although I have intervened and felt alarmed when others have been. My personal experience may be grounded in some combination of "masculine intellectual credentials" (it was worth mastering quantitative methods) and "acceptable femininity" (I might want to think about this some more). My experience has not always felt to me as if it is "about gender," but I have quietly resisted gender stereotypes throughout my life, in many ways, without really knowing why. I guess I see my "ground project," especially at the moment, as "finding a way to restore the value and meaning of the world, its qualitative richness, and its particularity without denying the power and success of scientific methods of quantitative analysis and causal generalisations" (Haldane, 2020, p. 5). I like this way of putting it. The "dual nature" of our world—manifest in art, imagination and empirical social science—requires equal attention to be paid to the "world of experience" and to the relationships between things.

Once or twice I have observed that I live like a man, as my much-admired George Eliot did. She understood the attractions of masculine authority—but she also understood that it could crush and exclude. Perhaps we become successful navigators of male power as we mature and grow stronger, learning to avoid or challenge its more overt manifestations, while learning to trust those men who forego it, or use it to nurture others. This can be a lifelong struggle. Maybe my experiences in prisons: the fact that prisoners say things out loud and are shrewd has helped me to "notice" my own power and own it.

Finally, how relevant is the gender-distorting setting in which we conduct research: our universities? The taxi driver cited earlier (one example of many such comments) was illustrating the background condition of our working lives. Professors are still mainly white older men. Inevitably, this shapes the kinds of institutions we work in, and the possibilities for us within them.

THE GENDER-DISTORTING POWER OF MODERN UNIVERSITIES

Two books capture my aspirations for and anxieties about University life: *The Slow Professor: Challenging the Culture of Speed in the Academy*, by Maggie Berg and Barbara Seeber (2016) and *What Are Universities For?* by Stefan Collini (2012). Both depict what I think we can describe as a "macho" or hypermasculine economic culture and argue that the role of the University should surely be intellectual, educational scientific and cultural, rather than narrowly economic. Berg and Seeber propose that inquiry requires "ungovernable play" and a distinctive (human, creative) kind of organization. As Collini writes:

> The distracted, numbers-swamped, audit-crazed, grant-chasing life of most contemporary academic departments is . . . far removed from classical ideals of the contemplative life. . . . The experience of being a senior academic now, especially one involved in chairing a department or directing a research center, may seem to more closely resemble that of being a middle-rank executive in a business organization than it does of being an independent scholar or freelance teacher, while the conditions of work of junior and temporary staff in some unflavoured institutions may . . . suggest comparisons with those of staff in a call centre. . . . We risk heading further toward that condition satirized long ago by Keynes in which we become "capable of shutting off the sun and the stars because they do not pay a dividend." (chapter 1)

His analysis is stark, but recognizable, and I worry, as many of us do, that the increasingly powerful ideological concept of knowledge as 'useful' is destructive. Berg and Seeber remind us that good books take five years to write. Their analysis is more explicitly gendered, so they characterize the contemporary environment as corporate and remasculinized—what gets noticed, and promoted is swagger, long hours, individual competitiveness, combativeness, assertive polemic taken as evidence of intelligence, and prizing productivity over collegiality (all fired up by the neoliberal economy). They argue that universities are still highly sexist institutions and that the new economy privileges macho practices, culture, and style. Men's voices just seem louder. Berg and Seeber, both women, argue that "when we are rushed, we are simply not the people we are capable of being." They call for a "Slow Professor" movement, in which we act with purpose, taking the time for deliberation, reflection, and dialogue, cultivating emotional and intellectual resilience (I prefer "aliveness" to resilience). Intellectual enquiry should not be instrumental; we are not delivering knowledge outputs; we are engaged in original, creative research and thinking, and in nurturing the intellectual lives of others. This kind of work has the bonus that it is a joy to engage in. Its opposite—the knowledge widgets game—is soul destroying. The colleagues who I have managed to have "joyful." contemplative, dialogic and hierarchy-free research experiences with have, with certain key exceptions, tended to be women. One of them has edited a relevant book herself, advocating, as I do, the "slow science" movement (Beyens et al., 2013).

REFLECTIONS ON RE-WILDING THE FIELD

I haven't answered all the questions that I started with. Writing this chapter has been a kind of "thinking out loud" process that, now started, will go on. Women have a different relationship with freedom, with authority, and with power, meaning that of course our lives are different from the lives of men (whether we are in prison, or hold positions of relative power in ancient institutions). Women have less access to all of these, particularly in some parts of the world. Even from a powerful vantage point, women doubt themselves, and need affirmation. I need it. With my colleague, Ben Crewe, we always invite every student in our optional MPhil course (*the Sociology of Prison Life*) to say a few words about the reading, to structure our dialogue, knowing that the quieter students, who are often sharp but shy, would otherwise not contribute as willingly. I still get nervous about teaching, something my students often find surprising. Berg and Seeber interpret this as "eagerness" (so, when women theories our universe, they do it kindly). Of course, healthy nervousness needs to be distinguished from feelings of unworthiness and shame—the intensely painful feeling of believing that we are flawed. Women disproportionately express these feelings, directly and indirectly, whether they are in prison or in the university.

I have considerable faith in the younger generation, who seem more switched on, resistant, and challenging than I was, as well as more mutually supportive as larger numbers of women make it into academic life. I am proud to have been part of the professional development of several outstanding prison scholars and other professionals. My advice to my younger women colleagues is: trust yourselves, find your voices, make them authentically yours, support each other, grow good friends, take men with you on this journey, be creative, and change the world. And as Helen Mirren said, "get wilder."[7]

NOTES

1. I would like to thank Yvonne Jewkes, for encouraging me to accept this invitation, and for reading and responding so positively to the almost final version of my chapter. It was a joy to "swap notes" as we were writing.

2. https://www.law.ox.ac.uk/research-subject-groups/centre-criminology/centreborder-criminologies/blog/2019/11/still-field.

3. The university now produces a fairly informative annual *Equality & Diversity Information Report* (since 2010, in accordance with the Equality Act) and is active in these areas. In it, the following statement is made: "The University of Cambridge is committed to providing the highest quality environment for employment, research and study and to ensuring the well-being of over 11,000 staff and 19,000 students. Our institutional values of freedom of expression and freedom of thought are underpinned by the principles of mutual respect and inclusivity, and celebration of the rich diversity of all in our community."

4. I have realized over the years that I tend to select students who have "deep," if under-articulated, relationship with their topic because I believe that when the work is (uniquely) meaningful at a personal level, it can be done exceptionally well. Getting this right—combining deep meaning with self-critique and rigour—can be a tightrope act. There are many tightropes in our field.

5. George Eliot's endlessly supportive life partner.

6. I asked a Prison Service senior manager who has known me for most of my career why I haven't been resisted, discriminated against, or terminally bullied or frozen out by the organization (as some other women I know have). He said, "The answer to this is that you were so obviously good at research and also really good at explaining what the results might mean. You dealt with all grades of prison staff as though they might have a contribution to make rather than, as was sometime the case with academics, looking down at them. We prisons people like working with those who are good at what they do and who are interested in us and our work. I don't think gender even remotely enters into this equation" (Senior manager).

7. "I think midlife is when the universe gently places her hands upon your shoulders, pulls you close, and whispers in your ear: I'm not screwing around. All of this pretending and performing. . . . It's time to stop growing up, stop growing older and start growing wiser—and wilder" (Mirren, H. various sources).

REFERENCES

Auty, K., & Liebling, A. (2020). "Exploring the relationship between prison social climate and reoffending." *Justice Quarterly*, *37*(2), 1–24.

Berg, M., & Seeber, B. K. (2016). *The slow professor: Challenging the culture of speed in the academy*. Toronto: University of Toronto Press.

Beyens, K., Christiaens, J., Claes, B., De Ridder, S., Tournel, H., & Tubex, H. (Eds.). (2013). *The pains of doing criminological research*. Brussel: VUB Press.

Collini, S. (2012). *What are universities for?* London: Penguin.

Drake, D. (2014). "Researching prisoner experiences with prison officers: An action research-inspired approach." *Action Research*, *12*(1), 94–109.

Felski, R. (2015). *The limits of critique*. Chicago: University of Chicago Press.

Frances-White. (2019). *The guilty feminist*. London: Virago.

Haldane, J. (2020). "Roger Scruton: Burkean and Bohemian." *First Things*, 1–6. https://www.firstthings.com/web-exclusives/2020/01/roger-scruton-burkean-and-bohemian.

Howe, A. (1999). *Punish and critique: Towards a feminist analysis of penality.* London: Routledge.

Liebling, A. (1992). *Suicides in prison.* Routledge: London.

Liebling, A. (2001). "Whose side are we on? Theory, practice and allegiances in prisons research." In E. Stanko & A. Liebling (Eds.), *Methodological dilemmas of research, British Journal of Criminology, Special Issue*, *41*(3), 472–484.

Liebling, A. (2010). "Finding George Eliot in prison: Reflections on its moral life." *George Eliot Review,* 51, 80–88.

Liebling, A. (2015a). "Appreciative inquiry, generative theory, and the 'failed state' prison." In J. Miller & W. Palacios (Eds.), *Advances in criminological theory* (pp. 251–270). New Brunswick, NJ: Transaction Publishers.

Liebling, A. (2015b). "Description at the edge? *I-It/I-Thou* relations and action in prisons research." *International Journal for Crime, Justice and Social Democracy,* *4*(1), 18–32.

Liebling, A., assisted by Arnold, H. (2004). *Prisons and their moral performance: A study of values, quality and prison life.* Oxford: Clarendon Studies in Criminology, Oxford University Press.

Liebling, A., Arnold, H., & Straub, C. (2015). "Prisons research beyond the conventional: Dialogue, 'creating miracles' and staying sane in a maximum security prison." In D. Drake, R. Earle, & J. Sloan (Eds.), *International handbook of prison ethnography* (pp. 59–79). Basingstoke: Palgrave McMillan.

Liebling, A., Crewe, B., & Hulley, S. (2011). "Conceptualising and measuring the quality of prison life." In D. Gadd, S. Karstedt, & S. F. Messner (Eds.), *The Sage handbook of criminological research methods* (pp. 358–372). London: Sage Publishing.

Liebling, A., Laws, B., Lieber, E., Auty, K., Schmidt, B. E., Crewe, B., Gardom, J., Kant, D., & Morey, M. (2018). "Are hope and possibility achievable in prison?" *The Howard Journal of Crime and Justice*, *58*(1), 104–126.

Liebling, A., & Price, D. (2001). *The prison officer.* Leyhill: Prison Service & Waterside Press.

Liebling, A., Price, D., & Elliot, C. (1999). "Appreciative inquiry and relationships in prison." *Punishment and Society: The International Journal of Penology*, *1*(1), 71–98.

Warr, J. (2020). *Forensic psychologists: Prisons, power, and vulnerability.* United Kingdom: Emerald Publishing.

Chapter 11

"You've Got a Hard Edge!"

The Gender Politics, Complexities, and Intimacies Undertaking Prisons Research at the "Edge"

Kate Gooch

INTRODUCTION

I stood to leave the interview room, thanking Graham again and drawing the final pleasantries of the interview to a conclusion. For the last two days, Graham and I had sat entombed in an interview room in the depths of a CSC (close supervision center)—one of the most secure wings within the English prison system. Graham now hovered tentatively at the door, seemingly uncertain or reluctant to end the conversation, or perhaps simply trying to decide what "ending" was appropriate. He reached out his hand, inviting me to shake it. As I did, Graham commented, "My old man taught me that you can tell a lot about a man by his handshake. You need a stronger grip. Let me show you." He took my hand again, but more firmly this time. I too gripped harder, shaking his hand more forcefully. This time Graham was satisfied, "That's better. You need a strong handshake." I stepped forward to exit through a door which Graham was now holding open for me. The prison officers stood as the door opened, their eyes darting to me to check I was okay. I gestured to Graham that he should go first, but wanting to be the "gentlemen," he suggested that I should. The juxtaposition was stark: the demand for a "strong manly handshake" coupled with the chivalrous act of opening a door for me. I had learnt not to step in front of prisoners, not to stand in front of cell doors, to keep my back against the wall, to quickly assess body language and to be aware of where prisoners were. Yet I was also acutely aware that ignoring Graham's gesture would reinforce the assumptions of "risk" and dangerousness that were already so deeply embedded in the habits, rituals, and routines of everyday life as to be taken for granted. During the interviews, I had been at pains to do quite the opposite—to reveal his humanity, his dignity and his capacity for good, for hope, for love, for kindness—so I stepped forward, aware that this might have breached some informal rules in the minds of the prison officers.

As I walked up the stairs to the staff office, I joked with the officer escorting me who was playfully goading me to tease "Gee Whizz." The previous day, I had been met with a degree of curiosity by the officers, but also some trepidation. How many prisons had I been to? Was the prison homicide study part of my studies? Did I agree with the death penalty? Did I want an officer in the interview room with me? During lunchtime, an officer walked into the staff office and, noticing my presence, quickly replaced the swear word he was just about to say with "Gee Whizz" leading to an uproar of laughter. Others were less censored—another officer had walked into the staff office and remarked, "He's been a little shit!" (although it was not clear who "he" was). The officer who preferred "Gee Whizz" as an expression was nicknamed such, and mercilessly teased for the rest of the day. This morning, I had arrived to find the staff office plastered with A4 posters of a cartoon bearing the title "Gee Whizz." I had been included in their social world, albeit briefly, very partially, and in a seemingly small way. Jokes about "Gee Whizz" later gave way to more personal gossip, conversation about workplace politics, discussion (between themselves) about who was or was not more attractive amongst their colleagues (with all the sexual innuendo, subtle sextual undertones and not so subtle gender politics that this implied). I had seemingly secured some form of approval when one officer announced, "you're one of us now." Perhaps this was a defensive safeguard, mitigating the likeliness of any unboundaried comments being reported to senior managers, but it seemed to be an affirmatory remark, suggesting an openness to conversation.

On entering the staff office, I was quickly asked, "How did the interview go?" I replied positively but without giving details. The officer replied, "He only spoke to you because you were a woman." His comment seemed to be more of an observation than an accusation; I wasn't quite sure how to respond but was prevented from needing to do so when another officer walked in and warmly said, "He [Graham] said you were a lovely lady." Both officers quickly bustled away to start locking the men in their cells before the lunchtime roll check. Only the custodial manager and I remained in the office, but the atmosphere had changed. We stood together, staring at the multiple screens mounted on the wall and watching the various comings and goings. The custodial manager was on edge, pensive and tense as he watched and waited. For several minutes, we didn't speak, and it was clear that this wasn't the time to initiate conversation. The custodial manager eventually pierced the silence with, "You never know what will happen," but he was not inviting a response. As he spoke, a slab of butter slid underneath the food servery hatch and his hawk-like gaze fixed first on the butter and then the nearby prisoners. He was on high alert, commenting "This is why we need so many staff." The butter, he explained, could easily ignite a fight. Without turning to me, he added, "People get killed here over nothing." Within seconds, officers intervened, guiding the prisoners to their cells and moving them away from one another. We stayed still, watching silently as the men slowly disappeared from view, hearing the gates and doors bang shut and lock, hearing the burst of loud music as a radio was turned on, and waiting for each officer to return. Finally, the custodial manager returned to his desk seemingly content, grabbing the box of snacks as he did and offering me a chocolate bar. The mood had relaxed, as had he. The conversation quickly turned to lunch. The danger had seemingly passed, for now. (June 2019)

As I drove away from the prison, blinking as my eyes slowly adjusted to natural light and reveling in the brightness and beauty of a summer day unnoticed within the prison, I reflected on the ironies, complexities, and contradictions deeply embedded in my interactions with Graham, with other prisoners in the CSC, with psychologists, and with prison officers and managers. Female, in my thirties, and with more than a decade's experience undertaking prisons research, the time spent in the CSC in June 2019 had once again brought to the fore the realities of being a woman in a man's world.

When I met Graham, I was in the early stages of an empirical project examining prison homicide in England and Wales. The project expanded upon earlier and ongoing research regarding prison violence, gangs, ongoing criminality, organized crime, drug use and drug dealing—research that sought "deep engagement in criminal worlds" (Ferrell, 1998, p. 20) within the prison walls. In addition, I was researching (and continue to research) prison leadership, occupational cultures, organizational resilience, styles of governance, and staff-prisoner relationships. I had visited prisons that had been rated by Her Majesty's Inspectorate of Prisons as some of the worst in the country, sometimes because prison senior leaders asked me to do so (and were interested in my observations) and at other times because this was the chosen research site. Throughout this time, I sought multiple perspectives, including those of prisoners, staff, "middle managers," and senior leaders, attempting to navigate the political and ethical complexities of "taking all sides seriously" (see Liebling, 2001). For me, prisons research has been "edge work," not necessarily because deep engagement has carried the risk of legal infractions (e.g., see: Adler, 1993; Hobbs, 1998; Ferrell, 1998), but because it has taken me to "the very edge of being human" and the "borders of life and death" (McDonald, 2014, p. 195)—confronting me with the brutal and unimaginable acts that one person can do to another, as well as the human capacity for compassion, forgiveness, kindness, grace, and mercy. It has raised moral, sociological, criminological, and philosophical questions about confinement, but it has also caused me to question what it means to *be* human and how easily humanity and inhumanity can sit together.

When we enter a prison as a researcher, our presence inevitably changes it; sometimes dramatically, sometimes imperceptibly (see Goffman, 1959). We cannot, therefore, "conveniently distance [ourselves] from [our] subjects of study" (Ferrell, 1998, p. 25). The "reflexive turn" in social sciences (e.g., see: Gurney, 1985; Coffey, 1999; Gelsthorpe & Morris, 1999; Lamsden, 2009; Rice & Maltz, 2018), and more latterly in prisons research (Phillips & Earle, 2010; Liebling, 2001; Jewkes, 2011; Drake et al., 2015; special issue 8(1) of *Qualitative Inquiry*), reflects an ambition to make more explicit the role of our identities, emotions, and autobiographical accounts in shaping and influencing our choices about the research we undertake, the performance of self within the field, how we establish rapport, and how we navigate the often "messy" realities of empirical research. It also reflects a desire to mitigate against the tendency toward "intellectual abstractionism" (Crewe, 2009, p. 488) and the production of "inhuman data" that is "cold, calculated, surgical," carefully distanced from the painful and emotionally raw aspects of prison life (Bosworth, 1999, p. 259; also see Liebling, 1999). In very deliberately writing myself into the text, this chapter seeks to yield greater insights into the prison world, the realities of conducting prison research, and to collapse the distinction between my "criminological [life] and human [life]" (Liebling, 1999, p. 148). This chapter calls for a more nuanced analysis of gendered identity, arguing that the performance and construction of gender is situational, neither binary nor fixed, and is bound up in other aspects of our identity, biography, character, and morality. Undertaking long-term prisons research has required something more than an ability to navigate sometimes opaque and amorphous gender politics; it has also required integrity, courage, resilience, social dexterity, political astuteness, discretion, discernment, emotional intelligence, and, crucially, the ability to hold seemingly competing moral and philosophical positions competently and simultaneously. Prisons are moral places, and it is therefore unsurprising that the most critical part of prisons research is, as this chapter argues, our "research morality" (Ferrell, 1999, p. 25).

HOLDING UP A MIRROR: HOW CLEAR IS THE REFLECTION?

A reflexive and critical examination of our positionality, the "biographical underside" (Gelsthorpe, 2007, p. 518; Phillips & Earle, 2010, p. 374) and the theoretical underpinnings to our research have been described as a "methodological imperative" (Gelsthorpe, 2007, p. 518)—one that gives greater transparency to the interpretive process (Phillips & Earle, 2010, p. 374), produces new forms of knowledge, and provides an instructive guide or "benchmark" for others (Jewkes, 2011; Crewe, 2014). Our choice of topic, participants, and prison undoubtedly influence the construction and performance of gender. Prison occupational cultures are not homogenous: there are differences across different categories of prison (e.g., high security cf. an open prison, remand cf. training prisons), depending on the population (e.g., mainstream cf. men convicted of sex offences), depending on the gender and age (women cf. men, the elderly cf. children), and depending on leadership styles and values (Gooch, 2020). How I present as a female, heterosexual, white, middle-class academic in a men's prison may be different to how I present, or are received, in a women's prison (see Rowe, 2015). Motherhood has also been of interest, such as in a New Zealand prison where whānau (extended family) and parenthood are highly esteemed (Gooch et al., 2020). Other decisions—including the decisions made by gatekeepers about access—also influence our experiences. We may choose to maintain some social distance from the prison landings, by either subconsciously or deliberately retreating to staff offices when prisoners are unlocked (e.g., see: Jewkes, 2002, p. 83), by eliminating participant observation or ethnographic approaches, or by choosing to interview participants in relatively sterile environments, such as a visits hall. That said, retreat is not an option if our desire is to understand the realities, intimacies, and complexities of the everyday prison social world. My decision to look closely, engage deeply, and tread slowly has almost certainly meant that I have been more exposed; you cannot help but reveal something of who you *really* are when spending months or years in the field. Yet, as a lone researcher, it can be incredibly difficult to establish the possible relationship, if any, between our gendered performances (and other aspects of the self) and the quality or nature of the data (also see Phillips & Earle, 2010; Crewe, 2014). There have, however, undoubtedly been occasions when prisoners themselves have alerted me the significance of my status as a woman.

In 2016–2017, I was undertaking research in a Category C (medium security) prison exclusively holding male sex offenders with a (male) doctoral research student who was attached to the study but working on a separate topic. During one visit, Peter questioned me as to why I would come to a *place like this* where I was on public view to *all these men*. The question was expressed sadly and mournfully rather than in combative or hostile terms, and possible explanations about why some male prisoners may find it profoundly difficult to interact with women later came during an interview with Billy:

> *I don't feel like a man anymore. I promise you, I don't. I really don't. I will probably never have a relationship again ever. . . . I will always be on edge and I won't trust another woman. I could never. . . . I would never go out now*

and try and chat up a woman. No way, never. That is how I feel. I will never do that now. That's me done. . . . Because I am classed as a rapist, I feel like every woman will look at me as if to say, is he looking me up and down? It's awful. It's an awful thing. It really is awful. I will not look at a woman.

The profound sense of shame, emasculation, and stigma that accompanied his conviction for rape not only generated fears about his relationships with women on release but also how any attempts to engage in normal social interactions with female prison officers might be misinterpreted, reframed as "offence paralleling behavior" or be recorded as an indicator of "risk"—a pejorative term that can quickly be emptied of meaning just as much as it can neatly encapsulate very real concerns about the likely possibility of harm. As Billy explained:

You have to be careful what you say as I was telling you earlier on. It is very hard to speak to a female. While the female officers will sit down and listen, you feel intimidated like you are doing something wrong. I said to you, I don't like giving eye contact with them because just in case they turn round and say, "Why are you staring at me like that?"

His fears about interacting with female prison officers translated to the research interview, and even though I was accompanied by a male colleague, Billy was still concerned about my assessment of him:

I'm paranoid that [you have] looked at me and thought that he is just another sex offender . . . that's how I come across because I am in this sort of environment. I am sure you feel the same way in a certain point of view.

Despite my best efforts, my reassurances that I did not see him as *just another sex offender* were woefully insufficient. While the interview had been instructive, it came at an unpalatable cost. I had inadvertently reminded Billy of unwelcome, painful, and intrusive thoughts, and it was for this reason I chose to draw back a little and ask a male colleague to have a more extensive role. Billy's response was not uniform within the prison. For the elderly and retired men within the prison (over half of the prison population), the tendency was to relate to me as they would a daughter or, more typically, a granddaughter. Thus, it was the intersection of my gender and age (then thirty-two to thirty-three years old) that appeared relevant, inviting war stories, nostalgic accounts of their *best years*, and, particularly for those convicted of historic sex offences, emphatic attempts to explain how attitudes toward women and sex had changed, expressing something of the perceived illegitimacy of their convictions many decades later.

Female researchers may find themselves positioned in respect of their sexuality, becoming the target of catcalling, heckling, or "hustling" (Gurney, 1985). I have both experienced and observed such behavior and while "there are 'no ready prescriptions for female researchers' coping with such situations" (Gurney, 1985, p. 49), I have always been relatively tolerant, only challenging such behavior when it became too personal or explicit and appreciating that such behavior was performative and often aimed at a wider audience. Crucially, any such experiences have always been instructive, revealing something about the experience of imprisonment, the occupational culture, and the prisoner social world. As Ugelvik (2014, p. 477) argues, "The fact that I was positioned in the field as a specific person with a specific gendered body made the various strategies prisoners use to counter the emasculating effects of imprisonment directly observable." For example, an interview with a twenty-one-year-old in a New Zealand prison ended with Taika asking whether he would see me again and commenting that I was a *pretty chick*. For me, such flirtatious behavior is far less interesting than what it reveals about the prison experience, culture, and environment. Earlier in the interview, I noticed that Taika had a rather angry red rash spreading over his neck and arm. After he had been aggressively scratching the rash for several minutes, I stopped to ask him if he was uncomfortable and whether he needed to see the nurse. The conversation continued:

Kate: And have they given you anything for it?

Taika: Ointments to put on it, I think I just found out, it's not usually like this, I'm usually good looking after myself.

Kate: I'm sure, I was more saying it out of worry for you that you know, you weren't in pain or anything or uncomfortable.

Taika: Yes, I've never had anyone care about me like that for ages, they [the officers] just look at it and don't even care.

Kate: I'm really sorry to hear that.

Taika had responded quickly to the kindness of a stranger, and it was the demonstration of care that contrasted strongly with its absence within the prison. By asking about the ointment, I had, however, inadvertently prompted him to reassert his masculinity, revealing the subtlety of what is at stake, even in a 1:1 interview away from the prison wing, and how easily female researchers are inadvertently drawn into such performances.

Gender politics may reveal themselves in various forms of initiations, "tests" (Ugelvik, 2014, p. 474) and "character checks" (Crewe, 2000, p. 465). Prisons are low-trust environments where misjudging someone's character, skill or strength can have profound consequences. It is unsurprising then, that it is an environment, which is prone to forms of subtle and informal testing.

My earliest introduction to this was as a PhD student observing the daily life of a segregation unit in a young offender institution (YOI) for children aged fifteen to eighteen years old. Tar-pooling had been erected in the segregation unit to shield officers from the urine and feces being thrown at them. The YOI was one of the most violent, and the segregation team were keen to move away from its relatively checkered history. Initially, the all-male team of officers seemed curious about the research but content to let me remain. The conversation was easy but regularly interrupted by competitive exchanges about the "best" (primarily blonde and sexist) jokes. I laughed, remaining relatively relaxed but knowing that these jokes were designed to test my reaction. Shortly before lunch, one of the officers went on all fours and re-enacted sexual activities and positions in some sort of odd expression of his sexual conquests. At one point, and most bizarrely, another officer, went over licked the bald head of the officer on the floor. The whole thing was so bizarre, words and actions utterly escaped me. No one seemed to question this unusual behavior, and I decided to ignore. During the staff changeover, an officer explained to the incoming staff that I was "Alright!" and they could "tell me things." I had seemingly "passed" some unwritten test, and the endorsement appeared to ease access to the interviewees and encourage disclosures about daily prison life. This encounter was unusual; I have rarely been tested in such an extreme, sexualized manner. Typically for prison staff and managers, the most critical issue was whether I would "tell the governor" what had been disclosed in informal conversation or observed on the wing. As with "Gee Whiz," staff have often been keen to establish whether we understand them and their concerns, priorities, values, and dark humor. With senior managers, I have not always known until many months later how I was being evaluated. For example, in one study, a senior manager subsequently disclosed that the research project would have ended after a fortnight had a colleague and I not engaged effectively with the rest of the senior management team. This was not apparent to us at the time, and it was never clear how we had secured their approval, but we were pleased to have done so.

Conducting research in teams and with male colleagues (also see Crewe, 2014, p. 393; Phillips & Earle, 2010) has created an obvious counterpoint and the possibility of critically exploring any similarities or differences in our observations or experiences. For example, while working with James Treadwell, there were some noticeable differences in the topics of conversation that young men (aged eighteen to twenty-one years old) chose to pursue. James was very actively involved in boxing and martial arts, and during one visit, James and two young men (Joshua and Dean) quickly engaged in a conversation about boxing—a topic I knew little about. The conversation developed into a competitive exchange about Joshua and Dean's tattoos, scars, and the various examples of their physical prowess and conquests. Later that day, as Joshua was cleaning the office and I was working (but with neither James nor Dean present), Joshua described his grief when his partner gave birth to a stillborn child, and subsequent worries when a second child was born—details he had not shared with James. Such differences could be explained with reference to gender and the need to publicly perform and rehearse masculine scripts with other men—a demand that Joshua may have felt temporarily relieved from when alone with me. Yet, it was almost impossible to establish precisely how and to what extent individual differences had changed or influenced the data, if at all (Damsa & Ugelvik, 2017, p. 8). Would our interactions have been different if I had been interested in boxing, martial arts, or weight training? Would Joshua have made similar disclosures to James given privacy and time? Was it our biographical experiences that were making a difference? James had an easy, intuitive understanding of Birmingham's inner-city estates and the street cultures from which the young men were drawn (see Treadwell, 2018)—a familiarity that I could not claim with a middle-class upbringing in an affluent part of Birmingham. Together, our differences were a strength, producing useful reference points for analysis and reflection.

The most effective way of better understanding ourselves is not, however, gleaned by simply peering longer or closer at our own reflections, but by deliberately asking others to "hold up a mirror." As Crewe argues: "Often, as researchers, we cannot see what is placed before our eyes, focusing too closely to catch the detail of the very things we want to see. . . . We are all blind to our blind spots" (Crewe, 2014, p. 401). I am indebted to my mentor, Ben Crewe, who, even when I was very junior and inexperienced academic, was willing to invest his time and energy without any obvious benefit or compensation in return. It is undoubtedly true that my progress could have been faster and further had I heeded a little earlier some of the lessons he endeavored to share with me. Yet, his mentoring has been the most significant contribution to my development, allowing me to: work through the "knotty" aspects of prisons research, discuss our moral and philosophical orientations to our research, think critically about the "data," determine where I would draw boundaries, develop my writing skill, think more carefully about the theoretical contribution of my work, and better understand what was important to me and why. I am also indebted to the Governing Governors and senior managers who spent many an hour answering my (often naïve) questions, walking around the prison and discussing our observations, inviting me to attend or contribute to senior management meetings, and digesting the research findings. It is this that has sharpened my skill, fostered a more intuitive understanding of operational realities, and helped me to understand how to navigate the often highly politicized prison world. In inviting the input of others, my shortcomings have been readily apparent, but it has strengthened me. I am also grateful to Katherine Doolin, Erika Rackley, Yvonne Jewkes, and Alison Liebling whose examples have greatly influenced me. Thus, reflexivity is not an end in itself—it should not only cause us to reflect critically on the data we have gathered and how we have understood it but also how we can sharpen our skills as researchers and critically examine how and why we engage in prisons research.

"WHY DO YOU SURROUND YOURSELF WITH VIOLENCE?" WHEN MOTIVES AND INTERESTS MATTER

> Why do people do research in prisons? Any research is usually driven by personal curiosity, but often the particular world selected or (landed upon) and the particular topic chosen resonates with some conscious or unconscious value or interest which pre-date the research project. . . . Prisons are dangerous places. What makes some people (like me) seek them out and other people shun them? (Liebling, 1999, p. 151)

Liebling's questions offer something more than an opportunity for self-indulgent naval gazing; they ask us to render explicit the motives and interests that inform how we approach the field, why we do so at all, and how we make sense of what we see, hear, and feel. We can easily forget how critical these questions are to gatekeepers, but also to our participants—something I was keenly reminded of during Liam's interview for the prison homicide study. Liam had been convicted of several offences of murder and attempted murder, and was facing at least another fifty years in prison, if he lived that long. At the time I interviewed him, he was living in a CSC (or "the sink" as it was dubbed). Prison staff warned me that he might attempt to control the interview or disclose intimate details of his offence to scare me or gauge my reaction. This I had been prepared for, but what I had not expected was the two threshold moments that fundamentally shifted the nature of our interaction: (1) addressing questions about why I chose to interview men about violence within prison; and (2) determining I had a "hard edge" (see below). The interview was designed to invite an appraisal and retelling of what had led up to the murder or attempted murder (including their emotional state, physical state, relationship to the victim and with others, their *mens rea*, and the extent to which they had considered the consequences to them or others), what was happening immediately prior to the act, how they experienced the act, and the aftermath. It had already become clear that Liam enjoyed the planning and reliving of the killing just as much, if not more, than the act itself. It was at this point in the interview that his attention turned to why I was interested in violent crime perpetrated by men:

Liam: Why do you keep examining men? You must get some kind of thrill out of it, do you know what I mean? There must some emotional connection with you somewhere, in violence, do you know what I mean? Because it's your job to stare at it all day. And you have to think about it all the time. So you are in some way quite taken in. . . . Have you never explored on a deeper level why you feel like that?
Kate: What, you mean, with a psychologist or something? Or just generally?
Liam: Generally, generally.
Kate: No, I haven't.
Liam: Why don't you examine it with a psychologist? Is there something in your past that makes you want to examine it?

. . .

Liam: You know, if you don't feel that kind of mechanisms around jumping out of planes or skydiving or fucking bungee jump, you have to get that feeling from somewhere, do you know what I mean? You have to get that thrill in life. Maybe you just like to get yours by observing other people's achievements.

This exchange was revealing in terms of the links he had made between his tragic childhood and his subsequent criminality, how he sought to present his violent offences as "achievements," his constant references to the "thrill" of violence, and how he had rationalized the role of psychologists in his own life. In seeking to reassure him that I had not been victimized as a child, nor did I gain some perverse "thrill" from interviewing men about violence, I explained why I engaged in prison research.

I cannot remember the exact moment when I decided to focus on prison research; in truth, it always felt somehow inevitable. There was no "lightbulb" moment, nor did I cherish such aspirations as a child; the question, "What do you want to be what you grow up?" never yielded the answer, "to research prisons." Yet, as I started to do so, I knew that it somehow "fit" and that I wanted to continue in the "messy" business of immersive prison research with all its complexities, dangers, tragedies, politics, humor and joys. In unconscious, subtle, and unintentional ways, much of my childhood has prepared me for what was to come. My father was a police officer, and this was inevitability part of my consciousness growing up, as were patrol cars, police stations, and, as I became a law student, an awareness of the demands of policing and occasional jokes about duty solicitors. As a child, I participated in child interview training, watching scenes of the Bodyguard and then being interviewed by trainee officers. Those scenes are etched in my memory and I am reminded of the interview training whenever I watch the film. My paternal great-uncle was a well-regarded Psychiatrist who assessed notorious, serious offenders. As a child, and without being able to fully appreciate it, his work had seemed important, significant, and demanding. His preciously guarded evening rituals—including whiskey and the undisturbed, silent viewing of the BBC News—I now understand to be his decompression zone, allowing him to separate and digest the day's events, scenes, and conversations. My paternal grandmother filled my childhood with books, murder mysteries, and puzzles, encouraging me to have a curious mind and fostering my intellectual development. She modeled a combination of fortitude and a "stiff upper lip" with a very well-preserved feminine charm and appearance. As a teenager, a maternal uncle was a prison officer for a short period, leading to conversations about his training on how sex offenders groomed their victims. These experiences had undoubtedly shaped my interest in law, crime, and order. It had introduced a healthy realism, that sometimes bordered on cynicism, but it was also coupled with faith, hope, and compassion. My mother worked in a women's refuge for several years, and meeting these women and children taught me about empathy, the desperate lives some women endure, the need for compassion, and the need to help the less fortunate. My Christian upbringing furnished me with a resolute belief in the power and need for (many) second chances, the need for unmerited grace and mercy, a deep and unwavering desire for truth and justice, and a sense that "there but for the grace of God go I"—something that I am often reminded of as I repeatedly hear the tragic stories of those who fill our care and criminal justice system. My formative years established the foundations of a moral framework that would guide me in later years.

During my undergraduate law degree, I began working with children who were remanded to local authority care. I then moved to the Youth Offending Service, and then for a short period during my master's degree, managed a NACRO center for young people not in education, employment, or training. This work was incredibly varied, including: supervising contact between parents and children after enforced separation by the courts, escorting children to appearances in the courts and police stations, visiting children in children's homes and YOIs, drafting written documents for the criminal and family courts and giving evidence in court proceedings, supporting children and parents during lengthy child protection proceedings while also working with social workers to achieve the best outcomes for the child (and therefore navigating complex moral, ethical and political terrain). It was during this period that my desire to understand the experiences of children in prison crystallized in my mind—a topic that would become the focus of my doctoral research.

As a PhD researcher, I was very much serving an apprenticeship and learning my craft. The first time I stood on a prison wing conversing and playing pool with young men, I was nervous but never daunted by the task; rather I welcomed the experience, viewing it as a privilege to meet, and listen to, young prisoners and prison staff. In subsequent years, as I have trained doctoral students and research assistants, it became clear that there are aspects of prisons research that cannot be taught. Not all who want to enter the prison world can do so competently, carefully, or safely. This is not to privilege the topics or modes of study that require close and sustained engagement, but to acknowledge that it requires an innate sense of courage, and "nerve." You can neither be reckless with risk nor hyper-vigilant. To do the former puts both ourselves and others in danger. To do the latter, not only makes the full appreciation of the prison and the "full use of ourselves" (see Liebling, 2001, p. 473) difficult, but also it can inadvertently imply a degree of vulnerability that some may attempt to exploit. Negotiating access alone meant that I learnt very quickly that prison managers appreciate honesty, clarity, transparency, and, crucially, discretion. Trust is hard won and easily lost. Knowing what to reveal and to whom, as well as when certain details are "not for the notes," requires political astuteness, emotional intelligence, and discernment. In one case, the decision to preserve the anonymity of the research site when directly asked for its name by a governing governor earned sufficient trust to prompt an invitation to develop a research project. Consequently, I have always been mindful about what I share with the media (including how I interact with social media), primarily because I did not want to cause unnecessary scrutiny and work for those who had shown me great trust. This does not mean that I have not been honest about the research findings, but I have preferred to share any uncomfortable truths with the governing governor first. For me, prison research has never been about voyeurism or bravado—it is and has always been motivated by "human curiosity" (Liebling, 2001, p. 474) and intellectual curiosity (Gooch, in press), grounded in an awareness that the stakes are high and, as a prisons researcher, we bear a great responsibility to "call it" accurately, to engage in "thick description" (Damsa & Ugelvik, 2017, p. 9) and to "get the description right" (Liebling, 2015).

My autobiographical disclosure to Liam, brief as it was and concentrated on the headlines (that I had a safe, middle-class Christian upbringing) prompted discussion about justice and injustice—including why I felt so strongly about justice—and questions of power and powerless—whether I had "power" to influence "change" (or indeed if that was what the research was for) and in his case, why Liam felt a sense of power when he killed and how he negotiated power with staff (albeit it within conditions of strict and coercive confinement). The exchange shifted the interview from a superficial "question and answer" session—a deliberate tactic by Liam to unsettle and test me—to a relatively reflective and detailed discussion. Authenticity mattered, and although I was not naïve enough to believe that his questions were wholly innocent nor divorced from a narcissistic desire to revel in the harm he had caused, he later commented on its importance:

Liam: Yeah, it's nice . . . a lot of these interviews are very systematic. So it's just kind of, get to know the person and then they leave, like, they get to know things and then they leave. Their work dictates your fate. And it dictates the regime and how it works in jail. . . . The thing is, they're [prison psychologists and researchers] whacking their walls up, and they say, "Well, it's unprofessional if I tell you anything about me," do you know what I'm saying? So it's a bit fucking cold, innit? It doesn't build a relationship. And anything they do say is really fucking tedious, man, "Oh, I like this on the telly," I don't care what you like on the telly. That's not telling me nothing about you as a person, do you know what I'm saying? Are you going to be a regular in this jail?

Liam, like so many other prisoners I have met, desired a human connection and interaction that recognized his "personhood" (Liebling, 2014) in its fullness and complexity, and not narrowly in terms of his flaws and failures. To be "seen" as something more than his criminal behavior. To be capable of more. To have a conversation that would not be written down, rehearsed, and repeated time and time again. To find warmth, not fear. To find human relationships that were not always held at a distance or separated by physical or metaphorical walls, even if they were good reasons for some of those walls.

"YOU'VE GOT A HARD EDGE": FINDING A COMFORT WITH MORAL COMPLEXITY AND DUALITY

Negotiating gender politics within the prison, and indeed within the academy, is far from straightforward. Calls for critical accounts about gendered positionality have often served to reinforce gendered stereotypes. Women may, for example, find themselves criticized for "exploiting" gender and sexuality to their advantage (Jewkes, 2002, p. 83). Conversely, an ease with hypermasculine environments may also risk criticism that a female researcher has fallen "prey to a macho, gung-ho mentality" (Jewkes, 2011, p. 65). Thus, to adopt more masculine traits and to, for example: find the pressures of the prison environment less overwhelming; to enjoy the company of men and engage in their often-performative conversations about sports, women, drinking habits and accumulated wealth (both prisoners and managers); and to understand the rationale for male aggression and violence (even if we do not view it as morally "right") might create some relational and cultural ease within the prison, but it risks overstepping conventional views of how female academics should behave. Yet, for me, the construction of gender within prison has not easily conformed to this "binary model" of femininity or masculinity. Rather, in my experience, navigating the prison environment involves the complex display of both stereotypical aspects of femininity and stereotypically masculine traits. As Graham illustrated, it is the ability to both "shake hands like a man" and to be cast as the "lovely lady" that has been important. It requires emotionally warmth and authenticity but also emotional fortitude and resilience in the face of considerable demands, challenges, and strains (or, as I heard expressed to others, both men and women, the ability to "man up" when required).

Gaining credibility in discussing certain aspects of prison life and criminality requires something of a combination of "toughness," "nerve," warmth, and emotional intelligence. For example, the second "turning point" in my interview with Liam came when, having tried and failed to scare me, he concluded that I had a "hard edge":

Liam: I think you have more of a harder edge than they [researchers and psychologists] do, do you know what I mean? Which is a really good quality.

Kate: I have a harder edge?

Liam: Yeah. Because I think a lot of people who are afraid, just, like, quite scared by their nature. . . . I think, to be successful, you kind of have to do groundbreaking work. So that means you have to work at the deep end, do you know what I'm saying, you can't fucking ask the same tired old questions everyone's asked.

Liam's apparent approval was linked to the willingness to both confront serious and fatal violence without fear (and demonstrate "hardness") but also foster a human connection, and express warmth, empathy, and respect. The point here is not to lay claim to some superior skill, but to illustrate that we cannot and should not shy away from carefully addressing serious harm, and how these realities inform our thinking about the experience and role of imprisonment. Although Liam's actions and attitudes may be viewed as extreme, accounts of self-interested, harmful, merciless, and calculated behavior have regularly emerged in prisoner's interviews. We cannot gloss over narratives, nor the values, cultures, desires, and masculine expressions that they impute. To do so risks building theory and scholarship with several of the jigsaw pieces missing. In seeing to understand violence and criminality within prison, my desire has never been to glorify, valorize, or sensationalize such acts, nor to engage in "thrill seeking" (also see Treadwell, 2018; Winlow et al., 2001). Rather, it is to understand the intricacies, difficulties, and exacting realities of prison life that often defy easy description. The expansion of British prison research over the past twenty years has largely focused on the multifaceted harms experienced by prisoners and their families, as well as the ways in which the exercise of state power can be capricious, excessive, careless, and punitive. There has been a tendency to romanticize prisoners, and to neatly overlook the harms done *by* prisoners, either in the community or in the prison. Confronting the latter requires a moral framework that allows for an honest appraisal of why some individuals engage in serious criminality while recognizing that such acts might offer the only means of surviving desperate circumstances. Recognizing "personhood" is not always "easy or straightforward to honour" (see Liebling, 2014, p. 482) but it is necessary. The art of prisons research therefore rests upon a complex moral duality that combines seemingly competing positions: compassion and realism, vigilance and ease; emotional investment without being overcome with emotion; a belief in the capacity to change with an awareness that people may not change; an appreciation of first impressions with a healthy skepticism and willingness to look beyond the superficial; an awareness of the need to breathe life and hope into a prison while safeguarding others from harm; creating human connections but without unprofessional and unfettered intimacies; a desire to reduce the role of imprisonment and the size of the prison population while also recognizing that imprisonment is necessary in some circumstances (and that even some prisoners recognize that should not be released very soon); and, a recognition that while there are abuses of power, few staff and managers set out to deliberately brutalize prisoners.

CONCLUDING THOUGHTS: IS GENDER WHAT REALLY MATTERS?

Good prisons research is a curious combination of craft, skill, instinct, art, and "slow science" (Liebling, 2014). It employs a vision of personhood that is not easy to achieve, a moral framework that is complex and contradictory, and it requires fine judgments about a diverse range of things, including ethical dilemmas, the culture, atmosphere and "feel" of a prison, the ability to determine between the particular and the generalizable (i.e., whether what is observed is true only for that wing on that day, or whether it is also observable across the prison and over time), the ability to record the minutiae of daily life while also suspending judgment, and the ability to "read people" (and, e.g., whether to go ahead with a planned interview or reschedule, to respond to cues in the interview). We are chiefly employed in sensing and sense-making. When we enter the prison, we affect the world around us, but are also affected by it. Undertaking prisons research has changed me in ways that I perhaps do not yet fully understand. I do know, however, that conducting prisons research "at the edge" has been "the making of me" (Treadwell, 2018, p. 290). I am still learning how to conduct research skillfully, sensitively, intuitively, artfully, systematically, rigorously, and in ways that authentically connect with the person sat before me with all their frailties, fears, imperfections, eccentricities, passions, triumphs, and afflictions. This pursuit of excellence will undoubtedly last the rest of my career; it is a quest where there are no shortcuts (or no effective shortcuts at least).

In the hypermasculine prison environment, my status as a heterosexual, white female academic has undoubtedly been relevant to how I presented myself and how I was received, although it was not always clear what—if any—effects this had on the nature or quality of the data I gathered, or whether a male researcher would have achieved different or better results. Women's experiences are not uniform, and may evolve over time if, for example, they have children and as those children age, as they take on more managerial responsibility, and as they take on caring responsibilities for elderly parents (see, for example, Bosworth, 2019). As Gelsthorpe argues:

> Women are never just women—they are old or young, mothers or daughters, black or white, partnered or unpartnered, employed in public life or employed at home, and so on, and all these "positions" or standpoints made for uniquely "valid insights." (1992, p. 215)

There is no one way of performing gender. I suspect that the way I currently present myself may change as I age, become more established as a scholar, adopt new interests, lead more projects, supervise more students and research assistants, and is therefore less likely to be questioned about how my studies are progressing (at thirty-six, I still get asked this question). In addition, it is very likely that decisions about, for example, which topics to pursue, which prisons to base myself in, and how long to remain there have informed both how I have presented and how I have been received. Thus, the construction and performance of gendered identity is "fluid and multi-dimensional" (Earle, 2014, p. 429), subject to change and situationally dynamic. In conducting prisons research at *the deep end*, it has been necessary to embody both feminine and masculine traits—to combine a "hard edge" and "toughness" with an authentic and empathetic warmth and compassion.

We should, however, be careful not to exaggerate the role of gender, or to conclude that this is the only complexity that as women, especially young women or early career researchers, we need to grapple with. As Crewe argues, while men's prisons are "suffused with masculine discourse, their social structure [can] not be reduced to themes of gender" (2009, pp. 465–466). Questions about gender—and other aspects of our identity or biography—may be less important than our character, values, work ethic, and moral disposition, although it can be difficult to detach the former from the latter. Over the long haul, though, it is our integrity, the rigor and quality of the work, and the willingness to develop meaningful relationships that sustains us in the field. As prisons researchers, we have a great responsibility to hold ourselves to the highest standards. Reports and publications that are based on thin or carelessly (perhaps even barely) interrogated data risk being converted into poor policy and practice, and therefore may do more harm than good. Too little attention has been paid to the importance of our moral framework when determining why, how, and on what terms we enter and understand the prison, prisoners, and prison reform. There has been too great a tendency to romanticize prisoners, to focus disproportionately on state power and harm, and to conceptualize prison security concerns as excessive and overbearing. Yes, prisons harm more than the heal. Yes, there is often more injustice than justice. Yes, prisoners are too often drawn from the backgrounds of sharp social, educational, and economic inequality. Yes, we should critically evaluate concepts such as "risk" and "security," but while recognizing that these notions and practices may have a valid role. In undertaking prison research, we must be prepared to appreciate and critically examine the prison in all its complexity. We must look beyond what first appears and "see"—as best an outsider can do—the prison as it really is. It is to look beyond the superficial and take the metaphorical dusting brush of the archaeologist to slowly but gradually dust away what lies beneath. It is only in the being there day and day that we can only begin to understand the prison, but it requires the full use of ourselves, and in that, we must get "up close and personal."

REFERENCES

Adler, P. (1993). *Wheeling and dealing: An ethnography of upper-level drug dealing and smuggling community*. New York: Columbia University Press.

Bosworth, M. (1999). *Engendering resistance: Agency and power in women's prisons*. Aldershot: Ashgate.

Bosworth, M. (2019). *From the field: Still in detention, 10 years on*. Retrieved January 4, 2020. https://www.law.ox.ac.uk/research-subject-groups/centre-criminology/centreborder-criminologies/blog/2019/10/field-still.

Coffey, A. (1999). *The ethnographic self: Fieldwork and the representation of identity*. Berkeley: University of California Press.

Crewe, B. (2014). "Not looking hard enough: Masculinity, emotion, and prison research." *Qualitative Inquiry*, *20*(4), 392–403.

Crewe, B., & Ievins, A. (2015). "Closeness, distance and honesty in prison ethnography." In Drake, D., Earle, R., & Sloan, J. (Eds.), *The Palgrave handbook of prison ethnography*. London: Palgrave, 124–142.

Damsa, D., & Ugelvik, T. (2017). "A difference that makes a difference? Reflexivity and researcher effects in all-foreign prisons." *International Journal of Qualitative Methods*, *16*, 1–10.

Drake, D., Earle, R., & Sloan, J. (2015). "What ethnography tells us about prisons and what prisons tell us about ethnography." In Drake, D., Earle, R., & Sloan, J. (Eds.), *The Palgrave handbook of prison ethnography*. London: Palgrave, 1–16.

Ferrell, J., & Hamm, M. S. (1998). *Ethnography at the edge: Crime, deviance and field research*. Boston: Northeastern University Press.

Fleetwood, J. (2009). "Emotional work: Ethnographic fieldwork in prisons in Ecuador." In *E-Sharp, Special Issue: Critical Issues in Researching in Hidden Communities*, 28–50.

Gelsthorpe, L. (1992). "Response to Martyn Hammersley's paper 'on feminist methodology.'" *Sociology*, *26*(2), 213–218.

Gelsthorpe, L. (2007). "The jack-roller: Telling a story?" *Theoretical Criminology*, *11*(4), 515–542.

Gelsthorpe, L., & Morris, A. (1999). *Feminist perspectives in criminology*. Milton Keynes: Open University Press.

Goffman, E. (1959). *The presentation of self in everyday life*. Garden City: Doubleday.

Gooch, K. (in press, 2020a). "'Just don't wear prison issue': Material deprivation, material machismo and the illicit economy." In Crewe, B., Goldsmith, A., & Halsey, M. (Eds.), *Power and authority in the modern prison: Revisiting the society of captives*. Oxford: Clarendon Press.

Gooch, K. (2020b). "The opportunities, challenges and politics of prison leadership." *Prison Service Journal*, *247*, 14–24.

Gooch, K., Doolin, K., & Barkham-Perry, B. (2020). *A comparative analysis of prison violence in England, Australia and Aotearoa New Zealand* (Report available on request).

Gooch, K., & Treadwell, J. (2015). *Prison bullying and victimisation*. Birmingham: University of Birmingham. IBSN: 978-0-7044-2859-1 (birmingham.ac.uk/prison-bullying).

Gurney, J. N. (1985). "Not one of the guys: The female researcher in a male-dominated setting." *Qualitative Sociology*, *8*(1), 42–60.

Hobbs, D. (1998). *Doing the business: Entrepreneurship, detectives and the working class in the east end of London*. Oxford: Oxford University Press.

Jewkes, Y. (2002). *Captive audience: Media, masculinity and power in prisons*. Cullompton: Willan.

Jewkes, Y. (2005). "Men behind bars: 'Doing' masculinity as an adaptation to imprisonment." *Men and Masculinities*, *8*(1), 44–63.

Jewkes, Y. (2011). "Autoethnography and emotion as intellectual resources: Doing prison research differently." *Qualitative Inquiry*, *18*(1), 63–75.

Lamsden, K. (2009). "Don't ask a woman to do another woman's job: Gendered interactions and the emotional ethnographer." *Sociology*, *43*(3), 497–513.

Liebling, A. (1999). "Doing research in prison: Breaking the silence?" *Theoretical Criminology*, *3*(2), 147–173.

Liebling, A. (2001). "Whose side are we on? Theory, practice and allegiances in prisons research." *British Journal of Criminology*, *41*, 472–484.

Liebling, A. (2014). "Postscript: Integrity and emotion in prison research." *Qualitative Inquiry*, *20*(4), 481–486.

Liebling, A. (2015). "Description at the edge: I-It/I-Thou relations and action in research." *International Journal for Crime, Justice and Social Democracy*, *4*(1), 18–32.

Liebling, A., Price, D., & Shefer, G. (2011). *The prison officer* (2nd ed.). Cullompton: Willan.

MacDonald, H. (2014). *H is for hawk.* London: Penguin.

Phillips, C., & Earle, R. (2010). "Reading difference differently: Identity, epistemology and prison ethnography." *British Journal of Criminology*, *50*, 360–378.

Rice, S., & Maltz, M. D. (Eds.). (2018). *Doing ethnography in criminology.* Germany: Springer.

Rowe, A. (2015). "Situating the self in prison research: Power, identify and epistemology." In Drake, D., Earle, R., & Sloan, J. (Eds.), *The Palgrave handbook of prison ethnography.* London: Palgrave, 347–370.

Sparks, R. (2002). "Out of the 'digger': The warrior's honour and the guilty observer." *Ethnography*, *3*(4), 556–581.

Treadwell, J. (2018). "Doing ultrarealist ethnography: Romanticism and running with the riotous while buying your round." In Rice, S., & Maltz, M. D. (Eds.), *Doing ethnography in criminology*. Germany: Springer, 289–301.

Ugelvik, T. (2014). "Prison ethnography as lived experience: Notes from the diaries of a beginner let loose in Oslo prison." *Qualitative Inquiry*, *20*(4), 471–480.

Winlow, S., Hobbs, D., Lister, S., & Hadfield, P. (2011). "Get ready to duck: Bouncers and the realities of ethnographic research in violent groups." *British Journal of Criminology*, *41*, 536–548.

Index

About the Contributors

Jennifer A. Schlosser is an assistant professor of sociology at Coastal Carolina University. Her work looks critically at prison policy, particularly in-prison classes designed to reduce recidivism. She engages critical theory and reflexive methodologies to examine the role of the researcher in prison studies and the co-construction of inmates' narratives. She has published in *Qualitative Inquiry*, *Critical Criminology*, and the *Journal of Theoretical and Philosophical Criminology*. Her book is titled *Inmates Narratives and Discursive Discipline in Prison: Rewriting Personal Histories through Cognitive Behavioral Programs* (Routledge, 2015).

Dallas Augustine is a doctoral candidate in the Department of Criminology, Law, and Society at the University of California, Irvine. Her work examines issues of punishment and inequality for people living at the margins of the criminal justice system, such as formerly incarcerated people, people in long-term solitary confinement, and those living at the intersections of homelessness and injection drug use. She has been published in venues including *Criminology*, *Law and Social Inquiry* and the *American Journal of Public Health.*

Melissa Barragan is an assistant professor at California State Polytechnic University, Pomona. She focuses broadly on understanding the nature and impact of violence, policing, and punishment for individuals and communities. She has conducted research on illicit gun transactions and behavior, perceptions of policing and safety, gun violence patterns and prevention strategies, and solitary confinement practices in American prisons. Her work has been published in *Criminal Justice & Behavior*, the *American Journal of Public Health*, and *Injury Prevention* journals.

Kelsie Chesnut is a research associate with the Center on Sentencing and Corrections at the Vera Institute of Justice. Her work focuses on conditions of confinement, prison administration, and the role of corrections staff in policy reform. Her work appears in venues such as the *Annual Review of Law and Social Science* and *American Journal of Public Health.*

Beth Easterling is an associate professor of criminal justice and sociology and the director of the Criminal Justice Program at Mary Baldwin University. Her research interests include the impact of incarceration on the family, social stratification, and qualitative research methods.

Lindsey Raisa Feldman is an assistant professor of anthropology at the University of Memphis. Her work centers on lived experiences of imprisonment, identity, and masculinity. She utilizes a variety of methodologies, including photography, to critically examine the ways incarcerated men create meaning and uphold dignity in their daily lives.

Kathryn J. Fox is a professor of sociology at the University of Vermont. Her research has been in the arena of Corrections for more than twenty years. She has studied prison therapy for violent offenders and reentry practices, and her current research is part of a five-state network of research partners with Departments of Correction to transform prisons. She is also the founder and director of the University of Vermont's Liberal Arts in Prison Program.

Kate Gooch is senior lecturer at the University of Bath. Her primary research interests lie in prison research, youth justice, and criminal law. She employs qualitative and ethnographic methods to understand a range of topics, to include: prison leadership, culture, violence, homicide, drugs and the illicit economy, serious and organized crimes, the opening of new prisons, and the needs and experiences of particular prisoner groups (children, young people, care leavers, and veterans). To date, her research has focused on England and Wales, Australia, and Aotearoa New Zealand. Kate regularly presents her research to practitioners and policy makers.

Gabriela Gonzalez is a doctoral candidate in the Department of Criminology, Law, and Society at the University of California, Irvine. Her research focuses on the nature and consequences of punishment and the production of "illegality" as mechanisms for stratification that shape social inequality. She is a Newkirk Fellow and a Ford Foundation Diversity Fellow. Her work has been published in the *American Journal of Public Health.*

Tobi Jacobi is professor of English at Colorado State University where she directs the University Composition Program and teaches courses on writing and literacy theory with a specialization in the experiences of incarcerated women writers. Since 2005, she has directed the Community Literacy Center and trains student/community volunteers to facilitate SpeakOut! writing workshops with incarcerated adults and at-risk youth. She has published on community literacy and prison writing in journals such as *Community Literacy Journal*, *Feminist Formations*, and the *Journal of Correctional Education* and her coedited collection, *Women, Writing, and Prison: Activists, Scholars, and Writers Speak Out* (Rowman & Littlefield, 2014). Her current research focuses on examining narratives of representation from a Progressive Era training school for girls in upstate New York and the possibilities of engaging historical prison narratives in contemporary carceral classrooms.

Yvonne Jewkes is professor of criminology at the University of Bath. She conducted her first piece of prison research, a PhD under the supervision of Alison Liebling at the University of Cambridge Institute of Criminology in 1997–2000. That work was published under the title *Captive Audience: Media, Masculinity and Power in Prisons* (Willan, 2002) and led to a continuing fascination for prison research, which has most recently developed into an interest in prison architecture and design, and the extent to which the built environment can help to rehabilitate people. Yvonne has published widely on various aspects of imprisonment and is editor of *The Handbook on Prisons* (with Ben Crewe and Jamie Bennett; Routledge, 2016) and the new SAGE journal *Incarceration* (with Ben Crewe and Thomas Ugelvik). She is also a series editor of *Palgrave Studies in Prisons and Penology*, *SAGE Key Approaches to Criminology*, and *Emerald Studies in Culture, Criminal Justice and the Arts*.

Abigail Kolb is an assistant professor at the University of West Georgia. Drawing upon her background as a clinical social worker and her experience working within the Latinx community in East Los Angeles, her current research interests include Latinas/Chicanas in gangs, gendered politics of incarcerated women, identity politics, and qualitative research methods.

Alison Liebling is professor of criminology and criminal justice at the University of Cambridge and director of the Institute of Criminology's Prisons Research Centre. She conducted her first piece of prison research as a research assistant for Professor Keith Bottomley at the University of Hull in 1986, where she had been awarded the University's first distinction for her MA in criminology (part-time). This involved interviewing young men and women in five prisons for young offenders. She was captivated by the experience, and on Keith Bottomley's advice, applied to the Cambridge Institute of Criminology to do a PhD under the supervision of Dr. Adrian Grounds during 1987–1990. That work was published as her first book, *Suicides in Prison* (Routledge, 1992) and was followed by a long series of subsequent projects on, for example, suicides and suicide attempts among adult prisoners, small units for difficult prisoners, public-private sector comparisons, the work and role of prison officers, and the nature and quality of staff-prisoner relationships. These projects led to the development of her interest in conceptualizing and measuring the moral quality of prison life (published as *Prisons and their Moral Performance*, in 2004, assisted by Helen Arnold), and to a long series of projects on the role of trust in prison life, the changing nature of high security prisons, and the role of values in survival and personal development in prison.

Natalie Pifer is an assistant professor of criminology and criminal justice at the University of Rhode Island. Her work takes a socio-legal approach to examining how criminal justice policies are developed by stakeholders and implemented by frontline workers, with an emphasis on reforms to extreme punishment practices and the system's treatment of vulnerable groups. Her research appears in venues such as *Law and Social Inquiry* and the *Cambridge Handbook on Policing in the United States*.

Keramet Reiter is an associate professor in the Department of Criminology, Law, and Society at the University of California, Irvine. She studies prisons, prisoners' rights, and the impact of prison and punishment policy on individuals, communities, and legal systems. She has evaluated the impacts of medical experimentation on prisoners, gun control laws, and long-term solitary confinement in the United States and internationally. She is the author of two books: *23/7: Pelican Bay Prison and the Rise of Long-Term Solitary Confinement* (Yale University Press, 2016) and *Mass Incarceration* (Oxford University Press, 2017).

Shenique Thomas-Davis is an assistant professor at the City University of New York (CUNY) Borough of Manhattan Community College. Her research sits within a criminology and human development framework and examines the social consequences of mass imprisonment efforts on individuals, family systems, and communities, race-related stress, and public policy. She has conducted related work on incarcerated individual's familial ties, prison visitation, and reentry.

www.ingramcontent.com/pod-product-compliance
Ingram Content Group UK Ltd.
Pitfield, Milton Keynes, MK11 3LW, UK
UKHW041842031026
15587UKWH00002B/960

9 781793 600608